THE DEVELOPMENT OF LIABILITY BETWEEN NEIGHBOURS

Cases arising from disputes between neighbours (what English law would describe in terms of the law of nuisance) fall towards the edge of the law of tort, on its boundary with the law of property. They, therefore, provide a good example of how the categorisation of a case can affect the liability rule: tort law is typically concerned with fault, property law with strict liability. The aim of this book is to examine the importance of these category shifts, as well as the extent to which statutory interventions, planning control and the like have had an impact on the analysis of tortious liability.

JAMES GORDLEY is Shannon Cecil Turner Professor of Jurisprudence at the University of California, Berkeley.

COMPARATIVE STUDIES IN THE DEVELOPMENT OF THE LAW OF TORTS IN EUROPE

Series editors
John Bell and David Ibbetson

THE DEVELOPMENT OF LIABILITY BETWEEN NEIGHBOURS

Volume 2

Edited by

JAMES GORDLEY

Comparative Studies in the Development of the Law of Torts in Europe

CAMBRIDGE
UNIVERSITY PRESS

CAMBRIDGE
UNIVERSITY PRESS

University Printing House, Cambridge CB2 8BS, United Kingdom

Cambridge University Press is part of the University of Cambridge.

It furthers the University's mission by disseminating knowledge in the pursuit of education, learning and research at the highest international levels of excellence.

www.cambridge.org
Information on this title: www.cambridge.org/9780521199537

First published 2010
First paperback edition 2014

A catalogue record for this publication is available from the British Library

Library of Congress Cataloguing in Publication data
Gordley, James.
The development of liability between neighbours / Jim Gordley.
p. cm. – (Comparative studies in the development of the law of torts in Europe ; v. 4)
ISBN 978-0-521-19953-7 (hardback) 1. Adjoining landowners–Europe.
2. Premises liability–Europe. 3. Nuisances–Europe. 4. Boundaries (Estates)–Europe.
I. Title. II. Series.
KJC1337.G67 2009
346.403'6–dc22
2009009024

ISBN 978-0-521-76766-8 Hardback
ISBN 978-1-107-47563-2 Paperback

Harback only available as:
ISBN 978-0-521-19953-7 6-volume set hardback

CONTENTS

SERIES EDITORS' PREFACE

The European Legal Development series has arisen from a project funded by the AHRC from January 2005 until February 2008.

The aim of the project as a whole was to examine the nature of legal development in Western Europe since 1850, focusing sharply on liability for fault. Behind this there is a more abstract purpose, to attempt to cast some light on the factors which have influenced the way in which the law has changed over this period. Legal historians have looked at the general question, usually focusing on the rather facile distinction between the English common law and continental European legal systems. Though rooted in the sources, these works have been marred by a somewhat unsophisticated methodology and an inevitably selective use of evidence. Comparative lawyers have developed far more sophisticated methodologies, but their theoretical perspectives have too often borne little relation to empirical data. Over the last twenty years, tort lawyers have looked at the same types of question; but their analysis has invariably been at a high level of generality and has rarely looked at the historical component. By bringing together experts with different disciplinary backgrounds – comparative lawyers and legal historians, all with an understanding of modern tort law in their own systems – and getting them to work collaboratively, we have aimed to produce a more nuanced comparative legal history, and one which is theoretically better informed.

The topic of legal development is broad and, to make it manageable, we have undertaken a programme of work which has built up from a number of case studies and has moved towards a more general analysis and conclusions. Although we have been concerned with the development of the law, and although many of those involved in the project have been lawyers, we have also been concerned to include and benefit from the insights of historians and scholars in other disciplines.

Liability for fault between 1850 and 2000 has been our major area of study. Around 1850, there were many similarities in approaches to liability for fault across the legal systems of Western Europe. But since then, there has been significant divergence. Our method has been first to chart the changes and then to seek the explanations for what happened. Although there have been many changes in tort and delict laws over the period, the idea of liability for fault remains central to private law approaches to the compensation of victims of harms caused by the actions of others.

As a first stage, the project worked on six case studies which illustrate the general theme of liability for fault and its development within the period:

legal doctrine
medical liability
product liability
relations between neighbours
technological change
traffic and railways

This research involved scholars from a range of countries, in particular, England and Scotland, Spain, the Netherlands, Germany, France, Sweden, Austria and Italy. Each working group drew on the expertise of both senior and more junior scholars familiar with different European legal systems, and contained a mixture of comparative lawyers and legal historians.

A second stage has involved further groups examining a number of salient factors in legal development. The topics covered at this stage are:

institutions and professions
social and political ideas
the economy (including the impact of insurance)

A final strand to the work is an overview book.

This book, edited by James Gordley, provides us with a good example of the benefits of this approach. We gain a clear insight into the way in which a well-established area of tort liability was adapted to changes in society and in the economy. The topic also reveals the extent to which legal change occurred not in tort law, but through an increase in state regulatory law and through private regulation. The factors for legal development identified in this book are ones which will be developed in later volumes.

John Bell
David Ibbetson

ABBREVIATIONS

AC	Appeal Cases
AC Aud.	Archivo civil Audiencias
Am. J. Comp. L.	American Journal of Comparative Law
App Cas	Law Reports Appeal Cases
APS	Acts of Parliament of Scotland
ARB	Administratieve en rechterlijke beslissingen betrefende het openbaar bestuur in Nederland
Ar civil	Archivo civil
Art.	Article
B (Scots)	Bell
B & S	Best & Smith's Queen's Bench Reports
BGB	Bürgerliches Gesetzbuch
BGH	Bundesgerichtshof
BGHZ	Bundesgerichtshof in Zivilsachen
BImSchG	Bundesimmissionsschutzgesetz
BVerwG	Bundesverwaltungsgericht
BVerwGE	Entscheidungen des Bundesverwaltungsgericht
BW	Burgerlijk Wetboek
CA	Court of Appeal
Cass. civ.	Cour de Cassation, Chambre civile (France)
Cass., ch. réun	Cour de cassation, combined chambers (until 1967)
CC	Civil Code
CLJ	Cambridge Law Journal
Conv	Conveyancer and Property Lawyer
CP	Common Pleas (Law Reports)
CR	Conveyancing Review
D	Dunlop, Bell & Murray's Reports, Second Series Session Cases
D	Digest (of Justinian)
D or DC	Recueil Dalloz
DLR	Dominion Law Reports
D.P.	Dalloz Périodique
DS	Recueil Dalloz-Sirey

DVB	Deutsche Verwaltungsblatt
EG	Estates Gazette
EGLR	Estates Gazette Law Reports
ER	English Reports
EUP	Edinburgh University Press
EWCA	England and Wales Court of Appeal
FR	Fuero Real
GenTG	Gentechnikgesetz (gene technology law)
GewO	Gewerbe Ordnung (Germany)
GG	Grundgesetz
GP	Gazette du Palais
H & C	Hurlston & Coltman's Exchequer Reports
HL	Judicial Committee of the House of Lords
HLC	House of Lords Cases
HR	Hoge Raad
ICLQ	International and Comparative Law Quarterly
IR	Informations rapides
JC	Jurisprudenzia civil
JCP	Juris-Classeur Périodique, la Semaine Juridique
JLS	Journal of Legal Studies
JR	Judicial Review
JW	Juristische Wochenschrift
KB	King's Bench
LGR	Local Government Reports
LQR	Law Quarterly Review
LR	Law Reports
LS	Legal Studies
LT	Law Times
LuftVG	Luftverkehrsgesetz
M	Macpherson's Reports (Scotland)
MLR	Modern Law Review
MR	Master of the Rolls
Murr	Murray's Jury Court Cases
NBW	Nieuw Burgerlijk Wetboek
NJ	Nederlandse jurisprudentie
NJW	Neue juristische Wochenschrift
NJW-RR	NJW-Rechtsprechungsreport Zivilrecht
NoR	Novísima Recopilación
NSWR	New South Wales Law Reports
NVwZ	Neue Zeitschrift für Verwaltungsrecht
OAG	Oberamtsgericht
OG	Obergericht

OJLS	Oxford Journal of Legal Studies
OLG	Oberlandsgericht
OUP	Oxford University Press
OVG	Oberverwaltungsgericht
OVGE	Entscheidungen der Oberverwaltungsgerichte
P & CR	Property, Planning & Compensation Reports
Pat App	Paton's Scotch Appeals House of Lords
PC	Judicial Committee of the Privy Council
PrOVGE	Prussian Oberverwaltungsgerichtsentscheidungen
QB	Queen's Bench
R	Rettie's Session Cases
RD	Revista de Derecho e Jurisprudencia y Ciencias Sociales
RG	Reichsgericht
RGD	Revista General de Derecho
RGZ	Reichsgericht, Zivilsachen (Ger)
RVR	Rating & Valuation Reporter
SAP	Sentencias Audiencia Provincial
SAT	Sentencias Audiencia Territorial
SC	Session Cases
Sh Ct Rep	Sheriff Court Reports
SLR	Scottish Law Review
SLT	Scottish Law Times
STS	Sentencias del Tribunal Supremo de Justicia en Materia Civil
TCPA	Town & Country Planning Act
TMA	Tijdschrift voor Milieuschade en Aansprakelijkheidsrecht
UmweltHG	Umwelthaftungsgesetz
WLR	Weekly Law Reports
YR	Year Book
ZEuP	Zeitschrift für europäisches Privatrecht
ZRG RA	Zeitschrift der Savigny-Stiftung fur Rechtsgeschichte Rechtsarchiv

1

Disturbances among neighbours: an introduction

JAMES GORDLEY

1.1 Introduction

The chapters of this volume describe how various legal systems deal with disturbances among neighbours. They pay particular attention to changes in the law and legal thinking since the mid-nineteenth century. This chapter discusses what general conclusions can be drawn, based on these studies.

My conclusion is that much of the doctrinal development in the nineteenth century described in these chapters had little to do with reaching new results in practice, results that would bring the law into line with the great economic and social changes of that century. The debate and reformulation of doctrine was addressed to a problem that can be simply stated. If fault is the general basis for liability in tort, then what should be the result if one person without negligence, and without the intent to hurt his neighbour, interferes with his neighbour's use of property? The continental jurists inherited that problem from earlier jurists. The English and Scots faced it when, for the first time, in the nineteenth century, they regarded fault as the general basis of liability in tort.

Urbanisation and industrialisation did put new strains on the problems of living in proximity. Legal systems responded by breaking with the past by created systems of land use regulation which vested great power in administrative authority. As we will see, however, the response was much the same throughout modern Europe.

If this interpretation is right, it rules out two others: that the differences among modern legal systems are the product either of different cultural proclivities or of different policy choices as to how to confront new problems such as industrialisation. That might be an encouraging conclusion, at least for those who regard law as a transnational rather than a national product. It is not the case that the law of different systems responds to differences in national culture and national policy. Rather, the problems are the same everywhere. If the solutions are different – and often they are not – the reason is not a difference in culture or policy but that the problems are difficult and there is an understandable confusion as to how they might best be solved.

1.2 Disturbances among neighbours in private law: continental law

1.2.1 An historical baseline

If we are to understand the changes our authors describe, we need to know what the law was like before the nineteenth century. That gives us a baseline. If we find the law has changed, we can ask why. If we find it has not, we can rule out accounts which presume the law did change, and then try to explain the change by the industrialisation, urbanisation and changes in political and economic thought of the nineteenth century. If we find that the law did not change, but that jurists explained or discussed it in a different way or by applying different doctrines, we can then ask why that change occurred.

1.2.1.1 The problem in Roman law

Suppose someone harms another's property through his own fault, that is, by acting negligently or intentionally. Under Roman law, the owner could recover under the *lex Aquilia*. On the continent, liability for fault came to be recognised wherever Roman law was adopted. It was the law in the nineteenth century. It is the law today. In England, it became the law, but only when an action for negligence was recognised in the nineteenth century.

Suppose, however, someone interferes with another's use of his property. The aggrieved party could recover, not under the *lex Aquilia*, but for *iniuria*. His right to do so was dealt with in a few brief texts. Here are the most important:

> Aristo states in an opinion given to Cerellius Vitalis that he does not think that smoke can lawfully be discharged from a cheese shop onto the buildings above it, unless they are subject to a servitude to this effect, and this is admitted. He also holds that it is not permissible to discharge water or any other substance from the upper onto the lower property, as a man is only permitted to carry out operations on his own premises to this extent, that he discharge nothing onto those of another; and he adds that one can discharge smoke just as well as water. Thus, the owner of the upper property can bring an action against the owner of the lower, asserting that the latter does not have the right to act in this way.[1]

[1] D. 8.5.8.5.

> A doubt is raised by Pomponius in the 41st book of his *Readings*, as to whether a man can bring an action alleging that he has a right or that another has no right to create a moderate amount of smoke on his own premises, for example, smoke from a hearth. He says that the better opinion is that such an action cannot be brought, just as an action cannot be brought to maintain that one has a right to light a fire or sit or wash on one's own land.[2]

> If the owner of the lower premises creates smoke to fumigate those of his neighbour above, or if the owner of the upper premises throws or pours anything on to those below, Labeo says that the action for *iniuria* does not lie. I think this wrong, if it were done with the intention to offend.[3]

These texts deal with two situations: (1) the defendant caused the disturbance because he intended to offend his neighbour, and (2) the defendant disturbed his neighbour without such an intention.

1.2.1.2 The search for an explanation of the Roman texts

In the first situation, medieval and early modern jurists did not look for any further explanation. It was clear the defendant is liable because his purpose was to offend. The second situation was more difficult. Sometimes the defendant could not recover and sometimes he could. He could not recover when, for example, the defendant created a moderate amount of smoke from his own hearth. He could when, for example, he ran a cheese shop and disturbed his neighbours by smoking the cheese. The Romans did not explain the principle that distinguishes these two kinds of cases.

Distinguishing them proved to be difficult. Medieval and early modern jurists suggested three ways of doing so. Odofredus said that one cannot use one's land in a way that bothers others.[4] Blackstone eventually gave the same solution, although the Latin phrase was a bit different: *sic utere tuo ut neminem laedere* (use what is yours so as not to injure another).[5] That maxim has been repeated countless times by common law judges. As Professor Thier notes in his chapter on German law,[6] this argument has reappeared periodically in Germany. Critics claim it is meaningless.[7]

[2] D. 8.5.8.6. [3] D. 47.10.44.

[4] *Lectura super digesto veteri* to D. 8.5.8.5 (Lyon 1550) (*unusquisque debet facere in suo quod non officiat alieno*).

[5] W. Blackstone, *Commentaries on the Law of England* (Chicago, University of Chicago Press, 1979), vol. 2, p. 306.

[6] Below, p. 90.

[7] E.g., W. V. H. Rogers, *Winfield and Jolowicz on Tort*, 14th edn (London, Sweet and Maxwell, 1994), p. 404.

According to the chapter on English Law, the same objection has been made in England.[8] Everything that bothers another person is not actionable, and the maxim does not tell us which ones should be.

Later in the thirteenth century, Iacobus de Ravanis said that one cannot discharge anything onto another's property that disturbs the owner. He was picking up on Aristo's remark that one must 'discharge nothing onto [the premises] of another'. His solution was repeated by the great fourteenth century jurist Baldus de Ubaldis[9] and was popular among the Dutch and German jurists of the seventeenth and eighteenth centuries.[10] But it did not explain why the owner of the hearth was allowed to discharge smoke on his neighbour's property.

Still another explanation was given by Bartolus of Saxoferato, who may have been the greatest medieval jurist. Here is his commentary to D. 8.5.8.5:

> The owner of the lower premises cannot discharge smoke into the upper premises by the law of servitudes, and the owner of the upper premises cannot discharge water into the lower unless there is an agreement to the contrary, and for these interferences they can bring actions and the possessory interdicts [Roman actions available to one whose possession has been disturbed]. It may be objected that one is permitted to make a fire in his own premises, and one is not bound if the smoke ascends to those of another unless that happens with an intention to offend. D. 8.5.8.5....
> I think the following is to be said: Sometimes the owner of the lower premises makes fire in the usual way for the ordering of his family, and then he may do it lawfully, and he is not liable if the smoke ascends unless he acts with an intention to offend. In the same way, if the owner of the upper premises lets water flow as is normal, for his water clock, he is not liable if some descends unless he acts with an intention to injure. But if the owner of the lower premises wants to make a shop or inn where he is continually making a fire and a great deal of smoke, he is not allowed to do so, as in this text (D. 8.5.8.5). In the same way, if the owner of the upper premises lets

[8] This has been criticised as lacking in accuracy: see Lord Wright in *Sedleigh-Denfield* v. *O'Callaghan* [1940] AC 880, p. 903.

[9] Baldus de Ubaldis, *Commentaria Corpus iuris civilis* to D. 8.5.8.5 (Venice, Iuntas, 1577).z

[10] E.g., Johann Brunnemann, *Commentarius in quinquaginta libros Pandectarum* (Genoa, Sumptibus fratrum Cramer, 1762)('in suo enim cuique facere licet, quatenus nihil in alienum immitit'); Dionisius Gothofredus, *Corpus iuris civilis ... cum notis integris Dionysii Gothofredi, Antonii Anselmo, Simonis von Leuwen* (Antwerp, 1726) to D. 8.5.8.5 n. 37 ('immittere ... vel ... projicere non licet'); Johannes Voet, *Commentarius ad Pandectas* (The Hague, Petrus de Hondt, 1726) lib. VIII, tit. 5 ('cuius ire liceat in suo facere ea, quibus vicino nocet, si prosit sibi; observandum tamen, cuique in suo hactenus facere licere, quatenus nihil in alienum immittit').

> water flow beyond what is normal, he is not allowed to do so, as this text says.[11]

Thus, what mattered to Bartolus was the amount of smoke and the normal or abnormal character of the activity.

All three of these solutions not only endured but sometimes can be found side by side in the same author. Here is how the eighteenth-century French jurist Robert Pothier described the proprietor's rights:

> Being neighbours obligates each of the neighbours to use his property in such a way that it does not injure the other neighbour ....
>
> This rule must be understood in the sense that, whatever liberty each one has to do what seems good on his own land, he may do nothing that may result in something going on the land of his neighbour which is injurious. (Citing D.8.5.8.5)

Because of this same principle, one is not allowed to do anything on one's land that would send into a neighbouring house smoke that is too thick or too much of an interference, such as that which issues from a lime kiln or a furnace for burning the dregs of wine (citing D.8.5.8.5.).[12]

1.2.1.3 A further complication: the relationship to negligence

Nothing in the Roman texts suggested that in cases like the cheese shop, the defendant was liable because he was negligent in the sense that he neglected some precaution or should have located the cheese shop elsewhere. Fault or negligence (*culpa*) mattered only if he had caused physical harm to the plaintiff's property and the plaintiff sought to hold him liable under the *lex Aquilia*.

Confusion set in with the emergence of a unified conception of tort liability in the sixteenth century. During this period, as I have shown elsewhere, a group of jurists known as the 'late scholastics' tried to synthesise the rules of Roman law with the philosophical principles of their intellectual heroes, Aristotle and Thomas Aquinas. Aristotle had said that distributive justice entitles each citizen to a fair share of honour or wealth. Commutative justice preserves that share. If another involuntarily deprives one citizen of resources, commutative justice requires the person

[11] *Commentaria in Corpus iuris civilis* to D. 8.5.8.5 (Venice, Iuntas, 1615).

[12] R. Pothier, 'Traité du contrat de société App. 2, Du voisinage' 235, 241, in *Oeuvres de Pothier annotées et mises en correlation avec le Code civil et législation actuel*, 2nd edn by Bugnet (Paris, Marchal et Billard, 1861).

who did so to compensate the victim.[13] Aristotle and Aquinas thought this principle applied even in cases of wounding or striking another in which the defendant did not financially gain. Aquinas explained that he gained in the sense of fulfilling his will at another's expense. Aquinas, though not Aristotle, also said that a party who harmed another negligently but not intentionally must also make compensation. He had also made a choice: he chose to act imprudently or to neglect cultivating the virtue of prudence.

Consequently, the late scholastics explained that commutative justice was the principle underlying the Roman actions in what we would call delict or tort. The distinctions among them were mere matters of Roman positive law. As Aristotle said, whatever belonged to a person should be protected, be it his person, his property or his honour. The *lex Aquilia* protected a person's property and (according to medieval jurists) his person. The action for *iniuria* protected his 'honour'.

In many situations, the action of *iniuria* did protect honour, as, for example when the defendant beat the plaintiff's slave,[14] insulted him by composing or reciting a song,[15] denounced him in a petition to the emperor,[16] or assembled people at his house to raise a loud and offensive clamour.[17] Nevertheless, as we have seen, however, the action for *iniuria* not only protected a person's honour. Inter alia, it protected a person against smoke from another's cheese shop. The late scholastics and the northern natural lawyers neglected the case of the cheese shop and did not explain how it fitted with their general principle that one who harms another's property, person, or honour owes compensation.

That general formula resting liability on fault outlasted the Aristotelian ideas that had inspired it. Grotius, who borrowed heavily from the late scholastics, said in a famous passage:

> From … a fault, if damage is caused, an obligation arises by the law of nature, namely, that the damage be made good. … Damage … is when a man has less than what is his whether by mere nature or by some human act in addition such as ownership, agreement, or statute. Things which a man may regard as his by nature are life …, his limbs, fame, honour, and his own acts.[18]

[13] *Nicomachean Ethics* V.ii 1130^{b} – 1131^{a}. [14] D. 47.10.15.34. [15] D. 47.10.15.27.

[16] D. 47.10.15.29. [17] D. 47.10.15.2.

[18] H. Grotius, *De iure belli ac pacis libri tres*, B. J. A. de Kanter-van Hetting Tromp (ed.) (Leiden, Brill, 1939), II.xvii.21.

The formula was repeated by many seventeenth- and eighteenth-century jurists, including Robert Pothier, although Pothier did not enumerate the rights that constituted damage. The drafters of the French Civil Code, who were greatly influenced by Pothier, replicated it in Arts. 1382–3. Versions of it, with various modifications, passed into virtually all modern civil codes. But the French Code included no provision dealing with interferences among neighbours like that of the cheese shop, even though they had been mentioned by Pothier, albeit only in an appendix to his *Traité du contrat de société*.[19] Other codes, such as the Dutch Code of 1838, did contain a provision mentioning disturbances among neighbours but never explained how that provision related to the general formula.

So, in addition to the ancient problem of how to limit actions for disturbing neighbours, continental jurists faced another problem as well, one which had been long neglected. They had to explain how the general formula which provided for liability based on fault was related to protecting neighbours against disturbances. Much of the development of modern law can be understood as a thrashing out of that problem.

1.2.2 The development of modern law

1.2.2.1 German law

In Germany, much confusion was avoided because the Germans did not simply model their Code on the French or on the work of the seventeenth- and eighteenth-century authors. While the French Code came into force in 1804, the German Code did so in 1900, and only after a revival of academic interest in the Roman texts. Consequently, their Code included not only a general provision governing liability for fault (§ 823(1)), which the Germans modelled on the *lex Aquilia*, but also special provisions governing disturbances among neighbours which they modelled on the action for *iniuria*. Because disturbances among neighbours were governed by these special provisions, there was no effort to apply the general formula to them, and consequently, no confusion about how it might apply.

The German jurists knew that, under Roman law, one could recover for *iniuria* if one interfered with a neighbour's use of land simply in order to disturb him. This rule was eventually adopted in a generalised form in § 226 of the German Civil Code which provides that 'The use of a right is not permitted when it can only have the purpose of causing harm to another.'

[19] Below, p. 68.

The German jurists also knew that one might be liable in Roman law even if the purpose of interfering with one's neighbour was not to disturb him. They gave considerable thought to when, in this second case, one should or should not be liable. The classic discussion was by Rudolph von Ihering. He pointed out that property rights would be worthless if a property owner either could disturb his neighbour at will or could not disturb him at all. An owner who could disturb his neighbours at will could make their land valueless by some pestilential use of his own. An owner who could not disturb them at all could not cook or use heat if they objected to the odours or the smoke. Ihering concluded that the owner's rights must depend on the degree of interference and the normal use of land.[20] As the German report observes, a similar solution was adopted by German courts in the nineteenth century. It passed into § 906 of the German Civil Code which reads (as amended in 1960):

> The owner of land may not prohibit the discharge upon it of gas, steam, odours, smoke, soot, heat, noise, vibrations, and any similar interferences from the operations conducted on other land insofar as the use of his own property is not impaired or not substantially impaired. …
> The same applies insofar as a substantial impairment is caused by a use of other land that is normal for the area and cannot be reasonably prevented by measures which are commercially feasible for activities of this type. If the owner must suffer some interference on this account, then he can require an appropriate compensation in money from the person using the other land when the interference prevents a use of his own land or its product that is unreasonable in degree.

Taken together, these provisions govern interferences among neighbours in much the same way as Roman law as interpreted by Bartolus. Courts give relief in two types of cases: against one who deliberately bothers his neighbours (§ 226), and sometimes against one who disturbs them even without fault as in the Roman case of the cheese shop (§ 906). In the second case, § 906 limits recovery for a disturbance in the same way German courts did in the nineteenth century, French courts have done since the nineteenth century, and Roman law did according to Bartolus. What matters is whether the disturbance is abnormal in kind or in degree for the locality.

[20] R. von Ihering, 'Zur Lehre von den Beschränkungen den Grundeigenthümers im Interesse der Nachbarn', (1863) 6 *Jahrbücher für die Dogmatik des heutigen römischen und deutschen Privatrechts* 81, at 94–6.

1.2.2.2 French law

Articles 1382–3 of the French Civil Code contained the general formula imposing liability on those who cause harm through fault. No provisions like the Roman rules of *iniuria* governed disturbances among neighbours. Yet, French courts avoided the confusion of how this formula might apply to such disturbances by, in effect, creating new actions for which the Code did not provide. As the chapter on French law points out, they gave relief when the defendant acted in order to disturb the plaintiff, and when, as French courts put it, the interference went beyond those normal among neighbours.[21] Although the terminology was not uniform, French commentators usually described the first case as an 'abuse of right' (*abus du droit*) and the second as an interference among neighbours (*trouble de voisinage*), although the latter expression was sometimes used to encompass cases of 'abuse of right'.

In the second case, to quote the chapter on French law, 'he is liable if the disturbance exceeds that which is "normal" among neighbouring properties'.[22] What is normal is judged by the character of the locality. The defendant is liable if the interference is normal in kind but abnormal in degree so that the defendant is causing more of a disturbance than others engaged in the same activity. He is liable whether or not he is at fault for causing the interference. For example, if his factory emits fluorine gas he is liable even if there is no measure he should have taken to prevent the emission. In such a case, however, a court may allow him to continue his operations but require him to pay damages for the harm they cause.[23]

Thus, the French resolved the problems they inherited by, in effect, recognising an action the Romans would have given for *iniuria* alongside the general formula of Arts. 1382–3. As in Roman law, this action lies in two types of cases: when one deliberately bothers one's neighbours and when one disturbs them even without fault as in the Roman case of the cheese shop. In the second case, the French cleared up the ancient question of when one can recover – of what makes smoke from a cheese shop different from smoke from a hearth – in much the same manner as Bartolus: it all depends on whether the disturbance is abnormal in kind or in degree for the locality. In short, in France as in Germany, it is hard to see much difference between the law governing disturbances among neighbours and the Roman law as interpreted by Bartolus.

[21] Below, pp. 70–71. [22] Ibid. [23] Ibid.

1.2.2.3 Dutch law

The Dutch Code of 1838 also contained a general formula like that of Arts. 1382–3. Indeed, as the chapter on Dutch law points out, Art. 1401 of the 1838 Code was a translation of Art. 1382, although it specified that the defendant's conduct must be 'unlawful' since merely to mention 'fault' was thought to be too vague.[24] In the new Dutch Code of 1992, the old Art. 1401 has been replaced by Art. 6:162 but without a change of substance.

The old Dutch Code also provided in Art. 625 'that an owner may not use his property in such a way that he causes nuisances to the rights of others'. What this provision meant was unclear. Had the Dutch courts wished, they could have construed it to mean that a neighbour could bring an action for a disturbance without having to bring his case within the general formula of Art. 1401. French courts had allowed such an action even though their Code did not contain a text like Art. 625, which spoke of nuisances.

As the chapter on Dutch law notes, 'The Supreme Court at first seemed to sanction the fact that plaintiffs based [their action] on art 625 CC, but later on it made clear that the relations between neighbours were governed by the law of torts', that is, by Art. 1401.[25] Consequently, a neighbour had to be at 'fault' and act 'unlawfully' to be liable. This approach has been taken by Art. 5:37 of the Dutch Civil Code of 1992. It provides that the owner of land is not allowed to cause nuisance to his neighbour that amounts to negligence within the meaning of Art. 6:162. It mentions specific examples of nuisances: noise, disgusting smells, smoke, and deprivation of air, light and support. But it does not clarify the question that remained unresolved under the old Dutch Code: what does it mean to say that one is liable for causing such disturbances only if one is at fault and acted unlawfully?

The closest the Dutch courts have come to answering this question is to lay down a list of factors that judges should take into account in order to decide whether a certain type of behaviour was unlawful or not.[26] To quote the chapter on Dutch law:

> The list of factors … was the following: 1) the chance that others would not pay attention, 2) the chance that as a result damage would ensue, 3)

[24] Below, p. 108.

[25] Below, p. 110, citing, as the first instance in which this earlier tendency was rejected, HR 14 May 1886, W. 5288, along with subsequent decisions reaffirming this position.

[26] Below, pp. 114–15.

the seriousness of that damage, and 4) the extent to which precautionary measures are burdensome.[27]

Those factors, as the author of the Dutch chapter observes, are much like those which American courts have used to define negligence.[28]

But does that mean that one can disturb one's neighbour whenever the damage caused is less serious than the burden of taking precautionary measures? The answer to that question is obscured by a list of additional factors which the Supreme Court has since mentioned. Again, according to the chapter on Dutch law, to resolve the question whether or not a certain behaviour constituted a nuisance, the list of factors provided by the Supreme Court has grown over the years. In the beginning, the seriousness of the nuisance and the circumstances under which it took place were the only ones listed.[29] Later on it became more specific. Relevant were the nature, the seriousness and the duration of the nuisance.[30] In a later decision it was said that whether or not a nuisance was unlawful depended on the nature, the seriousness, and the duration of the nuisance and the damage thus caused on their relation to the further circumstances of the case including local circumstances.[31] This formulation seems to be standard now although the Supreme Court is not always consistent. Sometimes added to this are the costs of and willingness to take precautionary measures.[32][33]

Consequently, one is led to wonder whether a person is liable for disturbing his neighbours if he was not at fault in the ordinary sense, that is, if he behaved as a reasonable person should. The answer is that Dutch law is not clear. In a letter to Prof. Verheij, who wrote the chapter on Dutch law, I asked how Dutch law would resolve the Roman case of the cheese shop if we assume that the shop was well managed and located in an appropriate area. He answered that he could only be held liable for 'fault' under Art. 6:162 of the 1992 Civil Code. Whether he would be is unclear: the only thing that can be said about the example with certainty is that it all depends on the circumstances. That is an open door but the fact is

[27] Ibid. p. 115.

[28] Below, n. 31. (There is a clear similarity with the Learned Hand Formula in *United States v. Carroll Towing Co* [1947] 159 F. (2d) 169.)

[29] HR 10 March 1972, NJ 1972, 278 (*Vermeulen/Lekkekerker*).

[30] HR 23 September 1988, NJ 1989, 743 (*Kalimijnen*).

[31] HR 3 May 1991, NJ 1991, 476 (*De Jong/Van Tol*).

[32] This factor was listed in HR 15 February 1991, NJ 1992, 639, nt. CJHB (Staat/OVB), but, for example, not listed in HR 18 September 1998, NJ 1999, 69, nt. ARB (Luykx/Bastiaansen).

[33] Below, p. 115.

that if neighbours suffer greatly, then judges will possible reason that the shopkeeper acts unlawfully (and therefore negligently).[34] Professor Verheij is describing Dutch law accurately. Once the problem of disturbances among neighbours is brought under the general formula of liability for fault, one faces two unpleasant alternatives: to use the word fault in its ordinary sense, and deny recovery if the cheese shop is properly located and well managed, or to blur the concept of fault, so that an action could succeed even in this case. Since 1838, Dutch law has not decided between these alternatives or even recognised that a decision must be made.

There is a similar confusion even in the more straightforward case in which a person disturbs his neighbour with no other purpose than to offend him. As the chapter on Dutch law points out, in the 1930s, Dutch courts held that in these cases at least the defendant would be liable for 'fault' under Art. 1401.[35] Yet under the 1992 Code, even this conclusion has been thrown into doubt. As the chapter on Dutch law points out, since Art. 5:37 only refers to negligence (Art. 6:162), there is doubt as to whether these older cases still express Dutch law.[36]

The problem is whether and how to separate the general formula that imposes liability for harm caused by fault from the problems the Romans addressed separately by granting an action for *iniuria*. As we have seen, that is not a problem the Dutch jurists made but one they inherited.

Nor can we conclude, from the confusion just described, that cases in the Netherlands are actually decided in a different way than in Germany or France. One can only say that the rules in force do not tell us how they are decided. To find out, one would have to look at each individual case.

1.2.2.4 Spanish law

In Spain, unlike the Netherlands, the distinction between liability for negligence and liability absent fault for disturbing one's neighbours has been clearly understood since the nineteenth century. As the chapter on Spanish law points out, the difficulty is that neither the jurists nor the courts have consistently committed themselves to one approach or the other.

Article 1902 of the Spanish Civil Code contains a general formula like that of Arts. 1382–3 of the French, s. 823(1) of the German and Art. 6:162 of the New Dutch Code. A person is liable for negligently or intentionally harming another. Article 1908 provides:

[34] Letter from A. J. Verheij, 3 February 2007. [35] Below, p. 112. [36] Below, p. 114.

> ... Equally, occupiers of property are liable for harm caused:
> 2. By excessive smoke which is harmful to people or property...
> 4. By emanations from sewers and contact with infectious material which had been dealt with without adequate precautions for the location.

Smoke (*humo*), as the chapter on Spanish law notes, covers other forms of emissions such as smells, noise, vibrations, toxic gases and others.[37]

Based on these passages, it would have been perfectly possible for the courts to recognise two distinct actions: one for harm caused by fault (like the Roman *lex Aquilia*, Arts. 1382–3 of the French Civil Code and § 823(1) of the German Civil Code) and one for disturbances to neighbours caused without fault (like the Roman action for *iniuria*, the French actions for *abus du droit* and *troubles de voisinage* and the German action under § 906).

As the chapter on Spanish law notes, there is some authority for applying Art. 1908 to distubances among neighbours with no requirement of fault. 'The problem is', the author adds, 'that in many cases [liability for emissions] is solved, not by applying article 1908, but by wrongly applying article 1902.'[38] He concludes:

> Spanish jurisprudence has shown an evolution towards an objective interpretation of the article 1902 without asserting, however, that this rule can support a fully strict liability, but without abandoning totally the criterion of fault liability.
>
> We can conclude that courts are moving in a blurred zone between strict and fault liability, without knowing if many judgments defend one or the other or if the basis of the judgment is fault or risk. This also happens with nuisance: there are judgments convicting in a basis of fault (fault liability) and others in a basis of the theory of liability of risk (strict liability), by this means who does an activity which is able to produce some risk and obtains an economic benefit from it ([t]ypical case of polluting industries) has to respond of the damage produced by the activity even if there is no fault at all.[39]

The problem is not that Spanish jurists fail clearly to distinguish these two bases for liability. They do, as the chapter on Spanish law shows at length. The problem is that the courts waffle between them, so that one cannot say what the law is. One might say that the confusion in the Netherlands is due to an attempt to square the circle by merging these two bases for liability into one. The confusion in Spain is due to the failure of the courts to make up their minds.

[37] Below, p. 178, n. 19. [38] Below, p. 191. [39] Ibid.

1.3 Disturbances among neighbours in private law: Scotland and England

When we turn to the development of Scots and English law, we again encounter confusion but for a different historical reason. As the chapter on Scots law points out, the law of nuisance was developed in Scotland largely on the model of English law. As we will see, English law never developed an action for negligence until the nineteenth century. The English and Scots began the nineteenth century with rules on disturbances of neighbours that did not depend on negligence, much like the Roman action for *iniuria*. As we will see, by and large, these rules are in force today. But confusion set in when, in the nineteenth century, courts in Scotland began to consider whether negligence was, in principle, the basis for an action in delict, and the English recognised an action for negligence for the first time. As we have seen, one source of confusion in continental law had been uncertainty about the relationship of an action for negligence and an action for disturbing a neighbour's use of property. But the historical debate occurred in a different context. The nineteenth-century continental jurists inherited a general formula according to which liability depended on fault. They then had to relate that formula to disturbances among neighbours. The English and Scots began with a rule imposing liability on neighbours that did not depend on negligence. They then had to relate that rule to the action for negligence which became of concern only in the nineteenth century.

1.3.1 Scots law

As the chapter on Scots law notes, in a note appended to the report on *Kinloch* v. *Robertson* in 1756,[40] in which the Dean of Guild had been petitioned for the removal of a blacksmith's workshop on the second floor of a building separated from the petitioner by a mutual gable, Lord Kames noted that the close proximity of neighbours gave rise to a need for a legal rule that would protect the comfortable habitation of property against extraordinary disturbances.[41] He did not mention negligence.

Similarly, Baron Hume discussed the problem in terms of mutual interference among neighbours: 'Every individual comes to see, that, if he were to insist on the absolute disposal of his own, he might indeed

[40] (1756) Mor. 13164. [41] See quote given at p. 156 below.

incommode his neighbours, but that he would be liable to be equally molested by them in return. He contracts too in time some degree of regard for them.'[42]

Today, according to the chapter on Scots law, the rule governing such disturbances depends, not on negligence, but on what disturbances go beyond what a neighbour should be expected to tolerate. The standard that has emerged is that of reasonable tolerability.[43] This standard was formalised in 1954 by Lord President Cooper in the case of *Watt* v. *Jamieson*. Lord Cooper's dictum in that case provides what is now regarded as the modern definitive statement of nuisance in Scots law:

> I deduce that the proper angle of approach to a case of alleged nuisance is rather from the standpoint of the victim of the loss or inconvenience than from the standpoint of the alleged offender: and that if any person so uses his property as to occasion serious disturbance or substantial inconvenience to his neighbour or material damage to his neighbour's property, it is in the general case irrelevant to plead merely that he was making a normal and familiar use of his own property. The balance in all such cases has to be held between the freedom of a proprietor to use his property as he pleases and the duty on a proprietor not to inflict material loss or inconvenience on adjoining[44] proprietors or adjoining property; and in every case the answer depends on considerations of fact and degree. The critical question is whether what he was exposed to was *plus quam tolerabile* when due weight has been given to all the surrounding circumstances of the offensive conduct and its effects.[45]

The *plus quam tolerabile* requirement introduced into the law a mechanism by which the competing interests of the parties may be balanced.[46] The defender's interest in the free use of his land yields to the pursuer's interest in the comfortable enjoyment of hers at the point at which the interference becomes more than reasonably tolerable, having regard to the circumstances. The test of tolerability is objective inasmuch as reasonable tolerability is considered from the point of view of the reasonable occupier in the locality of the pursuer.

[42] Below, p. 139. [43] Below, p. 139.

[44] 'Neighbouring' might have been a better word than 'adjoining', since there is no requirement that properties be adjoining.

[45] 1954 SC 56, 57 B 58. See also *Maguire* v. *Charles McNeil Ltd* 1922 SC 174 per Lord Skerrington, p. 190.

[46] The view that nuisance proceeds on a balance of interests has been a consistent theme in writing on nuisance in Scotland. See e.g. D. Hume, *Lectures 1786–1822*, 3 (Edinburgh, Stair Society, 1939), p. 207; T. B. Smith, *Short Commentary on the Law of Scotland* (Edinburgh, W. Green, 1961), p. 530.

The relevant circumstances that may be considered are: the nature and extent of the alleged harm or interference; the sensitivity to harm of the pursuer or the pursuer's property; the character of the locality; the purpose of the respective parties' land use; the ability of the pursuer to effect protective measures; and the ability of the defender to abate the nuisance.[47]

Thus, we again see an action like that which the Romans gave in the case of the cheese shop although it was not based on Roman authority.

The one rule that they did seem to have taken from the Romans governed recovery when an activity was done simply to bother a neighbour. Here, they retained a doctrine they referred to as *aemulationem vicini* in which, to recover, B must prove malice on A's part. The chapter on Scots law mentions that this action has been 'marginalised' by the action of nuisance, presumably because pure malice is both rare and hard to prove. In a letter to me, one of the authors, Mr Cameron, explained:

> It appears that this doctrine was generally accepted as part of Scots law, certainly during the eighteenth century though there was no real discussion of it in Court before 1808. While *aemulationem vicini* could have served as a basis for developing a doctrine equivalent to nuisance, the courts did not take a creative approach. The requirement of malice meant that actions could be easily defended where the defender could show that the activity was conducted / located for his own convenience and not to spite his neighbour (see *Dewar v Fraser* [1767] Mor 12803). The doctrine remains part of Scots law, but it has been marginalised by nuisance. *More v Boyle* [1967] SLT (Sh Ct) 38 is a 'recent' example in which a homeowner cut off the water supply to his neighbours who had refused to contribute to the cost of repairs. This doctrine is perhaps as close as Scots law gets to a doctrine of abuse of rights. Scotland never developed a doctrine of abuse of rights of general application.[48]

Still, it is close enough to cover cases like the Roman one in which a person makes smoke with the sole purpose of bothering his neighbour.

Thus, rules were developed like those in England or in Roman law: one is liable without negligence for disturbances that bother one's neighbour although Scots and English law, like Roman law, are not clear about the circumstances in which one is liable. One is also liable, at least sometimes, for disturbances which have the sole purpose of bothering him.

As the chapter on Scots law describes in detail, however, the story is complicated by a long and complex discussion of the role of fault. In

[47] Below, p. 140. [48] Letter from Cameron, 2 February 2007.

Scots law, the question of how fault was related to an action for nuisance surfaced only in the nineteenth century. The tension, as on the continent, was between regarding fault as the general basis for liability in delict and liability imposed without fault for disturbing one's neighbours. As the chapter on Scots law points out, some courts and authors used the term 'fault' to describe, not negligence, but actionable disturbance of another's use of property, or to claim that from such a disturbance, 'fault' in the sense of negligence can be inferred. Others used the term 'nuisance' to describe claims for physical damage to property which did, indeed, depend on proof of negligence. Yet, as the author points out, despite these complications, the Scots law can now be described succinctly.

Following *Kennedy* v. *Glenbelle* and a small number of subsequent cases, it is now possible to provide a coherent summary of fault in nuisance in Scots law. The first point to note is that, in any action grounded on nuisance, nuisance must first be established. This is sufficient if the remedy sought is not damages. Where damages are sought, fault must be proved in addition. Liability arises in respect of harmful acts or operations deliberately undertaken. Intention, in this context, means that the act is intentional. It does not mean that harm to the victim is intended. Motive is, in the general case, irrelevant in delict.[49] The conduct must be deliberate and carried out in the knowledge that harm would be the outcome, but knowledge may be established constructively. Actual knowledge is not required. Allowing the continuation of an activity or state of affairs in the knowledge that it is causing harm amounting to nuisance is likewise culpable.[50]

Thus, despite the confusion about the meaning of fault and its relation to nuisance, the end result is like that of Roman law. Fault in the sense of negligence must be shown in cases where property is harmed. It need not be in cases like that of the Roman cheese shop when one's neighbour's use of his property has been disturbed.

1.3.2 English law

Where it is simply a matter of 'nuisance' in the sense of interfering with one's neighbour by noise, smells, and the like, fault has never played a role. As the chapter on English law explains:

[49] It is relevant in use of land *in aemulationem vicini* in which liability is based on malice. It is also relevant in conspiracy.

[50] Below, p. 149.

> There is ... clear authority that negligence is not a necessary condition for a claim in private nuisance. The courts will examine the effect of the interference on the claimant and it is irrelevant whether the defendant had taken reasonable steps to prevent the nuisance or had been acting in good faith. In the leading case of *Rapier* v. *London Tramways Co.*,[51] a tramway company had built some large blocks of stables about forty-two yards[52] from the plaintiff's detached house and pleasure-grounds for the horses they used to draw the trams. The resulting smell of 200 horses can be imagined and the stables had capacity for some 440. The Court of Appeal held that it was no defence that they had taken all reasonable care to prevent it.[53]

The author describes the rule the court applies as follows:[54]

> The maxim is *sic utere tuo ut neminem laedas* (use your own in a way that does not harm another's).[55] The courts will focus on the impact to the claimant's proprietary rights, not on judging the conduct of the defendant[56] or the economic rationale in favour of the interference. If the defendant's actions are not considered 'reasonable', the defendant will be liable even if he is able to show that he exercised reasonable care and skill to avoid any interference to the claimant's use and enjoyment of land.[57]

Thus, we have a rule about interferences with one's neighbour's property that does not depend on fault where there is no intention to injure one's neighbour, like the Roman rule imposing liability for running the cheese shop. As in the Middle Ages, however, and unlike France or Germany, we have no clear standard as to when the rule applies. It applies if the defendant's conduct is not reasonable. Yet almost all we know is that conduct can be considered unreasonable even if it was not negligent and the plaintiff took due care.

If the defendant's conduct was intended solely to bother one's neighbour, then, again, it seems that the defendant may be liable, as in Roman,

[51] [1893] 2 Ch. 588. See also *Moss* v. *Christchurch Rural DC* [1925] 2 KB 750.

[52] About 38 metres. [53] Below, p. 34. [54] Below, p. 33.

[55] Although this has been criticised as lacking in accuracy: see Lord Wright in *Sedleigh-Denfield* v. *O'Callaghan* [1940] AC 880 at 903.

[56] The use of malice is, of course, inconsistent with this framework (see criticism, P. Giliker, *Tort*, 2nd edn (London, Sweet and Maxwell, 2005), p. 285) and serves to illustrate the court's inability to adhere to this distinction in practice.

[57] Lord Goff in *Cambridge Water Co* v. *Eastern Counties Leather Plc* [1994] 2 AC 264 at 299. See also Lord Symonds in *Read* v. *J. Lyons & Co Ltd* [1947] AC 156 at 183: 'negligence is not a necessary ingredient in this case. For if a man commits a legal nuisance it is no answer to his injured neighbour that he took the utmost care not to commit it. There the liability is strict.'

French and German law. And yet, the matter is not free from doubt. In *Christie* v. *Davey*,[58] the court enjoined the defendant from interrupting the plaintiff's music lessons by whistling, shrieking and banging on the walls of his apartment. In *Hollywood Silver Fox Farm Ltd.* v. *Emmett*,[59] the court held the defendant liable for firing guns during the season when the plaintiff's silver foxes were breeding in order to interfere with his business. But in *Bradford (Mayor of)* v. *Pickles*,[60] the defendant was not held liable even though he drained his own land to diminish the plaintiff's supply of water so he could buy the plaintiff's land more cheaply.

In a letter to the author of the chapter on English law, I asked the author how these cases could be reconciled. She replied:

> In *Hollywood Silver Fox Farm Ltd* [1936], Macnaghten J distinguishes *Bradford* and follows *Christie*. He focuses, notably, on the words of North J in *Christie* v. *Davey* that 'If what has taken place had occurred between two sets of persons both perfectly innocent, I should have taken an entirely different view of the case. But I am persuaded that what was done by the defendant was done only for the purpose of annoyance, and in my opinion it was not a legitimate use of the defendant's house to use it for the purpose of vexing and annoying his neighbours' (326–327). Such reasoning proved particularly helpful on the facts of *Hollywood Silver Fox Farm Ltd* where the defendant was shooting on his own land and the use of the plaintiff company might have been described as extra-sensitive. On this basis, *Christie* is considered the authority to follow in English law.
>
> This leaves, of course, *Bradford*. [This is a case in which the defendant was held not to be liable even though he lowered the water table for the sole purpose of lowering the value of the defendant's land so he could buy it more cheaply.] You state that you do not see how it can be reconciled with *Christie*. One argument, however, favoured by some academics (see Giliker & Beckwith 10–012; Winfield & Jolowicz 14–012) is that the plaintiffs in *Bradford* had no right to receive the water, and therefore no legally protected right or interest had been interfered with on which to found the nuisance.
>
> The courts, in any event, in practice will find malice sufficient to convert a reasonable user into an unreasonable user. I have commented elsewhere that this brings a subjective factor into the question of 'reasonable user' in contrast to the other factors which concentrate on the impact of the defendant's conduct on the claimant's use and enjoyment of land.[61]

[58] [1893] 1 Ch 316. [59] [1936] 2 KB 468. [60] [1895] AC 587.
[61] Letter from Paula Giliker, 28 December 2006.

One can conclude, then, that the liability in English law for bothering one's neighbour is much like liability in Roman law for *iniuria*. Only the rules are in some respects less clear.

In England, as in Scotland, however, the story is complicated by a discussion of the role of fault. England had nothing like the Roman *lex Aquilia*. As Milsom and Fifoot have pointed out, traditionally, the common lawyers did not clearly distinguish fault-based and strict liability even in the case of physical damage.[62]

Traditionally, if the plaintiff sued for physical damage, one of the trespass actions, he did not need to allege fault. For example, he might simply allege that the defendant shot him or struck him. The defendant might then 'plead the general issue' by answering with the set phrase 'not guilty'. Or he might set up a defence by making a special plea, in effect, admitting the trespass and offering some justification. It is hard to tell whether either course of action would allow a defendant to escape liability if he was not at fault in the sense in which civil lawyers or modern common lawyers understand fault. Suppose, for example, that the defendant struck the plaintiff because his horse bolted, either because the horse was highly strung or because it was frightened by a flash of lightning or a third party or an animal. If the defendant pleaded 'not guilty', the jury was supposed to decide whether this allegation was true or false, originally, without instructions from the judge as to what to consider. It is hard to know what juries did.[63] They may have found for the defendant if they believed that the bolting of the horse that he was riding was really not something he did, that he was the passive instrument of forces of nature, a third party or the animal he was riding. Possibly, they did so if they believed that he had not committed a trespass or wrong, whatever that might have meant to them. In the trespass actions, the common law did not really have a rule in such cases but a procedure: let the jury decide.

The defendant's other alternative was to plead, in justification, that he was not at fault. It was not clear what would happen then. Defendants did so in only a few cases, and the remarks of the judges are confusing and seem contradictory. Some judges said that the defendant was not liable

[62] S. F. C. Milsom, *Historical Foundations of the Common Law*, 2nd edn (London, Butterworths, 1981), pp. 392–8; C. H. S. Fifoot, *History and Sources of the Common Law Tort and Contract* (London, Stevens, 1949), pp. 189, 191.

[63] S. F. C. Milsom, above, n. 62, p. 393.

if he had done his best,[64] some said that he was,[65] and some said he could escape liability if his conduct was the product of 'unavoidable necessity'.[66] It is hard to know what these statements meant to the judges who made them. They may not have been thinking in terms of a clear distinction between fault-based and strict liability. For example, in *Weaver* v. *Ward*, when a company of part-time soldiers were drilling with muskets, one soldier injured another because his musket accidentally went off. He pleaded that it was not his fault. The court said that he would be excused if he were 'utterly without fault', if the accident were 'inevitable' and if he 'had committed no negligence to give occasion to the hurt'.[67] As Fifoot said of this case, '"[f]ault," "inevitable accident," "negligence" are words used indiscriminately without reflection and almost without meaning'.[68]

On account of these uncertainties, the plaintiff might sue, not in a trespass action, but in trespass on the case and allege that the defendant acted negligently in his statement of the facts that supposedly called for relief. Sometimes, the plaintiff did so.[69] But even then, it is not clear what the allegation meant.[70] It might or might not mean negligence in the modern (or ancient Roman) sense. Certainly, judges did not instruct the jury to ask themselves whether the defendant had behaved like a reasonable person. In any event, the defendants also brought actions of trespass on the case without alleging negligence.[71]

[64] E.g., *The Thorns Case*, YB Mich. 6 Ed. 4, f. 7, pl. 18 (1466) (Choke, CJ: 'As to what has been said that they [thorns] fell *ipso invito* [on another's land], this is not a good plea; but he should have said that he could not do it in any other manner or that he did all that was in his power to keep them out'); *Millen* v. *Fandrye* (1626) Popham 161 (defendant excused because he has 'done his best endeavour'); *Wakeman* v. *Robinson* (1823) 1 Bing. 213 (Dallas, CJ: 'If the accident happened entirely without default on the part of the defendant or blame imputable to him, the action does not lie').

[65] *The Thorns Case*, YB Mich. 6 Ed. 4, f. 7, pl. 18 (1466) (Littleton, J: 'If a man suffers damage, it is right that he be recompensed'); *Bessey* v. *Olliot* (1682) Sir T. Raym, 421, 467 (Sir Thomas Raymond: 'in all civil acts the law doth not so much regard the intent of the actor as the loss and damage of the party suffering'); *Leame* v. *Bray* (1803) 3 East. 593 (Grose, J: 'if the injury be done by the act of the party himself at the time or he be the immediate cause of it, though it happen accidentally or by misfortune, yet he is answerable in trespass').

[66] *Dickenson* v. *Watson*, (1682) Sir T. Jones 205 (defendant who had shot the plaintiff and pleaded accident not excused 'for in trespass the defendant shall not be excused without unavoidable necessity').

[67] (1616) Hobart 134. [68] C. H. S. Fifoot, above, n. 62, p. 191.

[69] S. F. C. Milsom, above, n. 62, p. 394.

[70] Ibid. 399; A. I. Ogus, 'Vagaries in Liability for the Escape of Fire', (1969) 27 CLJ 104, pp. 105–6.

[71] S. F. C. Milsom, above n. 62, p. 394.

In the nineteenth century, the forms of action were abolished. The plaintiff could merely plead the facts that entitled him to recover without naming a certain form of action. Supposedly, the substantive law remained the same. Yet much of it changed. One change was the rise of what we now call an action in negligence. A first step was to hold that the plaintiff could not recover for bodily injuries which the defendant caused accidentally and without negligence. In England, it was not taken until 1891.[72]

Before that action had been clearly recognised, however, English courts had decided the famous case of *Rylands* v. *Fletcher* in a series of opinions reported between 1865 and 1868. The owner of a reservoir was held liable without fault when the water escaped and damaged his neighbour's property. Lord Blackburn had said 'the person who for his own purposes brings on his land and keeps there anything likely to do mischief if it escapes must keep it at his peril'. Lord Cairns, in the House of Lords, had spoken of 'non-natural user'. In the United States, and for a long time in England, that case was thought to mean that if one caused physical harm (as distinguished from merely disturbing one's neighbour's use of his property), although one was normally liable only for negligence, in certain exceptional cases, one was strictly liable. Americans said that one is liable in these exceptional cases for carrying on an 'ultrahazardous activity'.

As the chapter on English law describes, the proper interpretation of *Rylands* was a matter of sustained controversy. The American interpretation of the case was called into question by *Read* v. *J. Lyons & Co Ltd.*[73] The House of Lords held that an employee in a munitions factory could not recover when injured by an exploding shell because nothing had 'escaped' from the property. The American interpretation of the case was definitively rejected by the House of Lords in 1994, in *Cambridge Water Co* v. *Eastern Counties Leather plc.*[74] There it was said that *Rylands* did not create a general principle of strict liability for dangerous or non-natural activities which sometimes trumped the law of negligence. Rather, *Rylands* applied the law of nuisance, which was not based on fault, to 'isolated escapes' from land as opposed to ongoing escapes of noise, smoke, smells and the like.

In one respect, the English court was correct historically. The judges in *Rylands* could not have intended to create an exception to a general rule of liability for negligence which was not recognised until a quarter of a century later. Yet, in other instances, cases have been read to include more general principles that were not faced squarely by the judges who

[72] *Stanley* v. *Powell* [1891] 1 QB 86. [73] [1947] AC 156 (HL). [74] [1994] 2 AC 264.

decided them. The result of confining *Rylands* to what might well have been its historical context has been that the English now use the word 'nuisance' to cover two different situations: 'isolated escapes' and ongoing disturbances. As to the latter, as we have seen, their law is not much different than that of the ancient Romans. As to the former, they must distinguish isolated escapes 'from land', for which the plaintiff need not prove fault, from other physical harms caused by the defendant, for which he must.

All that need be noted here is that the problem is particularly English, and that it concerns liability, not merely for disturbing one's neighbours, but for physically harming them or anyone else. It is like the problem other jurisdictions face when they distinguish liability for negligence from strict liability. That problem goes beyond the scope of this volume. Yet the English story cannot be told because the problem of strict liability for 'isolated escapes' from land causing physical harm has been regarded as one of limiting liability for nuisance. That story is told in detail in the chapter on English law, but it has no parallel elsewhere.

1.4 Disturbances among neighbours in private law: conclusion

Legal development can mean making new institutions or reshaping old ones to meet new problems or to utilise new capabilities in solving old ones. As we will see next, that may be the case with zoning. But it does not seem to be the case with the private law that governs disturbances among neighbours.

Everywhere we have looked, we have found jurists addressing the same problems as the ancient Romans: what if someone disturbs another's use of his land simply in order to bother him? What if he does so as a by-product of his own use of his own land? How are these grounds of liability to be distinguished from liability based on negligence? The Romans allowed recovery on the first two grounds in an action of *iniuria*, and in the case of negligence, under the *lex Aquilia*, provided there had been physical damage to property. Admittedly, they were not so clear about when one is liable who disturbs one's neighbour but in pursuit of one's own interests and not simply to bother him. They simply gave an example: the proprietor of a cheese shop was liable to those bothered by the smoke. The medieval jurists suggested several solutions.

The doctrinal problem around which much of nineteenth-century legal development centred arose because fault in the sense of negligence was considered as a general basis of a tort action. The continental jurists inherited that problem from the late scholastics and natural lawyers. The English and French confronted it with the significance they first attributed to negligence in the nineteenth century.

Solutions were varied. In Germany and France, the problem was handled by rules that clearly separate liability for negligence from others from liability for disturbing a neighbour's use of his land. In the Netherlands, the problem has been complicated by an attempt to amalgamate the rules governing disturbance to a neighbour with those governing fault in damaging his property. In Spain, although jurists have had no trouble distinguishing these two different bases for liability, Spanish courts have had trouble making up their minds in what way negligence matters. In Scotland, after wavering and debate, it has been decided that negligence need not be shown in an action for disturbing one's neighbour without causing physical harm. The same can be said for England, except there the question has been confused by using the term 'nuisance' to cover 'isolated escapes' that occur without fault and cause physical harm and then trying to determine the boundary between liability for this sort of 'nuisance' and liability for physical harm caused by negligence.

Despite the doctrinal confusion and the differences in the formulations of rules, still, so far as one can tell, it is hard to see any real difference in practice among the liability imposed in the legal systems we have examined, or, for that matter, between these systems and the law of the Romans. One who deliberately interferes with his neighbour's property simply to hurt him is liable, despite some doubts raised in England. One who disturbs his neighbour otherwise is liable without proof of negligence in the normal sense, despite some confusion in the Netherlands, Spain and Scotland about the meaning of fault and the failure, in England, to distinguish clearly between disturbances of a neighbour's use of his property, and occasional escapes which count as nuisance but give rise to strict liability. The differences we have seen do not reflect divergent policies but rather a common source of doctrinal confusion.

Some of our authors have suggested that the growth of industry was in some way important to the development of modern private law governing disturbances among neighbours. Of course, that is true, if one means that, with the rise of industry, it became more likely that the noise, smoke or smells emanating from one person's property would disturb his neighbours. But that shows an old problem that arose more often and became a matter of far greater concern. It does not show that the increasing frequency of the problem affected the development of the law. One is more likely in the modern world to be bothered by a manufacturing plant than a cheese shop. But that does not change the ancient problem of when one who is bothered should have relief. As the chapter on Scots law puts it:

> Clearly, the need was felt for a doctrine such as nuisance. It may be assumed that this need was driven by the twin processes of industrialisation and urbanisation. There may be some doubt, however, concerning the relative extent to which industrialisation operated as a driving factor. While the emergence of nuisance is broadly contemporary with the earliest stages of industrialisation, its origin in burghs precedes the textile boom that may be taken to indicate full blown revolution.[75] Moreover, the subject matter of complaint in the earlier cases tended not to be new or large scale industrial operations, but traditional crafts: blacksmithing, bleaching and dying, tanning, skinning, glue-making, boiling of tripe or whale blubber and so on. Noxious trades could have been no innovation in an economy in which the processing of dead animals had long played such an important role.[76]

That, then, has been the problem. It is universal and ancient. It has nothing to do with industrialism and different national responses based on different policies.

If that is so, we have reached a conclusion of some significance. If the differences among modern legal systems could be explained by differences in policy, then it would seem appropriate to evaluate the merits of the policies. If they could be explained by differences in legal culture, then we might conclude that the differences are embedded in culture, and must remain as long as distinct national cultures remain intact. But if the differences are due to a common doctrinal problem – the role of negligence – and if this problem is common and doctrinal in that it represents the attempts of all jurists to make sense of the law of torts, despite the fact that their courts may be reaching the same results, then we have learned a great deal. We have learned that problems of importance to jurists may not affect the law in practice. We have learned that these problems may lie more in a search for intellectual consistency than for the proper result. We have learned that the search for intellectual consistency is much the same, although for historical reasons, it was presented in different ways in different countries.

[75] While precise dates have been set for the Industrial Revolution this is considered by some historians to be problematic. Industrialisation may be better seen in terms of a lengthy process.

[76] The export of hides had been a major element of Scottish trade for centuries; below, p. 137.

1.5 Public land use regulation

There is no doubt that ancient and medieval cities appointed boards and passed regulations to ban or relocate certain unsanitary enterprises. In 1810, as the chapter on French law points out, an Imperial decree required government permission to carry on an activity that was deemed dangerous, unhealthy or particularly likely to disturb one's neighbours.[77] As the chapter on Dutch law notes,[78] the Netherlands adopted the provisions of this decree in 1810. Spain did so in 1813. The chapters on Scots law[79] and English law[80] describe a spate of legislation, beginning in the early nineteenth century, that, again, was meant to suppress particularly obnoxious activities.

In the late nineteenth century, however, we find a new phenomenon: land use regulation which was comprehensive in that it covered almost any activity that might interfere with neighbours, and which, in its final form, was based on the division of an urban area in zones in which certain activities were permitted or forbidden. In some countries, this form of regulation was adopted by degrees, and in others, all at once. The chapter on German law describes a steady development of administrative control over land use beginning in the latter nineteenth century.[81] The Constitution of the German Reich, adopted 16 March 1871, explicitly allowed the member states the power to adopt land use and building laws which became the basis for a modern system of urban planning. In 1865, Prussia adopted a law regulating streets and setback lines.[82] Bavaria adopted building and land use laws in 1863 and 1864. One of the most influential laws was adopted by Saxony in 1900.[83] In 1875, the Netherlands enacted the Industrial Nuisance Act (*Hinderwet*) of 1875.[84] As the chapter on Dutch law notes, this Act was changed many times before it was finally absorbed by the Environmental Management Act of 1993 (*Wet Milieubeheer*).[85] But 'the Industrial Nuisance Act and its successors created a preventive system' in which '[a]ctivities that could

[77] Below, p. 75. [78] Below, p. 124. [79] Below, pp. 167–169. [80] Below, pp. 52–53.

[81] Below, pp. 94–95.

[82] Gesetz betreffend der Anlegung und Veränderung von Strassen und Plätzen in Städten und ländlichen Ortschaften.

[83] Das Allgemeine Baugesetz für das Königreich Sachsen. For a history of the development of German land law see E. Zinkahn 'Introduction: Die Entwicklung der Baugesetzgebung', *Kommentar zur Bundesbaugesetz 1* (1986).

[84] Law of 2 June 1875, Stb. 95.

[85] See for this Act F. C. M. A. Michiels, *De wet milieubeheer* (Deventer, Kluwer, 2003). Licences required under various other laws were integrated in the Environmental Management Act as well: see Lindenbergh (looseleaf), titel 5.4, aant. 14.

cause nuisance had to apply for a licence'.[86] France did not enact a law providing for comprehensive land use regulation and zoning until the law 'Cornudet' of 14 March 1910 which required towns of over 10,000 inhabitants to approve plans of urban development.[87] It was modelled on Dutch, English and Swiss law.[88] In Spain, public land use regulation is governed by a law enacted in 1961 (Regulation for Annoying, Unhealthy, Harmful and Dangerous Activities). Yet, as the chapter on Spanish law notes, 'this law was a consolidated version of a patchwork of municipal ordinances. From the viewpoint of the material content, there was nothing new in the 1961 Regulation.'[89] As the chapter on the law of Scotland points out, '[p]lanning in the modern sense originated in 1909 with the Housing and Town Planning Act of that year. This and subsequent Acts empowered local authorities to draw up plans for land that was likely to be developed.'[90] As the chapter on English law points out, '[p]lanning legislation from the Housing, Town Planning etc Act 1909 onwards has sought to regulate potential land disputes by means of planning control. Prior to this date, there had been very limited intervention beyond legislation targeted at specific activities such as those endangering public health.'[91]

In short, in the late nineteenth and early twentieth centuries, the private law of nuisance and a public law directed at particularly dangerous, interfering or unhealthy activities was supplemented by a series of statutes which, however much they varied, had one thing in common: comprehensive public law which comprehensively regulated the permissible uses of land by zoning plans.

There are two plausible causes. One is that, with increasing urbanisation, problems of land use had become more complex. It was not simply a matter of the offending pigsty. It was a matter of fine-tuning the private law of disturbances among neighbours so that one could set clear limits to how high one could build, what activities in which neighbourhoods would be impermissibly disturbing, how much one must set back one's building from one's boundary. It was a more precise regulation of what counted as a disturbance.

The other feature was the emergence of states with the institutional power to enact policies which would then govern municipalities. By the late nineteenth century, the regulatory state was emerging throughout Europe.

[86] Below, p. 126, 5.13.
[87] P. Soler-Couteaux, *Droit d'urbanisme*, 3rd edn (Paris, Dalloz, 2000) n. 8.
[88] J. Morand-Deviller, *Droit d'urbanisme*, 6th edn (Paris, Dalloz 2003), p.4.
[89] Below, p. 200. [90] Below, p. 168. [91] Below, p. 54.

We can see, however, that this legislation, all enacted in the late nineteenth century and early twentieth century throughout Europe, was not a cultural phenomenon determined by the ideas or mores of particular states. We can also see its utility. It gave private law a fine-tuning that was needed in an age when more and more people lived in close proximity. The emerging regulatory states had the power to give the law that fine-tuning and to do so comprehensively.

So, in the end, we see a common story. The older part of it, dealt with by the private law of disturbances among neighbours, concerned problems that existed ever since people lived in proximity. In the nineteenth century, while this law became economically tmore significant, there was little change in the law itself except as a result of attempts, more or less successful, to resolve doctrinal problems inherited from the past or confronted for the first time. The newer part of the story was the resolution of more complex problems of living together that came with large-scale urbanisation. They required a more sophisticated approach than traditional private law could give, and that approach was made possible by the rise of regulatory institutions that could provide it. In both cases, it is a common and only incidentally a national story.

2

Relationships between neighbours: England and Wales 1850–2000

PAULA GILIKER

2.1 Introduction

The period 1850–2000 represents a time of great economic and social change in England and Wales. The Industrial Revolution, which began in the eighteenth century, and during 1760–1830 was largely confined to Britain, marked significant changes in both the living and working conditions of the population of Britain. It was inevitable that the existing mechanisms of tort law would be called upon to deal with harm consequential on such changes, but this period also marks the development of new forms of intervention, for example the rule in *Rylands* v. *Fletcher*,[1] and, in particular, statutory intervention, at first in the context of public health legislation. Traditionally, landowners had been able to use land in any way they wished, subject to the terms of the grant and common law regulation by means of nuisance or trespass. By the latter part of the nineteenth century, significant public health legislation such as the Public Health Acts 1848 and 1875[2] and the Nuisances Removal Acts 1855 and 1860 signified a movement towards greater state-based regulation.[3] Statute, however, was not solely protective, and private Acts of Parliament have been used to authorise developments regardless of the nuisance caused.

Nevertheless, a movement in tort law towards fault-based reasoning in the late nineteenth century may be identified. This received considerable impetus from the House of Lords judgment in *Donoghue* v. *Stevenson* in 1932[4] which laid the foundations for the modern tort of negligence. The increasing dominance of negligence in the English law of tort has inevitably

[1] (1865) 3 H & C 774 (Court of Exchequer); (1866) 1 LR 1 Ex 265 (Court of Exchequer Chamber); (1868) LR 3 HL 330 (House of Lords).

[2] An Act for consolidating and amending the Acts relating to Public Health in England.

[3] Note also Housing, Town Planning etc. Act 1909 (giving local authorities wide powers to build new houses and clear substantial housing) which was the first of many pieces of planning legislation (see below, p. 54).

[4] [1932] AC 562.

had an impact on other torts. One sees also a growing recognition of the social impact of industrialisation. McLaren, examining nineteenth-century nuisance cases, finds inconsistency in the courts' approaches, reflecting a divergence of views on the appropriate way of ordering society in general and the economy in particular.[5] Should exploitation of land be seen as a positive benefit to the community or a negative source of pollution and misery? The failure of nuisance to respond to the abuses of the Industrial Revolution is well documented,[6] notably in relation to claims for personal discomfort. Nevertheless, the central notion of 'reasonable user' was used as a means of providing the courts with flexibility, permitting consideration of a number of circumstantial factors in reaching its decisions.

This paper will examine developments in the law of tort in comparison with the parallel growth of regulation in determining the duties of neighbouring landholders to each other. In tort, the emphasis will be on the growth of fault-based liability in what has traditionally been regarded as an area of strict liability. This will be contrasted with legislative provisions which provide alternative means of recourse, and a general overview will be given of the impact of planning legislation. Finally, this paper will consider the role of the defence of statutory authority in permitting common law nuisances and the resultant priority given to progress above that of individual discomfort.

It is worthwhile stating at this stage, however, that the topic of relations between neighbours continues to be controversial in English law. In particular, one might question to what extent it is a private matter (resolved through individual litigation) or a public matter best dealt with by the legislature. Opinions continue to diverge and, as will be seen, the differing responses will additionally raise concerns of access to justice. One matter is, however, clear. Unless substantial discomfort and injury are caused, it will be risky to pursue the culprit, and the more serious the physical injury, the more likely a claim is to succeed.

The Human Rights Act 1998 will not be discussed in this paper. This came into force on 2 October 2000 (and hence outside the period of this

[5] J. P. S. McLaren, 'Nuisance law and the industrial revolution – Some lessons from social history', (1983) 3 OJLS 155 at 190. See also J. F. Brenner, 'Nuisance law and the industrial revolution', (1974) 3 JLS 403, who, at 415, alleges that 'strict nuisance liability would apply to John Doe down the street, but Doe Manufacturing Co Ltd would be judged by a more lenient rule'.

[6] McLaren *loc. cit.*; Brenner *loc. cit.*; A. W. B. Simpson, *Leading Cases in the Common Law* (Oxford, OUP, 1995) ch 7.

study) and its true impact has yet to be discerned in tort law, although it has already made some mark in determining privacy rights.[7] It may be noted, however, that this will provide a fresh influence on the development of these torts in future years.[8]

2.2 Remedies in tort

2.2.1 Private nuisance, trespass and the rule in Rylands *v.* Fletcher

Private nuisance, together with trespass, provides the primary tortious basis for protecting landholders from interference with their land by their neighbours. As a tort it can be traced back to the thirteenth century and derives from the Assize of Nuisance, a real property action supplementary to the Assize of *novel disseisin*, which sought to vindicate the claimant's right to the use and enjoyment of his land.[9] Although the action was initially confined to freeholders of land, it became available to other occupiers of land when the action on the case for nuisance superseded the earlier Assize of Nuisance.[10] Its foundations therefore lie in the protection of land interests and extend, as recognised by Lord Lloyd in the leading case of *Hunter* v. *Canary Wharf Ltd*, to three kinds of private nuisance: 'They are (1) nuisance by encroachment on a neighbour's land; (2) nuisance by direct physical injury to a neighbour's land; and (3) nuisance by interference with a neighbour's quiet enjoyment of his land.'[11] It will thus cover interference by tangible and intangible things, although the courts tend to treat tangible interference as more serious and therefore are more likely to find an actionable nuisance.[12] This will extend to interference with rights over land, including natural rights. All three forms seek to protect the claimant's use and enjoyment of land from an activity or state of affairs for which the

[7] *Douglas* v. *Hello! Ltd* [2001] 2 WLR 992, *Campbell* v. *Mirror Group Newspapers* [2004] 2 AC 457, but see *Wainwright* v. *Home Office* [2004] 2 AC 406.

[8] See *McKenna* v. *British Aluminium Ltd* [2002] Env. LR 30, *Dennis* v. *Ministry of Defence* [2003] Env. LR 34 and *Marcic* v. *Thames Water Utilities Ltd* [2004] 2 AC 42.

[9] See Lord Wright in *Sedleigh-Denfield* v. *O'Callaghan* [1940] AC 880, pp. 902–3.

[10] See D. J. Ibbetson, *A Historical Introduction to the Law of Obligations* (Oxford, OUP, 1999), p. 98; J.S. Loengard, 'The assize of nuisance: Origins of an action at common law', (1978) 37 CLJ 144; P. H. Winfield, 'Nuisance as a tort' (1930–2) 4 CLJ 189; F. H. Newark, 'The boundaries of nuisance' (1949) 65 LQR 480.

[11] [1997] AC 677, p. 695.

[12] See *St Helen's Smelting Co* v. *Tipping* (1865) 11 HLC 642.

defendant is responsible.[13] The House of Lords in *Hunter* v. *Canary Wharf Ltd*,[14] by a majority, confirmed the proprietary roots of private nuisance.

Trespass seeks to protect the claimant against direct and unjustifiable interference with his or her possession of land. It is 'essentially a wrong against possession, not against ownership'.[15] It may be defined as 'any unjustifiable intrusion by one person upon land in the possession of another'.[16] Interference with the land must be direct, immediate and intentional. It is no excuse that the act of entry was not intended to amount to a trespass. Provided one's actions are voluntary, one is deemed a trespasser irrespective of one's knowledge of trespass or not,[17] although the courts will not impose liability where one has been forcibly thrown or pushed onto the land.[18] Even if invited onto land, one must remain within the scope of the invitation and any act in excess of this will be deemed a trespass.[19] The tort is actionable per se. This is a historical legacy which remains, although a claimant is likely to receive only nominal damages without proof of loss. In relation to neighbours, it provides a useful function in determining boundaries to land (although claimants may alternatively seek a declaratory judgment), whilst also dealing with persistent trespassers by means of injunctive relief.

Both torts, thus, have traditionally imposed liability irrespective of fault. Trespass has been seen as a wrong without any question of negligence.[20] It is no defence to plead that the trespass occurred by mistake and even necessity provides only a limited defence. As Lord Denning MR commented in *Southwark LBC* v. *Williams*,[21] 'The doctrine so enunciated must, however, be carefully circumscribed. Else necessity would open the door to many an excuse.'[22] The voluntary act of the defendant will

[13] See the classic definition of private nuisance of Professor Winfield: 'unlawful interference with a person's use or enjoyment of land, or some right over, or in connection, with it': W. V. H. Rogers, *Winfield & Jolowicz on Torts*, 17th edn (Sweet and Maxwell, 2006) at 14–04: P. H. Winfield, 'Nuisance as a tort' (1930–2) 4 CLJ 189 at 190.

[14] [1997] AC 677. [15] *Simpson* v. *Fergus* (2000) 79 P & CR 398 at 401 *per* Robert Walker LJ.

[16] *Clerk & Lindsell on Torts*, 19th edn (Sweet and Maxwell, 2006), para. 19–01.

[17] *Conway* v. *George Wimpey & Co. Ltd* [1951] 2 KB 266 at 273–4; *Jolliffe* v. *Willmett & Co* [1971] 1 All ER 478.

[18] *Smith* v. *Stone* (1647) Style 65; 82 ER 533.

[19] As Scrutton LJ remarks in *The Calgarth* [1927] P 93 at 110: 'When you invite a person into your house to use the staircase, you do not invite him to slide down the banisters.'

[20] See Viscount Simon in *Read* v. *Lyons* [1947] AC 156 at 166. See also Coleridge CJ in *Ellis* v. *Loftus Iron Co* (1874) LR 10 CP 10 at 12.

[21] [1971] 1 Ch 734 at 743.

[22] The defence will thus only be available to an individual in cases of emergency where the individual is responding to immediate and serious danger to life or property in a manner which is reasonable in the circumstances. It will be especially difficult

therefore provide the intention to act and negligence is no excuse. On this basis, my entry onto your land will amount to a trespass even though I negligently believed that I had a right of way. The question of fault can, therefore, only arise as a distinct issue in relation to involuntary trespass when the defendant did not intend to enter the claimant's land, but was driven off course. Despite dicta that such claims should be brought in negligence,[23] it would seem that the courts have contemplated the use of trespass and thereby present litigants with the distinct advantage of not having to prove damage or establish a duty of care. For example, in *League against Cruel Sports* v. *Scott*,[24] staghounds had strayed onto the claimants' land during a hunt. Park J indicated that the owner of animals which enter onto his neighbour's land will be responsible for the damage they cause if he or she intended them to enter the claimant's land or, knowing that there was a real risk that they would enter, failed to take reasonable care to prevent their entry. Here, fault liability responds to the need to control animals by placing a more onerous duty on the owner. There is evidence, however, that if land adjoining the highway is unintentionally entered, for example following a road accident, the claimant must establish negligence on the defendant's part. Lord Blackburn in *River Wear Commissioners* v. *Adamson*[25] expressed the view that such property is liable to be subject to trespass by traffic on the highway and so the owner must bear his own losses unless he can establish that the other is at fault, be it intentionally or negligently. It may be questioned, however, whether, like other highway cases, it would be better classified as negligence rather than trespass in modern times.

There is, additionally, clear authority that negligence is not a necessary condition for a claim in private nuisance. The courts will examine the effect of the interference on the claimant and it is irrelevant whether the defendant had taken reasonable steps to prevent the nuisance or had been

to establish this defence where, as in *Monsanto plc* v. *Tilly* [2000] Env. LR 313, there exists a public authority responsible for the protection of the relevant interests of the public.

[23] *Letang* v. *Cooper* [1965] 1 QB 232 (albeit *obiter* in that the case concerned trespass to the person). See G. Dworkin, 'Trespass and negligence – A further attempt to bury the forms of action' (1965) 28 MLR 92.

[24] [1986] QB 240. See also the Animals Act 1971 which deals with liability of owners of animals which stray onto a neighbour's land, ss. 2 and 4 (trespassing livestock).

[25] (1876–7) LR 2 App. Cas. 743 at 767. See also *Fletcher* v. *Rylands* (1866) LR 1 Ex. 265 at 286 and *Esso Petroleum Co Ltd* v. *Southport Corp* [1956] AC 218 at 244–5 *per* Lord Tucker (HL), [1953] 3 WLR 773 at 778 *per* Devlin J (QBD). It was applied in *Gayler & Pope Ltd* v. *B Davies & Son Ltd* [1924] 2 KB 75.

acting in good faith. In the leading case of *Rapier* v. *London Tramways Co*,[26] a tramway company had built some large blocks of stables about forty-two yards[27] from the plaintiff's detached house and pleasure-grounds for the horses they used to draw the trams. The resulting smell of 200 horses can be imagined and the stables had capacity for some 440. The Court of Appeal held that it was no defence that they had taken all reasonable care to prevent it. Further, the court was not prepared to accept the economic arguments in favour of economy of scale:

> If the Defendants are right in saying that they cannot concentrate their stables to such an extent as is desirable without committing a nuisance to the neighbourhood, then they must not concentrate their horses to such an extent. It is a mere question of money; it is nothing but economy which requires them to crowd their horses together. In their attempt to economise, I think they have gone too far. If they cannot have 200 horses together, even when they take proper precautions, without committing a nuisance, all I can say is, they cannot have so many horses together. No doubt it is a serious matter to them; but I cannot bring my mind to say that I disagree with the learned Judge who tried the case in the Court below.[28]

The maxim is *sic utere tuo ut alienum non laedas* (use your own in a way that does not harm another's).[29] The courts will focus on the impact to the claimant's proprietary rights, not on judging the conduct of the defendant[30] or the economic rationale in favour of the interference. If the defendant's actions are therefore not considered 'reasonable', the defendant will be liable, even if he is able to show that he exercised reasonable care and skill to avoid any interference to the claimant's use and enjoyment of land.[31] It is a 'rule of give and take, live and let live'.[32] In *Bliss* v. *Hall*,[33] therefore, the fact that the defendant's business in the manufacture of candles

[26] [1893] 2 Ch 588. See also *Moss* v. *Christchurch Rural DC* [1925] 2 KB 750.

[27] About 38 metres.

[28] Lindley LJ above note 26 at 602, Bowen and Kay LJJ concurring.

[29] Although this has been criticised as lacking clarity and accuracy: see Lord Wright in *Sedleigh-Denfield* v. *O'Callaghan* [1940] AC 880 at 903.

[30] The use of malice is, of course, inconsistent with this framework (see criticism, Giliker, *Tort*, 2nd edn (London, Sweet and Maxwell, 2005), p. 285) and serves to illustrate the courts' inability to adhere to this rigid distinction in practice.

[31] See Lord Goff in *Cambridge Water Co* v. *Eastern Counties Leather Plc* [1994] 2 AC 264 at 299. Note also Lord Simonds in *Read* v. *J. Lyons & Co Ltd* [1947] AC 156 at 183: 'negligence is not a necessary ingredient in the case. For if a man commits a legal nuisance it is no answer to his injured neighbour that he took the utmost care not to commit it. There the liability is strict.'

[32] Bramwell B in *Bamford* v. *Turnley* (1862) 3 B & S 62 at 84.

[33] (1838) 4 Bing. NC 183, 132 ER 758.

(a noisy and odorous enterprise) had been operating for three years before the plaintiff moved next door was considered irrelevant. The plaintiff came to the land with all the rights which the common law affords and, in particular, the right to wholesome air.[34] The English courts' approach is therefore piecemeal.

Each case will turn on its facts, subject to guidance from previous caselaw which indicates that factors such as the nature of the locality,[35] the duration[36] and frequency[37] of the defendant's conduct and any malice[38] on his or her part will be considered relevant. Although there is some mixed authority as to the relevance of malice,[39] Macnaghten J in *Hollywood Silver Fox Farm Ltd* v. *Emmett*[40] favoured the approach in *Christie* v. *Davey* and, indeed, relied upon the words of North J in that case: 'If what has taken place had occurred between two sets of persons both perfectly innocent, I should have taken an entirely different view of the case. But I am persuaded that what was done by the defendant was done only for the purpose of annoyance, and in my opinion it was not a legitimate use of the defendant's house to use it for the purpose of vexing and annoying his neighbours.'[41] Such reasoning proved particularly helpful on the facts of *Hollywood Silver Fox Farm Ltd* where the defendant was shooting on his

[34] See Tindal CJ 4 Bing. NC 186. See also *Walter* v. *Selfe* (1851) 20 LJ Ch 433 (the fact that the defendant was making and burning bricks using his own soil in a manner common and useful did not justify the resultant air pollution).

[35] See Thesiger LJ in *Sturges* v. *Bridgman*: 'What would be a nuisance in Belgrave Square would not necessarily be so in Bermondsey': (1879) 11 Ch D 852 at 865. See also Veale J in *Halsey* v. *Esso Petroleum* [1961] 1 WLR 683 and *Miller* v. *Jackson* [1977] QB 966 at 986. Note, however, that this is not considered relevant where there is physical damage to neighbouring land: *St Helen's Smelting Co* v. *Tipping* (1865) 11 HLC 642.

[36] *Harrison* v. *Southwark and Vauxhall Water Co* [1891] 2 Ch 409.

[37] See Lawton J in *British Celanese* v. *AH Hunt Ltd* [1969] 1 WLR 959 at 969: 'Most nuisances do arise from a long continuing condition; and many isolated happenings do not constitute a nuisance. It is, however, clear from the authorities that an isolated happening by itself can create an actionable nuisance.'

[38] *Christie* v. *Davey* [1893] 1 Ch 316.

[39] Contrast *Bradford (Mayor of)* v. *Pickles* [1895] AC 587 to that of *Christie* v. *Davey* (above), where the House of Lords disregarded the fact that the defendant had drained his own land to diminish plaintiff's supply of water so he could buy plaintiff's land more cheaply. Lord Halsbury LC stated at 594: 'This is not a case in which the state of mind of the person doing the act can affect the right to do it. If it was a lawful act, however ill the motive might be, he had a right to do it. If it was an unlawful act, however good his motive might be, he would have no right to do it. Motives and intentions in such a question as is now before your Lordships seem to me to be absolutely irrelevant.' *Christie* was not cited in this case.

[40] [1936] 2 KB 468.

[41] *Christie* v. *Davey* [1893] 1 Ch 316, 326–7.

own land and the use of the plaintiff company might have been described as extra-sensitive.[42]

The courts are also wary of claims based on abnormal sensitivity on the part of the claimant. In *Robinson* v. *Kilvert*,[43] for example, the defendant operated a business in the lower part of a building, which required hot and dry air. As a result, the temperature of the floor of the plaintiff's premises above rose to 80°F,[44] which diminished the value of the brown paper stored there. The heat was not such as to affect ordinary paper or to cause discomfort to the plaintiff's workforce. The Court of Appeal refused to award the plaintiff damages. He had undertaken an exceptionally delicate trade and had not shown an actionable nuisance. Private nuisance will therefore not impose unduly onerous burdens on neighbours due to the sensitivity of the other. This would tip the balance unfairly in the claimant's direction. However, if the claimant can show that the defendant's conduct would have amounted to an unreasonable user in any event, then he or she may recover the full extent of his or her losses, even where they result from interference with an exceptionally delicate use of the land.[45]

A further form of protection appeared in 1865. The rule in *Rylands* v. *Fletcher*[46] derives from a case reported between 1865 and 1868 and therefore at the very start of the period of this study. Here, the courts approved strict liability on a millowner, who had employed independent contractors to build a reservoir on his land to provide water for his mill. During the course of building, the independent contractors discovered some old shafts and passages of an abandoned coal mine on the defendant's land, which appeared to be blocked. When the reservoir was filled, the water burst through the old shafts, which were subsequently found to connect with the plaintiff's mine. As a result, the plaintiff's mine was flooded and he sought compensation.

42 *Bradford Corp* v. *Pickles* [1895] AC 587 has been distinguished on the basis that the plaintiffs in *Bradford* had no right to receive the water, and therefore no legally protected right or interest had been interfered with on which to found the nuisance: see P. Giliker and S. Beckwith, *Tort*, 2nd edn (London, Sweet and Maxwell, 2004), pp. 10–012, W. V. H. Rogers, *Winfield and Jolowicz on Tort*, 17th edn (London, Sweet and Maxwell, 2006) at 14–012.

43 (1889) 41 Ch D 88. See also *Heath* v. *Mayor of Brighton* (1908) 98 LT 718.

44 Approximately 27°C.

45 *McKinnon Industries Ltd* v. *Walker* [1951] 3 DLR 577 at 581, PC.

46 (1865) 3 H & C 774 (Court of Exchequer); (1866) 1 LR 1 Ex 265 (Court of Exchequer Chamber); (1868) LR 3 HL 330 (House of Lords).

The case was finally resolved at House of Lords level, but the classic statement of principle was given by Blackburn J in the Court of Exchequer Chamber:

> We think that the true rule of law is that the person who for his own purposes brings on his lands and collects and keeps there anything likely to do mischief if it escapes, must keep it in at his peril, and, if he does not do so, is *prima facie* answerable for all the damage which is the natural consequence of its escape. He can excuse himself by shewing that the escape was owing to the plaintiff's default; or perhaps that the escape was the consequence of *vis major*, or the act of God; but as nothing of this sort exists here, it is unnecessary to inquire what excuse would be sufficient.[47]

This was approved by the House of Lords, although Lord Cairns used the term 'non-natural user' in explaining the principle.

It may be questioned, however, to what extent the courts have succeeded in divorcing fault and other external factors from their reasoning. Whilst the test of 'reasonable user' in nuisance has traditionally been distinguished from that of reasonable care, this does not prevent the courts from moving gradually towards a form of fault-based liability. Equally, the rule in *Rylands* v. *Fletcher* has been confined by subsequent caselaw, nervous of the extent of the strict liability rule. The defence of *vis major* or the unlawful act of a stranger was immediately used to limit liability where the escape was due to the unforeseeable act of a stranger over whom the defendant had no control.[48] The defendant will therefore not be liable if the escape is due to unforeseeable vandalism or unusual natural events – in fact, the most common reason for escapes. Lindley LJ in *Green* v. *Chelsea Waterworks Co*[49] noted in the late nineteenth century that the principle 'is not to be extended beyond the legitimate principle on which the House of Lords decided it. If it were extended as far as strict logic might require, it would be a very oppressive decision.' In *Sedleigh-Denfield* v. *O'Callaghan*,[50] the rule was rejected due to the fact that it required some special use of property bringing increased danger to others and did not therefore apply to ordinary uses of land.[51] The House in *Read* v. *J. Lyons & Co Ltd*[52] went further. In this case, an inspector of munitions had been injured by the explosion of a shell whilst inspecting the defendants' munitions factory.

47 (1866) LR 1 Ex 265 at 279–80; affirmed in (1886) LR 3 HL 330, HL.

48 See *Box* v. *Jubb* (1879) 4 Ex D 76 on similar facts to *Rylands*. See also *Rickards* v. *Lothian* [1913] AC 263, *Perry* v. *Kendricks Transport Ltd* [1956] 1 WLR 85.

49 (1894) 70 LT 547 at 549. 50 *Infra*, p. 39.

51 See Viscount Maugham [1940] AC at 888, relying on *Rickards* v. *Lothian* [1913] AC 263.

52 [1947] AC 156.

Their Lordships held that there had not been an 'escape' within the rule. An escape would only occur when the object moved from the defendant's premises to a place which was outside his occupation or control. Yet the decision is more than an application of the rule. The effect of the House confining the tort to injury caused by an escape from land under the control of the defendant was to prevent any further development of the tort and, indeed, the House went so far as to suggest that it should be limited to injuries to land and should not provide damages for personal injury.[53] It is therefore a rule regulating the mutual obligations of neighbours and not, as the first instance judge suggested, a strict liability rule for ultra-hazardous activities. In reaching this decision, the House indicated the exceptional nature of the rule.

2.2.2 The movement towards fault-based liability

Examination of this area of law demonstrates the increasing influence of negligence and distrust of strict liability rules from the nineteenth century onwards. As Friedmann recognised in 1943, 'the tort of nuisance demonstrates, in a particularly complex manner, the difficulties created by the grafting of modern conceptions of negligence on older actions'.[54] Indeed, as tort theory relies increasingly on fault-based justifications for liability, it becomes more and more difficult to continue to apply rules of strict liability. These questions continue to trouble lawyers today and go to the heart of one's conception of tort law itself. Professor Weinrib, for example, has argued that in seeking to balance the interests of interacting property owners, the courts are setting a 'common standard', consistent with the principle of corrective justice.[55] Whilst this may be questioned, the courts do appear reluctant at times to impose liability in excess of that demanded in the tort of negligence and seek evidence of fault before imposing liability.

An increasing body of case law can be identified which seeks to integrate fault-based concerns into traditional nuisance analysis. Such case law comes to the fore following Lord Atkin's judgment in *Donoghue* v. *Stevenson*, although the history of nuisance and negligence has long been intertwined.[56] Lord Atkin, in defining an obligation to one's neighbour

[53] See Lord Macmillan ibid. at 173.

[54] W. Friedmann, 'Incidence of liability in nuisance' (1943) 59 LQR 63, p. 63.

[55] E. Weinrib, *The Idea of Private Law* (Harvard University Press, 1995), p. 7.4.3.

[56] See P. H. Winfield, 'The history of negligence in the law of torts' (1926) 42 LQR 184, pp. 190 and 198.

beyond the protection of proprietary or possessory rights,[57] forced the courts to view the term 'neighbour' in a broader sense. If one owes one's metaphorical neighbour a duty of care, should this not also be applied to one's physical neighbour? Strict liability becomes difficult to justify when one's duties are seen in terms of fault.

The leading cases illustrating the use of fault-based reasoning in private nuisance and the rule in *Rylands* v. *Fletcher* are *Sedleigh-Denfield* v. *O'Callaghan*,[58] *The Wagon Mound (No. 2)*[59] and *Cambridge Water Co* v. *Eastern Counties Leather plc.*[60] In the first case, fault serves to extend liability, but in the second and third, it confines liability to the extent permissible in negligence. In all, however, negligence is used as a point of reference in determining the extent of liability.

2.2.2.1 Sedleigh-Denfield *v.* O'Callaghan *(Sedleigh-Denfield)*[61]

Here, a local authority, without the defendants' permission (and therefore as a trespasser), had placed a drainage pipe in a ditch on the defendants' land with a grating designed to keep out leaves. The grating had not been fixed in the correct position, with the result that, during a heavy rainstorm, the pipe became choked with leaves and water overflowed onto the plaintiff's land. The House of Lords held the defendants liable. They had adopted the nuisance by using the drain for their own purposes to drain water from their land. They had also continued the nuisance because their manager should have realised the risk of flooding created by the obstruction and taken reasonable steps to abate it.

The use of fault-based reasoning in this judgment is of considerable interest. A number of significant factors may be identified. Eight years had passed since *Donoghue* v. *Stevenson*[62] and the changing attitudes reflected in Lord Atkin's judgment in that case are clearly influential in the court's reasoning.[63] Lord Wright states:

> The liability for a nuisance is not, at least in modern law, a strict or absolute liability. If the defendant by himself or those for whom he is responsible has

[57] *Donoghue* v. *Stevenson* [1932] AC 562 at 580: 'The rule that you are to love your neighbour becomes in law, you must not injure your neighbour; and the lawyer's question, Who is my neighbour? receives a restricted reply. You must take reasonable care to avoid acts or omissions which you can reasonably foresee would be likely to injure your neighbour.'

[58] [1940] AC 880.

[59] (*Overseas Tankship (UK) Ltd* v. *Miller Steamship Co Pty Ltd)* [1967] 1 AC 617.

[60] [1994] 2 AC 264. [61] [1940] AC 880. [62] [1932] AC 562.

[63] As recognised by Megaw LJ in *Leakey* v. *National Trust* [1980] QB 485 at 515.

> created what constitutes a nuisance and if it causes damage, the difficulty now being considered does not arise. But he may have taken over the nuisance, ready made as it were, when he acquired the property, or the nuisance may be due to a latent defect or to the act of a trespasser, or stranger. Then he is not liable unless he continued or adopted the nuisance … This rule seems to be in accordance with good sense and convenience. The responsibility which attaches to the occupier because he has possession and control of the property cannot logically be limited to the mere creation of the nuisance. It should extend to his conduct if, with knowledge, he leaves the nuisance on his land.[64]

Liability is imposed not on the creator of the nuisance, but a third party – here the occupier of the land – and is justified by fault on his part. The House was not willing to impose liability merely by virtue of his occupation, but equally would not accept the Court of Appeal view that an occupier should not be liable for a mere failure to act and should only have a duty to permit the defendant access to his land to abate the nuisance.[65] The wider jurisprudence of public nuisance was also relied upon.[66] 'Fault' justifies an extension of liability and results in a rule of good sense and convenience in which the person best placed to deal with the nuisance has a clear incentive to do so. Control over land thus results in responsibility.[67] English pragmatism meets the prevalent 'fault' justification for liability.

This rule has since been extended to nuisances caused by natural events, such as a tree set on fire by lightning[68] or a mound rendered unstable due to extreme weather conditions.[69] Megaw LJ in *Leakey* v. *National Trust for Places of Historic Interest or Natural Beauty*[70] held that

[64] [1940] AC at 904–5. See also Lord Atkin himself, p. 897: 'The occupier or owner is not an insurer; there must be something more than the mere harm done to the neighbour's property to make the party responsible.'

[65] Rejecting the view of Bankes LJ in *Job Edwards* v. *Birmingham Navigations Proprietors* [1924] 1 KB 341.

[66] See *Attorney-General* v. *Tod-Heatley* [1897] 1 Ch 560 and *Barker* v. *Herbert* [1911] 2 KB 633. The law remains the same in public and private nuisance: *R* v. *Shorrock* [1994] QB 279.

[67] See Shaw LJ in *Leakey* v. *National Trust* [1980] QB 485 at 528; Lord Goff in *Smith* v. *Littlewoods* [1987] AC 241, p. 279.

[68] *Goldman* v. *Hargrave* [1967] 1 AC 645, PC.

[69] *Leakey* v. *National Trust* [1980] QB 485. See also *Green* v. *Lord Somerleyton* [2004] 1 P & CR 33, CA (duty to take reasonable steps to prevent flooding from natural flow of water) and a number of cases involving subsidence due to root encroachment from neighbouring land: *Russell* v. *Barnet* (1984) 271 EG 699, *Solloway* v. *Hampshire CC* (1981) 258 EG 858, CA and *Delaware Mansions Ltd* v. *Westminster City Council* [2002] 1 AC 321.

[70] [1980] QB at 524.

it would be a 'grievous blot on the law' if the law did not impose liability on the defendants in such circumstances, although Shaw LJ expressed substantial misgivings in imposing a further burden on landowners to deal with natural phenomena arising without any human intervention.[71] In *Page Motors Ltd* v. *Epsom and Ewell BC*,[72] this line of authority was applied where a local authority was found liable to the plaintiffs for failing to take reasonable steps to evict gypsies from its land when their activities had been harming the plaintiffs' businesses. Such reasoning was further applied in the 1999 case of *Lippiatt* v. *South Gloucestershire CC*.[73] Here, the local authority was found liable for travellers who had caused a nuisance in nearby farmland and whom the local authority had failed to evict within a reasonable time. Despite the fact that the local authority had clearly not authorised such conduct, it was found liable to the local farmers on the basis that it had permitted use of its land as a 'launching pad' for repeated acts of trespass to the claimants' land.

The nature of such liability is discussed in more detail in the Privy Council decision in *Goldman* v. *Hargrave* and by the Court of Appeal in *Leakey* v. *National Trust*. The standard of care is not the objective standard of care applied in negligence,[74] but rather a subjective one:

> The law must take account of the fact that the occupier on whom the duty is cast has, *ex hypothesi*, had this hazard thrust upon him through no seeking or fault of his own … [W]here the hazard could have been removed with little effort and no expenditure, no problem arises. But other cases may not be so simple. In such situations the standard ought to be to require of the occupier what it is reasonable to expect of him in his individual circumstances. Thus, less must be expected of the infirm than of the able-bodied: the owner of a small property where a hazard arises which threatens a neighbour with substantial interests should not have to do so much as one with larger interests of his own at stake and greater resources to protect them.[75]

Megaw LJ in *Leakey* confirms the application of this test to English law: 'The defendant's duty is to do that which it is reasonable for him to do. The criteria of reasonableness include, in respect of a duty of this nature, the factor of what the particular man – not the average man – can be expected

71 Ibid., 527. 72 (1982) 80 LGR 337.

73 [2000] QB 51, using the public nuisance case of *Attorney-General* v. *Corke* [1933] Ch. 89 to justify recovery and distinguishing *Hussain* v. *Lancaster CC* [2000] QB 1, CA.

74 *Blyth* v. *Birmingham Waterworks Co* (1856) 11 Exch 781; 156 ER 1047.

75 Lord Wilberforce [1967] 1 AC at 663.

to do.'[76] This is an important limitation. In *Goldman*, the costs would have been minimal – throwing buckets of water over a smouldering tree – and intervention would have prevented extensive damage by bush fire to neighbouring farms, of particular importance in Western Australia where the case originated. Equally, in *Leakey*, the Court of Appeal believed that the National Trust, a large organisation, should have intervened to prevent subsidence of a hill. More recently, however, the Court of Appeal rejected a claim that a local authority should protect a cliff-top hotel from a massive landslip which caused part of the hotel and grounds to collapse into the sea and the hotel to be demolished. Such losses were unforeseeable and the resources of the local authority were not unlimited.[77] In taking account of the fact that liability is 'thrust upon him',[78] the law will only require what is reasonable in the individual circumstances of the occupier.

It is thus possible to distinguish this duty of care from that of negligence, although some judges have expressed doubts as to the need for this distinction. In *Goldman* itself, Lord Wilberforce remarked that 'the present case is one where liability, if it exists, rests upon negligence and nothing else; whether it falls within or overlaps the boundaries of nuisance is a question of classification which need not here be resolved'.[79] Nevertheless, Megaw LJ in the subsequent case of *Leakey* v. *National Trust*[80] described the claim as one in nuisance, although it was not regarded as a matter of importance.

A further distinction may be drawn. *Sedleigh-Denfield* imposes liability on an occupier for his or her omission to act. Negligence remains reluctant to impose liability for omissions save where the defendant has assumed responsibility for a risk, for example by assuming responsibility for the security of a neighbour's land,[81] or for controlling the actions

76 [1980] QB at 526.

77 See *Holbeck Hall Hotel Ltd* v. *Scarborough BC (No 2)* [2000] QB 836, discussed further below, p. 43.

78 *Goldman* above, note 68, p. 663.

79 [1967] 1 AC 645 at 657. See also Lord Goff in *Smith* v. *Littlewoods* [1987] AC 241, 274: 'in *Goldman* v. *Hargrave*, such liability was held to sound in nuisance; but it is difficult to believe that, in this respect, there can be any material distinction between liability in nuisance and liability in negligence' and Lord Cooke in *Delaware Mansions* v. *Westminster CC* [2002] 1 AC 321, 333: 'The label nuisance or negligence is treated as of no real significance. In this field, I think, the concern of the common law lies in working out the fair and just content and incidents of a neighbour's duty rather than affixing a label and inferring the extent of the duty from it.'

80 [1980] QB 485 at 514.

81 *Stansbie* v. *Troman* [1948] 2 KB 48.

of a trespassing third party.[82] The most we can perhaps say is that it is 'negligence-like' liability – a variant of negligence liability adapted to meet the pragmatic concern of who should deal with a nuisance created by another on their land. The more esoteric questions of how this affects the strict liability character of nuisance have been neglected by all save academics.[83]

2.2.2.2 The Wagon Mound (No. 2)

This case gives perhaps the most obvious indication of the influence of negligence. The Privy Council, in finding the same rule of remoteness to apply to negligence, private and public nuisance, draws all three torts together. Lord Reid in *The Wagon Mound (No. 2)* was of the opinion that foreseeability must be an essential element in determining liability in both types of nuisance: 'It would not be right to discriminate between different cases of nuisance.'[84] To reach such a conclusion, his Lordship placed considerable emphasis on the clear influence of fault in public nuisance cases – notably in the obstruction to the highway cases – and in *Sedleigh-Denfield*. If foreseeability of damage was relevant in these cases, consistency would require it to be a necessary element of all types of nuisance. One might question this chain of reasoning. As seen above, *Sedleigh-Denfield* can be distinguished from the ordinary case of a private nuisance created by the defendant. Further, even if fault is a relevant factor in determining liability, it does not necessarily apply to the scope of damages awarded.[85] The case could also be distinguished in that it is a public nuisance case. Nevertheless, Lord Goff in *Cambridge Water* confirmed that the advice of the Privy Council has been taken to apply to private nuisance generally and gave his approval to this condition of liability.[86] On this basis, liability will only arise in all forms of nuisance if the harm suffered is of a kind which is reasonably foreseeable.

82 *Home Office* v. *Dorset Yacht Co Ltd* [1970] AC 1004. See, generally, *Smith* v. *Littlewoods* [1987] AC 241.

83 See, notably, C. Gearty, 'The place of private nuisance in a modern law of torts' (1989) 48 CLJ 214; R. J. Buxton, 'The negligent nuisance' (1966) 8 Malaya L. Rev. 1; J. M. Eekelaar, 'Nuisance and strict liability' (1973) 8 Ir. Jur. (N.S.) 191; and M. Lee, 'What is private nuisance?' (2003) 119 LQR 298.

84 *The Wagon Mound (No. 2)* [1967] 1 AC 617 at 640.

85 See R. W. M. Dias, 'Trouble on oiled water: Problems of the *Wagon Mound (No. 2)*', [1967] CLJ 62.

86 [1994] 2 AC 264 at 300.

2.2.2.3 Cambridge Water Co *v.* Eastern Counties Leather plc *(Cambridge Water)*[87]

In this case, subsequently confirmed by the House of Lords in *Transco plc* v. *Stockport MBC*,[88] Lord Goff assessed the role of *Rylands* v. *Fletcher* at a time when environmental concerns were largely dealt with by statute. In retaining the tort, his Lordship sought to identify its scope and concluded that it was, in reality, a form of private nuisance relating to isolated escapes from land.[89] As such, the principle of 'reasonable user' could be compared to the idea of non-natural use and, significantly for the case, the fault-based test of remoteness for private nuisance – reasonable foresight of the kind of harm suffered – would also apply to the rule.

Whilst *Cambridge Water* accepted the influence of fault-based reasoning on the rule, the House in *Transco* went further. Their Lordships concluded that the rule in *Rylands* v. *Fletcher* would serve only a residuary role in modern society where statutes and regulations now largely covered the area of dangerous escapes; for example, the discharge of water is now regulated by s. 209 of the Water Industry Act 1991.[90] The rule would be confined to exceptional circumstances where the occupier has brought some dangerous thing onto his land which poses an exceptionally high risk to neighbouring property should it escape, and which amounts to an extraordinary and unusual use of land. Lord Hoffmann is particularly scathing of its role in modern law: 'It is perhaps not surprising that counsel could not find a reported case since the Second World War in which anyone had succeeded in a claim under the rule. It is hard to escape the conclusion that the intellectual effort devoted to the rule by judges and writers over many years has brought forth a mouse.'[91]

2.2.3 *An assessment of fault*

Although the English courts have not gone as far as the Australian courts in absorbing the rule in *Rylands* v. *Fletcher* into the tort of negligence,[92] it is clear that its potential has not been recognised. The dominance of negligence has led the courts to favour the imposition of strict liability obligations by means of legislation rather than judicial intervention. Lord Goff

[87] [1994] 2 AC 264. [88] [2004] 2 AC 1.

[89] [1994] 2 AC at 306: 'It would moreover lead to a more coherent body of common law principles if the rule were to be regarded essentially as an extension of the law of nuisance to cases of isolated escapes from land.'

[90] See also s. 73(6), the Environmental Protection Act 1990 (pollution by escape of waste) and s. 7, the Nuclear Installations Act 1965 (radioactive matter).

[91] [2004] 1 AC at 19. [92] See *Burnie Port Authority* v. *General Jones Pty* (1994) 179 CLR 520.

in *Cambridge Water* observes that 'if such liability is imposed by statute, the relevant activities can be identified, and those concerned can know where they stand. Furthermore, statute can where appropriate lay down precise criteria establishing the incidence and scope of such liability.'[93] In reducing the scope of the tort and superimposing the restrictions of private nuisance in terms of who can sue and the scope of recovery on the tort, it is clear that this head of liability will rarely succeed. Indeed, as in *Cambridge Water*, it is normally pleaded in conjunction with private nuisance and negligence – the claimants pursuing the rule in *Rylands* v. *Fletcher* in the higher courts when it was clear that the other two claims would fail. In rejecting strict liability in this context in favour of state intervention, the courts recognise the dominance of negligence-based liability, but also the fact that hazardous escapes are now seen as a social problem to be regulated by Parliament rather than a matter to be resolved between private parties.

There is considerable authority which recognises the impact of negligence-based liability on the tort of private nuisance. Whilst fault is accepted as determinative of liability for landholders who do not create the nuisance in question and implicitly recognised in relation to remoteness, one notes increasing reference to the fact that, although private nuisance need not be created negligently,[94] this will often be the case. It remains a matter of debate to what extent fault has impacted on the tort of private nuisance generally.[95] Such discussion may appear at odds with the majority view of the House of Lords in *Hunter* v. *Canary Wharf* in 1997[96] that the tort of private nuisance is a tort to land. On this basis, only those with rights to land may sue. Any party wishing to sue for personal injury or without such a right must frame their claim in negligence. By restating the limited scope of private nuisance, their Lordships sought to distinguish nuisance from the tort of negligence, in terms of goals, objectives and standing to sue. This has received considerable criticism for its failure

[93] [1994] 2 AC at 305. This is followed in *Transco*: see Lords Bingham and Hoffmann respectively above, pp. 9 and 20.

[94] See *Rapier* v. *London Tramways Co* [1893] 2 Ch 588.

[95] Professor Conor Gearty, in C. Gearty, 'The place of private nuisance in a modern law of tort' (1989) 48 CLJ 214, has argued for a distinction between physical and non-physical damage, with the former to be dealt with in negligence, and only the latter brought in private nuisance as a distinctive strict liability tort. Maria Lee has concluded that 'private nuisance is a vulnerable tort: vulnerable to negligence but mainly vulnerable to its own uncertainty and unpredictability': 'What is private nuisance?' (2003) 119 LQR 298, 325.

[96] [1997] AC 677.

to adapt the tort to modern social conditions.[97] Lord Cooke, dissenting in *Hunter* v. *Canary Wharf*, more recently maintained his view that 'the concepts of reasonableness between neighbours (real or figurative) and reasonable foreseeability … underlie much modern tort law and, more particularly, the law of nuisance'.[98] *Hunter*, however, stands in the way of any greater degree of assimilation. In view of challenges brought under the Human Rights Act 1998,[99] one must wonder whether *Hunter* can continue to withstand the onward march of negligence and retain the individual identity of this tort.

2.2.4 Interference with natural rights in land and public nuisance

The courts' approach towards interference with natural rights in land has, until recently, been to exclude fault-based reasoning.[100] Such rights arise by virtue of ownership of land and do not require a legal grant.[101] Withdrawal of lateral support of the adjoining owner's land will give rise to an action for damages.[102] Although interference with a particular proprietary right, such as a right of way, is generally treated by analogy to trespass, in that provided a substantial degree of interference can be shown, the tort will be actionable per se,[103] where the right in question is simply a right to support, damage must be shown.[104] A form of strict or no-fault liability is thereby imposed on the neighbour[105] or independent

97 See Lord Cooke dissenting in *Hunter* v. *Canary Wharf*, above; J. Wightman, 'Nuisance – the environmental tort? *Hunter* v. *Canary Wharf* in the House of Lords' (1998) 61 MLR 870.

98 In his last House of Lords opinion in *Delaware Mansions Ltd* v. *Westminster City Council* [2002] 1 AC 321 at 332.

99 *McKenna* v. *British Aluminium Ltd* [2002] Env. LR 30.

100 See *Humphries* v. *Brogden* (1850) 12 QB 739, 116 ER 1048; *Backhouse* v. *Bonomi* (1861) 9 HL Cas 503, [1861–73] All ER Rep 424, *Darley Main Colliery Co* v. *Mitchell* (1886) 11 App Cas 127, J. F. Garner, 'Rights of support', (1948) 12 Conv (NS) 280.

101 Such rights extend to a right to be supported by subjacent strata of minerals (removal of underground salt: *Lotus Ltd* v. *British Soda Co Ltd* [1972] Ch. 123) and any adjacent bed of wet sand or running silt (*Stephens* v. *Anglian Water Authority* [1987] 1 WLR 1381 at 1384–5). This is also a natural right of support to strata of the subsoil, e.g. the support of gas pipes (*Newcastle-under-Lyme Corp* v. *Wolstanton Ltd* [1947] Ch. 92). This section will not deal with the natural right to water which is outside the scope of this study.

102 Or possibly injunctive relief, see *Redland Bricks Ltd* v. *Morris* [1970] AC 652.

103 *Nicholls* v. *Ely Beet Sugar Factory Ltd* [1936] 1 Ch. 343.

104 *Midland Bank* v. *Bardgrove Property Services* [1992] 37 EG 126.

105 It is no excuse that the work has actually been undertaken by subcontractors where the work requested will in the natural course of things give rise to damage: *Bower* v. *Peate* (1876) 1 QBD 321, pp. 326–7.

contractor, although, as shown in the leading case of *Dalton* v. *Henry Angus & Co*,[106] it is confined to lateral support for land. It does not include a right to support for a building on that land, which may only be acquired by means of the express or implied grant of an easement or an easement acquired by prescription.[107] In the words of Lord Penzance, 'it is the law, I believe I may say without question, that at any time within twenty years after the house is built, the owner of the adjacent soil may with perfect legality dig that soil away, and allow his neighbour's house, if supported by it, to fall in ruins to the ground'.[108] The only exception is where the land subsides due to loss of support and the claimant suffers consequential damage to a building on the land, provided that the weight of the building did not cause or contribute to the subsidence.[109] Such claims, often based on subsidence due to mining or excavation works on a neighbour's land in preparation for a new building development, were an obvious consequence of the Industrial Revolution. In more recent times, and in the light of mass urban development, the distinction between the right of support to land, and buildings built upon it, has been subject to considerable criticism.[110] It has been described recently as 'a petrified remnant of an outdated social policy that does not benefit from sound logical foundations'.[111] Indeed, it is hard to see why a building, being a fixture on land, should not also benefit from this rule.

It continues to be accepted that such interference will give rise to strict liability in nuisance regardless of fault. In *Ray* v. *Fairway Motors (Barnstaple) Ltd*,[112] the Court of Appeal considered whether the rise of negligence in the twentieth century would support a claim based on the failure of the neighbour to take reasonable care in undertaking works which might undermine the property, but rejected this possibility: 'I doubt whether the impact of *Donoghue* v. *Stevenson* is sufficient to have reversed the law in that regard.'[113]

106 (1880–1) LR 6 App Cas 740, HL.

107 See E. H. Bodkin, 'Rights of support for buildings and flats' (1962) 26 Conv (NS) 210.

108 (1880–1) LR 6 App Cas 740, p. 804.

109 *Brown* v. *Robins* (1859) 4 H & N 186, 157 ER 809; *Stoyan* v. *Knowles* (1861) 6 H & N 454, 158 ER 186; *Public Trustee* v. *Hermann* [1968] 3 NSWR 94, 109.

110 See K. and S. F. Gray, *Elements of Land Law* (OUP, 2005), pp. 33–5; T. H. Wu, 'The right of lateral support of buildings from the adjoining land', [2002] Conv 237, who relates the perhaps unsurprising Singaporean rejection of this principle in *Xpress Print Pte Ltd* v. *Monocrafts Pte Ltd* [2000] 3 SLR 545.

111 Wu above, note 110, p. 247.

112 (1968) 20 P & CR 261.

113 Russell LJ *ibid.*, p. 272. Fenton Atkinson LJ *ibid.* at 275 did, however, suggest that liability might arise if the claimant could show something beyond the mere removal of soil or a failure to take steps to prevent its effect, for example, by the adoption of an

However, fault has recently been found to be relevant where the claim is based on the failure of a neighbour to intervene to *prevent* loss of support. While liability will arise where the neighbour removes the support, merely sitting back and allowing part of his building to deteriorate, which he knows will provide support for his neighbour, did not in the past give rise to liability.[114] However, in *Holbeck Hall Hotel Ltd* v. *Scarborough BC*,[115] the Court of Appeal was prepared to impose a 'measured' duty in private nuisance on the landowner to intervene where he knew or should have known of the defect or condition on his land which might rise to the danger of subsidence. Here, the claimants owned a hotel at the top of a cliff; the local authority owning the undercliff between the hotel grounds and the sea. Following landslips in 1982 and 1986, some remedial works had been carried out, but no one had predicted a massive landslip in 1993 which caused a loss of support to the hotel grounds and part of the hotel, with the result that the entire hotel had to be demolished. The Court rejected the claim against the local authority. The 'measured' duty of care, identified in *Goldman* v. *Hargrave*[116] and applied in *Leakey* v. *National Trust*,[117] would apply, regardless of the fact that these two cases involved dangers escaping from the defendant's land rather than the natural erosion of land. However, the landslip had been far more extensive than anyone save a geological expert could have foreseen and the cost of abatement would have been large. The authority was therefore under no duty other than to warn the claimants of any risks they appreciated at that time.

Commentators have suggested that this duty may not be as onerous as it seems.[118] Where the losses are extensive, the means of the defendant will be taken into account and it would seem that a sympathetic account is taken of the limits of local authority funds. Insurers in general will still be left to bear the burden of such disasters.

In contrast, public nuisance readily accepts the relevance of fault. As a tort and crime, public nuisance serves to regulate conduct affecting the

unnecessarily dangerous method of removal causing collapse. This does not seem to have been followed. The approach of the Court of Appeal was approved in *Midland Bank plc* v. *Bardgrove Property Services Ltd* [1991] 2 EGLR 283.

114 *Bond* v. *Nottingham Corporation* [1940] Ch 429, 438 *per* Lord Greene MR.

115 [2000] QB 836. See M. P. Thompson, 'Coastal erosion and collapsing hotels' [2001] Conv 177, C. A. Hopkins, 'Slipping into uncertainty' (2000) 59 CLJ 438 and J. Wightman, 'Liability for landslips: Should landowners be responsible for the consequences of erosion?' [2000] Env LR 285. See also *Bradburn* v. *Lindsay* [1983] 2 All ER 408 (failure to take reasonable steps to support party wall).

116 [1967] 1 AC 645, PC. 117 [1980] QB 485. 118 See M. P. Thompson, [2001] Conv 177.

public at large.[119] By its very nature, this is a tort which does not focus on disputes between individual neighbours, but on wider social problems. Indeed, in recent years, public nuisance has been used by local authorities to deal with anti-social behaviour on housing estates.[120] In its classic formulation in *Attorney-General* v. *PYA Quarries*, 'any nuisance is "public" which materially affects the reasonable comfort and convenience of life of a class of Her Majesty's subjects'.[121] Individual claimants must show special damage to bring a civil action[122] or rely on the Attorney-General or, more usually, a local authority to bring a claim.[123] Buckley identifies two types of public nuisance: those which overlap with private nuisance but affect a much larger group of people, and those which do not but involve interference with the public generally, for example obstruction of the highway.[124] Notably, in cases involving Buckley's second category, fault seems to be necessary,[125] although there is not consensus on this fact.[126] In the highway cases, there is a clear overlap with negligence-based reasoning and a sense that negligence would logically be the best tort to deal with all such analogous claims. Similar difficulties have arisen in defining the nature of liability for dangerous objects projecting onto the highway.[127] Lord Denning MR attempted a compromise in *Southport Corp* v. *Esso Petroleum Co. Ltd*[128] by suggesting that for public nuisance, unlike negligence, once the nuisance was proved, the legal burden would fall on the defendant to prove that it occurred without his fault. This would serve to keep the torts logically distinct, but as the House of Lords on appeal did not deal with this matter, the view of Lord Denning MR is not authoritative. The courts therefore still experience difficulty in separating the question of whether there is a nuisance (i.e. an unreasonable obstruction of the highway) from the question of fault.

[119] See J. Spencer, 'Public nuisance – a critical examination' (1989) 48 CLJ 55.

[120] *Nottingham City Council* v. *Zain* [2002] 1 WLR 607, CA.

[121] [1957] 2 QB 169 at 184 *per* Romer LJ.

[122] See G. Kodilinye, 'Public nuisance and particular damage in the modern law' (1986) 2 LS 182.

[123] Under section 222 of the Local Government Act 1972.

[124] R. A. Buckley, *The Law of Nuisance*, 2nd edn (Edinburgh, Butterworths, 1996) ch 4.

[125] See Lord Reid in *The Wagon Mound (No 2) (Overseas Tankships (UK) Ltd* v. *Miller Steamship Co Pty)* [1967] 1 AC 617.

[126] *Dymond* v. *Pearce* [1972] 1 All ER 1142.

[127] *Tarry* v. *Ashton* (1876) 1 QBD 314 and *Wringe* v. *Cohen* [1940] 1 KB 229 suggest strict liability, whilst *Barker* v. *Herbert* [1911] 2 KB 633 and *Noble* v. *Harrison* [1926] 2 KB 332 favour fault-based liability. The general view now seems to favour fault-based liability: see Buckley *op. cit.*, p. 84.

[128] [1954] 2 QB 182 at 197.

Fault may thus be seen to play an increasing role in relation to private law remedies in the law of tort. Individual litigants may seek an injunction or damages from the defendant. Injunctions as an equitable remedy remain, however, at the discretion of the court. The courts are generally willing to grant an injunction, unless there are circumstances which indicate that damages are seen as the most appropriate remedy.[129] There is authority, however, that where the injunction would curtail an activity of benefit to the public, the courts will be reluctant to grant an injunction or will at least confine the remedy to an injunction on terms.[130]

Liability is, however, dependent on proof of damage[131] and will require each litigant to fund his or her own particular claim. The courts are increasingly conscious of the role of the legislature and local planning authorities in providing alternative remedies for the benefit of local residents.

2.3 Statutory regulation of nuisances and planning law

2.3.1 Statutory protection

It is important to recognise that a number of statutory provisions serve to protect the rights of neighbours. Statutory nuisances provide a very useful means whereby individuals can complain to their local authority about grievances affecting their enjoyment of their land. As Bell and McGillivray explain, 'the law of statutory nuisance represents a bridge between the private law of nuisance and the more characteristic

[129] See section 50 of the Supreme Court Act 1981 and *Shelfer* v. *City of London Electric Lighting Co* [1895] 1 Ch 287. It is important to understand the nature of the court's decision to give damages in lieu of an injunction, which permits a court to grant damages in full satisfaction of all damage (past and future): see *Jaggard* v. *Sawyer* [1995] 1 WLR 269. As Rogers (above, n. 42) acknowledges at 22–053, 'This is, in effect, to allow the defendant to purchase the right to commit a tort in the future.' Such damages will only, however, be given in the very exceptional circumstances outlined in *Shelfer*: see A.L. Smith LJ in that case at 322–3: 'whether the case be for a mandatory injunction or to restrain a continuing nuisance, the appropriate remedy may be damages in lieu of an injunction, assuming a case for an injunction to be made out. In my opinion, it may be stated as a good working rule that: (1) If the injury to the plaintiff's legal rights is small, (2) And is one which is capable of being estimated in money, (3) And is one which can be adequately compensated by a small money payment, (4) And the case is one in which it would be oppressive to the defendant to grant an injunction: then damages in substitution for an injunction may be given.' See also J. A. Jolowicz, 'Damages in Equity: A study of Lord Cairns' Act' [1975] CLJ 224.

[130] See *Miller* v. *Jackson* [1977] QB 966 and *Kennaway* v. *Thompson* [1981] AC 88.

[131] Save for trespass which is actionable per se.

statutory mechanisms'.[132] The best example in modern law is Part III of the Environment Act 1990, but the concept may be traced back to the Industrial Revolution.[133] Reforming social legislation in the nineteenth century sought to address public health problems[134] and the influence of this early legislation continued in the Public Health Act 1936 to the 1990 Act today. Part III deals with nuisances which are or are likely to be prejudicial to a person's health or interfere with their legitimate use and enjoyment of land. The list of 'statutory nuisances' in s. 79 is broad, and includes: (a) run-down premises; (b) smoke; (c) fumes or gases; (e) accumulations or deposits on one's land; and (g) noise.[135]

Statutory nuisances provide a remedy for individual claimants and possess a number of advantages above their common law counterparts. The claimant will usually ask a local authority to intervene, thereby avoiding the costs and burden of private litigation. The Act provides a special summary procedure for dealing with such nuisances by means of Abatement Notices.[136] Failure to comply with the Notice is a criminal offence. Section 80(4) provides that 'if a person on whom an abatement notice is served, without reasonable excuse, contravenes or fails to comply with any requirement or prohibition imposed by the notice, he shall be guilty of an offence'.[137] It is clear that the defendant bears the evidential burden to establish a 'reasonable excuse' and that the courts give very limited scope to this provision when the point should have been the subject of an appeal.[138] Such a mixture of administration and criminal law has little in common with the law of tort, but seeks to provide an efficient

[132] S. Bell and D. McGillivray, *Environmental Law*, 6th edn (Oxford, OUP, 2006), p. 404.

[133] See, generally, R. Malcolm and J. Ponting, *Statutory Nuisance: Law and Practice* (Oxford, OUP, 2002). See also the Clean Air Act 1993 and the Noise Act 1996.

[134] See Public Health Act 1848 and 1875 and Nuisances Removal Acts 1855 and 1860.

[135] See F. McManus, 'Noise law in the United Kingdom – a very British solution?' (2000) 20 LS 264.

[136] Section 80 (summary proceedings for statutory nuisances). Breach is unlikely to give rise to an action for compensation for breach of statutory duty: see *Hackney LBC* v. *Issa* [1997] 1 WLR 956.

[137] Section 80(5) provides that 'except in a case falling within subsection (6) below, a person who commits an offence under subsection (4) above shall be liable on summary conviction to a fine not exceeding level 5 on the standard scale together with a further fine of an amount equal to one-tenth of that level for each day on which the offence continues after the conviction'. Section 80(6): 'A person who commits an offence under subsection (4) above on industrial, trade or business premises shall be liable on summary conviction to a fine not exceeding £20,000.'

[138] See *Wellingborough BC* v. *Gordon* [1993] Env. LR 218; *A Lambert Flat Management Ltd* v. *Lomas* [1981] 2 All ER 280; *Butuyuyu* v. *London Borough of Hammersmith and Fulham* [1997] Env. LR D13; Malcolm and Ponting *op. cit.*, p. 265.

means of dealing with social problems. Courts may order the abatement of the nuisance and impose a fine, and a criminal court has some powers to award compensation.[139] Individuals may also instigate summary proceedings under s. 82 of the Act, and these will usually be brought against local authorities for failures, for example in their provision of housing.[140]

Use of statutory provisions to deal with specific social problems is common. In their text *Environmental Law*, Bell and McGillivray outline eleven areas of sectoral coverage ranging from statutory nuisance to legislation dealing with waste management, air pollution and water pollution. The history of waste management demonstrates the evolution of protection in English law: whilst there were no real problems prior to 1848, from 1848 the first real controls were introduced to safeguard health in the Public Health Act 1848, extended under the Public Health Acts 1875 and 1936. Planning restrictions were imposed by the Town and Country Planning Act 1947, and the first comprehensive system for regulating waste disposal by means of a licensing regime was introduced by the Control of Pollution Act 1974. Waste management is now governed by Part II of the Environmental Protection Act 1990 (as amended). The impact of EC Directives should also be noted from 1975 onwards.[141] Similarly, while control of pollution may be dated back to 1273 in London, legislation again appears on a regular basis post-1850 with the Alkali Act 1863,[142] the Sanitary Act 1866, the Public Health Act 1875 (as amended and extended), the Clean Air Acts 1956, 1968 and 1993, the Environmental Protection Act 1990 and the Environment Act 1995, together with a number of EC Directives and international conventions. Such examples illustrate the clear move towards legislative regulation of

[139] See Powers of the Criminal Courts (Sentencing) Act 2000, ss. 130–4.

[140] 'If the magistrates' court or, in Scotland, the sheriff is satisfied that the alleged nuisance exists, or that although abated it is likely to recur on the same premises ... the court or the sheriff shall make an order for either or both of the following purposes:
(a) requiring the defendant or, in Scotland, defender to abate the nuisance, within a time specified in the order, and to execute any works necessary for that purpose;
(b) prohibiting a recurrence of the nuisance, and requiring the defendant or defender, within a time specified in the order, to execute any works necessary to prevent the recurrence;
and, in England and Wales, may also impose on the defendant a fine not exceeding level 5 on the standard scale': section 82(2). Note also s. 82(12) [compensation for expenses properly incurred in the proceedings].

[141] See also the Waste Framework Directive (75/442) and Directive 91/156.

[142] Consolidated in the Alkali etc Works Regulations Act 1906. See B. Pontin, 'Tort law and Victorian government growth: the historiographical significance of tort in the shadow of chemical pollution and factory safety regulation' (1998) 18 OJLS 661.

health and pollution problems which gathers pace during the period of this study.

Further measures exist on a more localised level. The Noise Act 1996, for example, deals with the particular problem of noise emitted from dwellings at night. Section 4 provides that it is an offence where the noise exceeds the permitted level after service of a warning notice.[143] The Anti-social Behaviour Act 2003 Part 8[144] deals with disputes between neighbours over the height of a boundary hedge by means of remedial notices supported by criminal penalties.[145] The Party Wall etc Act 1996 additionally enhances the rights of owners of party walls, giving them the right to make good or repair a party structure or wall where the work is necessary due to a defect or want of repair,[146] and to require support when the neighbour is undertaking excavation work near the adjoining property.[147] There is also some statutory provision for loss of support. In certain cases of subsidence, the Coal Mining Subsidence Act 1991 renders the British Coal Corporation liable to take remedial action or to compensate for depreciation of property.[148]

Statute here is used as a form of 'macro-regulation'. Here, the focus is not on individual grievances, but larger social issues such as environmental

[143] 'A person guilty of an offence under this section is liable on summary conviction to a fine not exceeding level 3 on the standard scale': section 4(3). See section 4(2): 'It is a defence for a person charged with an offence under this section to show that there was a reasonable excuse for the act, default or sufferance in question.'

[144] It covers complaints which are made by an owner or occupier of a domestic property and which alleges that his reasonable enjoyment of that property is being adversely affected by the height of a high hedge situated on land owned or occupied by another person: section 65.

[145] Namely, a fine not exceeding level 3 on the standard scale (section 75) with the possibility under section 77 of entry by a person authorised by the relevant authority to take the required action.

[146] Section 2.

[147] Section 6 deals with adjacent excavation and construction where a building owner proposes to excavate within a distance of three metres from any part of a building or structure of an adjoining owner; and any part of the proposed excavation, building or structure will within those three metres extend to a lower level than the level of the bottom of the foundations of the building or structure of the adjoining owner: section 6(1). See also 6(2). In such circumstances, the building owner may, and if required by the adjoining owner shall, at his own expense underpin or otherwise strengthen or safeguard the foundations of the building or structure of the adjoining owner so far as may be necessary: section 6(3). Section 7(2) also provides that 'the building owner shall compensate any adjoining owner and any adjoining occupier for any loss or damage which may result to any of them by reason of any work executed in pursuance of this Act'.

[148] See sections 2 and 11, *Langley* v. *Coal Authority (No 2)* [2003] EWCA Civ 204, [2005] RVR 11; *McAreavey* v. *Coal Authority* (2000) 80 P & CR 41.

pollution,[149] flooding[150] and the control of hazardous waste.[151] Such regulation, which must be interpreted in the light of relevant EC law and international conventions, adopts a broader view of neighbourhood rights and signifies a movement from private to state regulation.

2.3.2 *Planning law*

The importance of planning law represents a further step towards regulatory control of the relations between neighbours. Its role in the tort of nuisance is tangential. Whilst a grant of planning permission is not a defence, it may, if it changes the nature of the locality, serve to render the defendant's interference with the claimant's rights 'reasonable'.[152] However, it does form a background to private law remedies, as recognised in *Hunter* v. *Canary Wharf* where Lord Goff notes that 'if a large building is proposed in a neighbouring area, it will usually be open to local people to raise the possibility of television interference with the local planning authority at the stage of the application for planning permission'.[153] Planning law thus seeks to control the development of land and imposes a limit on the landowner's traditional freedom to build as he or she wishes.

Planning legislation from the Housing, Town Planning etc Act 1909 onwards has sought to regulate potential land disputes by means of planning control. Prior to this date, there had been very limited intervention, although one does see the roots of modern legislation in the Public Health Act 1848 and the Nuisance Removal and Disease Prevention Act 1848 which were implemented in response to serious outbreaks of cholera and typhoid in the 1830s and 1840s.[154] Although the focus of such legislation

[149] See, for example, the Pollution Prevention and Control Act 1999, the Environmental Protection Act 1990 and the Nuclear Installations Act 1965.

[150] For example, the Water Industry Act 1991.

[151] See the Planning (Hazardous Substances) Act 1990.

[152] See *Gillingham Borough Council* v. *Medway (Chatham) Dock Co Ltd* [1993] QB 343 and *Wheeler* v. *JJ Saunders Ltd* [1996] Ch 19.

[153] Above at 686–7, although he also notes the limitations of regulation by planning permission: 'It has, however, to be recognised that the problem may well not be appreciated until after the building is built, when it will be too late for any such representations to be made. Moreover in the present case, in which the Secretary of State had designated the relevant area as an enterprise zone with the effect that planning permission was deemed to have been granted for any form of development, no application for permission had to be made.'

[154] See also the Nuisances Removal Act 1855, the Sanitary Act 1886, the Artisans' and Labourers' Act 1868, the Artisans' and Labourers' Dwelling Improvement Acts 1875 and 1890, and the Public Health Act 1875.

was public health, the model of using local boards or authorities to regulate the building of houses continues to this day. One must also recognise the importance of local Acts of Parliament during this period which were obtained by local municipalities by petitioning Parliament. As Duxbury states, 'These local Acts were of special significance in that they paved the way for the great Public Health Act 1875. This consolidated the earlier public general Acts and gave national application to provisions previously found only in local Acts. Local authorities were given power not only to secure proper standards of drainage and closet accommodation, but also to make bye-laws regulating the size of rooms, the space about the houses and the width of the street in front of them; provision was also made for the making up and sewering of unadopted streets at the expense of the frontages.' [155]

The foundations for modern planning law may be found, however, in the Town and Country Planning Act 1947. This repealed all previous law[156] and established a system of land use control. It was followed by a succession of statutes up to the much-amended Town and Country Planning Act 1990 ('TCPA 1990').[157] The key features are (a) regulation by means of local administration, and (b) the preparation of local development plans for each designated area. The result is that, in most cases, an application for planning permission will be necessary for any new development of land.[158] As Lord Hoffmann comments in *Hunter*, 'The

[155] R. M. C. Duxbury, *Telling & Duxbury's Planning Law and Procedure*, 13th edn (Oxford, OUP, 2006), p. 2. Duxbury also recognises (at 1) the importance of the population growth in Britain over the last 200 years from 10.5 million in 1800 to over 60 million today: 'such an increase could not fail to alter the physical appearance of the country and to bring in its train a whole host of problems'.

[156] With the exception of the Minister of Town and Country Planning Act 1943. The 1947 Act came into force on 1 July 1948.

[157] The 1990 consolidation also led to the Planning (Listed Buildings and Conservation Areas) Act 1990 and the Planning (Hazardous Substances) Act 1990, supplemented by the Planning (Consequential Provisions) Act 1990. This legislation has been subject to significant amendments and subsequent statutory instruments. Note, in particular, the Planning and Compensation Act 1991, the Environment Act 1995 and the Planning and Compulsory Purchase Act 2004.

[158] New buildings will additionally often need to comply with Building Regulations made by the Secretary of State with respect to the design and construction of buildings and the provision of services, fittings and equipment in or in connection with buildings for the purposes of securing the health, safety, welfare and convenience of persons in or about buildings and of others who may be affected by buildings or matters connected with buildings, furthering the conservation of fuel and power, and preventing waste, undue consumption, misuse or contamination of water: see the Building Act 1984 and the Building Regulations 2000 SI 2000/2531.

power of the planning authority to grant or refuse permission, subject to such conditions as it thinks fit, provides a mechanism for control of the unrestricted right to build which can be used for the protection of people living in the vicinity of a development. In a case such as this, where the development is likely to have an impact upon many people over a large area, the planning system is, I think, a far more appropriate form of control, from the point of view of both the developer and the public, than enlarging the right to bring actions for nuisance at common law. It enables the issues to be debated before an expert forum at a planning inquiry and gives the developer the advantage of certainty as to what he is entitled to build.'[159]

2.3.2.1 Regulation by means of local administration

The Town and Country Planning Act 1947 provided for regulation by local planning authorities, i.e. the county council or county borough council, with overall control by the Minister of Town and Country Planning. Each planning authority would prepare a development plan for its area, and no development would take place without planning permission.

This basic structure has continued in modern legislation. Section 57 of the Town and Country Planning Act 1990 provides that 'subject to the following provisions of this section, planning permission is required for the carrying out of any development of land'. Such permission will be sought from the relevant local authority, or, on appeal from refusal, from the relevant Secretary of State. 'Development' is defined in s.55 of the Act. Generally, 'development' means the carrying out of building, engineering, mining or other operations in, on, over or under land, or the making of any material change in the use of any buildings or other land.[160] This is a broad

[159] [1997] AC at 710.

[160] Section 55(1), TCPA 1990. Section 55(2) provides that: 'The following operations or uses of land shall not be taken for the purposes of this Act to involve development of the land:

(a) the carrying out for the maintenance, improvement or other alteration of any building of works which:
   (i) affect only the interior of the building, or
   (ii) do not materially affect the external appearance of the building,
   and are not works for making good war damage or works begun after 5 December 1968 for the alteration of a building by providing additional space in it underground;

(b) the carrying out on land within the boundaries of a road by a local highway authority of any works required for the maintenance or improvement of the road but, in the case of any such works which are not exclusively for the maintenance of the road, not including any works which may have significant adverse effects on the environment;

definition,[161] but will exclude marginal works of internal alteration or use incidental to the enjoyment of the home. Exclusions are additionally made for simplified planning zones,[162] enterprise zones (such as in *Hunter*),[163] development with government authorisation[164] and permitted developments.[165] Permission, when granted, may be outline, full or subject to conditions. It may be granted by a development order by the Secretary of State or by the local planning authority, with appeal to the Secretary of State. The grant has always been influenced by the local development plan which sets out the strategy for development in the area and which will involve a measure of public participation. If a development is undertaken without the requisite permission, the planning authority may issue an enforcement notice,[166] although the council may simply ask the householder to apply

(c) the carrying out by a local authority or statutory undertakers of any works for the purpose of inspecting, repairing or renewing any sewers, mains, pipes, cables or other apparatus, including the breaking open of any street or other land for that purpose;
(d) the use of any buildings or other land within the curtilage of a dwellinghouse for any purpose incidental to the enjoyment of the dwellinghouse as such;
(e) the use of any land for the purposes of agriculture or forestry (including afforestation) and the use for any of those purposes of any building occupied together with land so used;
(f) in the case of buildings or other land which are used for a purpose of any class specified in an order made by the Secretary of State under this section, the use of the buildings or other land or, subject to the provisions of the order, of any part of the buildings or the other land, for any other purpose of the same class. See also Town and Country Planning (Use Classes) Order 1987 SI 1987/764 (as amended);
(g) the demolition of any description of building specified in a direction given by the Secretary of State to local planning authorities generally or to a particular local planning authority.'

161 See Duxbury (see n. 155 above), ch. 6, who notes the two-fold nature of the definition which covers both 'operations' and 'uses'.

162 See section 82, TCPA 1990: '(1) A simplified planning zone is an area in respect of which a simplified planning zone scheme is in force.
(2) The adoption or approval of a simplified planning zone scheme has effect to grant in relation to the zone, or any part of it specified in the scheme, planning permission–
(a) for development specified in the scheme, or
(b) for development of any class so specified.
(3) Planning permission under a simplified planning zone scheme may be unconditional or subject to such conditions, limitations or exceptions as may be specified in the scheme.'

163 See section 88 of the Act.

164 See section 90 of the Act.

165 See Town and Country Planning (General Permitted Development) Order 1995/418 Art 3.

166 See s. 172, TCPA 1990, Issue of enforcement notice: '(1) The local planning authority may issue a notice (in this Act referred to as an "enforcement notice") where it appears to them:

retrospectively for permission. Subject to appeal,[167] a failure to comply will lead to criminal penalties.[168] Blackhall[169] reports that since the Town and Country Planning Act 1947, enforcement has been regarded as the weak link in the planning chain due to the problems of gathering evidence and its legal technicalities. Such difficulties would appear to originate in the fact that planning legislation does not regard a simple breach of planning control as an offence, but rather utilises discretionary enforcement notices which require the owner or occupier of land or premises to remedy the situation – essentially giving the owner/occupier a second chance to comply. Only if the enforcement notice is ignored may the planning authority proceed to prosecute the offender. One of the aims of recent legislation in 1991 and 2004 has been to improve the effectiveness of the enforcement system, but it does not overturn this procedural choice.

It should also be noted that due to changes in the nature of local government, the identity of the planning authority has changed over recent years. Until 1974, the local planning authority would be the county or county borough council, but the reforms of 1974 brought two tiers of local government dealing with planning: the county council and the

(a) that there has been a breach of planning control; and
(b) that it is expedient to issue the notice, having regard to the provisions of the development plan and to any other material considerations.

(2) A copy of an enforcement notice shall be served:
(a) on the owner and on the occupier of the land to which it relates; and
(b) on any other person having an interest in the land, being an interest which, in the opinion of the authority, is materially affected by the notice.

(3) The service of the notice shall take place:
(a) not more than twenty-eight days after its date of issue; and (b) not less than twenty-eight days before the date specified in it as the date on which it is to take effect.'

167 Section 174, TCPA 1990: '(1) A person having an interest in the land to which an enforcement notice relates or a relevant occupier may appeal to the Secretary of State against the notice, whether or not a copy of it has been served on him.'

168 Section 179, TCPA 1990: '(1) Where, at any time after the end of the period for compliance with an enforcement notice, any step required by the notice to be taken has not been taken or any activity required by the notice to cease is being carried on, the person who is then the owner of the land is in breach of the notice.

...

(8) A person guilty of an offence under this section shall be liable:
(a) on summary conviction, to a fine not exceeding £20,000; and
(b) on conviction on indictment, to a fine.

(9) In determining the amount of any fine to be imposed on a person convicted of an offence under this section, the court shall in particular have regard to any financial benefit which has accrued or appears likely to accrue to him in consequence of the offence.'

169 J. Cameron Blackhall, *Planning Law and Practice*, 3rd edn (London, Cavendish, 2005), p. 18.1.

district council. Further changes in 1986 again altered the structure and in recent years constitutional changes in Wales (see the Government of Wales Acts 1998 and 2006) and the return to a Greater London Authority (the Greater London Authority Act 1999) have altered the planning structure in Wales and London. The latest reforms are contained in the Planning and Compulsory Purchase Act 2004 by which the government seeks to speed up the planning system and increase the predictability of planning decisions.[170]

Further regulatory powers permit the protection of conservation areas, national parks, sites of special scientific interest, areas of outstanding natural beauty, trees and hedgerows, listed buildings[171] and scheduled monuments. By this means, relations between neighbours may be controlled, subject to local authority views on development and governmental schemes to encourage projects which stimulate economic growth.

2.3.2.2 Preparation of local development plans for each local area

As stated above, the development plan lies at the heart of the 1947 and 1990 legislation. Moore notes that 'development plans play a vital part in the system for the control of development. They constitute the main backcloth against which applications for planning permission are determined and decisions made on whether or not to issue an enforcement notice to terminate unauthorised development. The strength of the development plan system is that it ensures that there is both a rational and a consistent basis for making those decisions.'[172] They may be traced back to the Housing, Town Planning etc Act 1909 which authorised the preparation of planning schemes for suburban land. Section 54 of the 1909 Act granted local planning authorities the power to make town planning schemes 'as respects any land which is in the course of development or appears likely to be used for building purposes, with the general object of securing proper sanitary conditions, amenity and convenience in connection with the laying out and use of land and of any neighbouring lands'.[173] It is from 1948 that it has been a requirement that each

[170] See http://www.opsi.gov.uk/acts/en2004/2004en05.htm. This Act received Royal Assent on 13 May 2004, but will be implemented in stages. Such legislation is outside the period of the study and will therefore not be dealt with in this paper.

[171] See the Planning (Listed Buildings and Conservation Areas) Act 1990.

[172] V. Moore, *A Practical Approach to Planning Law*, 9th edn (Oxford, OUP, 2005) at 4.01.

[173] Practically, the impact of this section was limited due to its discretionary nature and need to obtain approval from the Local Government Board or in some cases Parliament.

planning area should have a development plan which states the manner in which land in their area should be used, by development or otherwise, and the ways in which any development should be carried out.[174] The nature of the plans has varied over time. The 1947 Act envisaged a comprehensive system of plans prepared by the county and county borough councils and approved at each stage by the relevant Minister, based on detailed maps. The Town and Country Planning Act 1968 provided for a two-tier system of structure plans (dealing with strategic issues and requiring, prior to the Planning and Compensation Act 1991, approval of the Secretary of State) and local plans (setting out detailed policies and specific proposals for the development and use of land which sought to guide planning decisions).[175] Both plans are based on the results of a survey. The structure plan stated the local planning authority's general policies and proposals in relation to the development and use of land and contained such diagrams, illustrations and other descriptive matter as might be prescribed.[176] The local plan under the 1968 system supplemented the structure plan, but tended to be patchy in coverage due to the fact that there was no requirement to prepare a plan for the whole of the local authority area.[177] Due to concerns about the delay in approving and adopting structure and local plans, the 1991 Act introduced fundamental reforms to streamline the procedure for adoption and imposed a duty on local planning authorities in non-metropolitan areas to prepare a single district-wide local plan.

Planning law thereby provides a sophisticated means by which land use is regulated in England and Wales. A number of government sites such as the Planning Portal (www.planningportal.gov.uk) and the Ministry for Communities and Local Government (www.communities.gov.uk), in addition to consumer protection sites, attempt to keep citizens aware of the impact of regulation on their lives. The early roots of regulation owe much to the problems of the expansion of cities due to the Industrial

The Housing, Town Planning etc Act 1919 sought to overcome these problems and section 47 of the 1919 Act required the council of every borough or urban district with a population of over 20,000 to prepare schemes for land in the course of development or likely to be used for building purposes.

[174] For a more detailed discussion of development plans prior to the Planning and Compulsory Purchase Act 2004, see Duxbury (n. 155), Ch. 4 and Moore (n. 172), Ch. 4.

[175] Note that structure and local plans were, for Greater London and metropolitan areas in 1986 (see the Local Government Act 1985) and Wales (due to the Local Government (Wales) Act 1994), replaced by unitary development plans.

[176] See Duxbury (n. 155), p. 52. [177] See Duxbury (n. 155), p. 57.

Revolution and planning law has responded to social difficulties such as post-war construction and urban development in the 1980s and 1990s. The 2004 Act demonstrates the ongoing importance of planning regulation. As the government stated in its 2002 Policy Statement entitled *Sustainable Communities: Delivering through Planning*:

> An effective planning system is essential to delivering the step changes we need to tackle the challenges of ensuring that everyone has the opportunities of a decent home, and the quality of life that goes with that. An effective planning system is essential to delivering our objectives for living communities; for urban and rural regeneration; for improving the country's infrastructure; and for achieving truly sustainable development. Without an effective planning system we risk constraining the economy, at a cost to everyone in the UK.[178]

2.4 The defence of statutory authority

This final section returns to the question of private law remedies and examines to what extent the courts will recognise a defence that the activity in question was authorised by an Act of Parliament, public or private. This defence is most prominent in the context of nuisance and the rule in *Rylands* v. *Fletcher* and permits Parliament to authorise an interference with a particular claimant's rights subject to any remedy specified by the relevant statute. Such a defence will be contentious in that it allows the statute to give priority to a particular activity – usually deemed of economic advantage to the state – above any harm suffered to the individual interests of nearby residents.

Much will depend on the wording of each particular statute. Parliament is presumed to have considered the competing interests, and to have determined which is to prevail in the public interest and whether or not compensation should be paid to those adversely affected. Thus, the defendant has a good defence if the statute expressly or by necessary implication authorises the nuisance, or the nuisance is the inevitable consequence of the performance of the authorised operations. A distinction must be drawn, however, between statutory duties and statutory powers. Whilst a statutory duty to act will protect the defendant against liability for the activity and its necessary consequences, a statutory power provides more limited protection.

[178] *Sustainable Communities: Delivering through Planning* (July 2002) (www.communities.gov.uk/index.asp?id=1143137). The 2004 Act aims to give effect to the Government's policy on the reform of the planning system, the principal features of which were set out in this policy statement.

The courts will generally assume, unless expressly stated, that the legislature does not intend to take away the private rights of individuals without compensation.[179]

The leading case is that of *Allen* v. *Gulf Oil Refining Ltd.*[180] Here, Gulf Oil had obtained its own private Act of Parliament (the Gulf Oil Refining Act 1965) to authorise its expansion in Milford Haven, South Wales. Section 5(1) of the Act provided specifically for the acquisition of all necessary land and the construction of a refinery, but no express provision was made for the use and operation of the refinery once it had been built.[181] Local residents complained about the noise and vibrations emitted by the refinery and *Allen* was brought as a test case. The House treated the matter as one of statutory construction. If the nuisance was authorised, expressly or implicitly, by the relevant statute, the defendant would not be liable. The burden was, however, on the defendant to satisfy the court that this was in fact so. On the facts, the majority held that the operation of the refinery was implicitly authorised by the Act, and the nuisances were inevitable. The nuisance would not be inevitable, however, if it had been caused by the negligence of the defendant. 'Negligence' here is used in a special sense, so as to require the undertaker to carry out the work and conduct the operation with all reasonable regard and care for the interests of other persons.[182] The plaintiffs would only have a remedy to the extent to which any nuisance exceeded the statutory immunity. Similarly, in *Green* v. *Chelsea Waterworks Co*,[183] the defendants, who were under a statutory duty to maintain a continuous supply of water, were not liable when, in the absence of negligence, the water main burst, damaging the plaintiff's premises, horse and stock. As stated by Lord Blackburn in *Geddis* v. *Proprietors of Bann Reservoir* in 1878, 'it is now thoroughly well established that no action will lie for doing that which the legislature has authorised, if it be done without negligence, although it does occasion damage to anyone'. [184]

In relation to statutory powers, acts within the scope of the statute (or intra vires) will be deemed to be authorised. Defendants will often have a choice how to exercise their power, and if they choose an option which

[179] *Manchester Corp* v. *Farnworth* [1929] 1 KB 533 at 556 *per* Lawrence LJ. This is now supported by the Human Rights Act 1998.

[180] [1981] AC 1001 (Lord Keith dissenting).

[181] Section 5(1): 'Subject to the provisions of this Act, the company may enter upon, take and use such of the lands delineated on the deposited plans ... as it may require for the purposes of the authorised works or for the construction of a refinery in the parish of Llanstadwell.'

[182] See *Wildtree Hotels Ltd* v. *Harrow L.B.C.* [2001] 2 AC 1 at 13 *per* Lord Hoffmann.

[183] (1894) 70 LT 547. [184] (1878) 3 App Cas 430, 455–6.

creates a nuisance when there are other options which would not have raised such problems, their actions are unlikely to be found to be authorised.[185] However, the Act may contain a 'nuisance clause', which provides that nothing in the Act should exonerate the undertakers from liability for nuisance. In such circumstances, the defendants will be liable even in the absence of negligence. For example, in *Charing Cross Electricity Supply Co* v. *Hydraulic Power Co*,[186] the defendants were operating under a statutory power to supply water for industrial purposes. They were held liable for damage caused by their burst water mains. This had occurred without any negligence on their part, but the mains had been laid under a private Act which contained a clause providing that nothing in the Act should exempt the company from liability for nuisance.[187] One may contrast this case with the later case of *Dunne* v. *North Western Gas Board*[188] where there was a series of forty-six explosions of coal gas in Liverpool, which resulted when a water main had leaked and water had washed away the soil supporting a gas main. The plaintiffs sued both the Gas Board and the Corporation which was responsible for the water main. The Gas Board had a statutory duty to supply gas and it had, in the absence of negligence, a good defence of statutory authority. The Corporation, in contrast, only acted under a statutory power. However, unlike *Charing Cross*, the Act did not contain a nuisance clause, and so the Corporation would not be liable in the absence of negligence.

The significance of this defence is considerable. In the absence of a 'nuisance clause', private actors or, more recently, public authorities or utility undertakers may be given authority to harm their neighbours and a right to compensation is dependent on the construction of the statute. The House of Lords in *Transco Plc* v. *Stockport Metropolitan Borough Council*[189] in 2003 rightly emphasised the significance of this defence in limiting the scope of common law remedies, notably in relation to high risk activities arising from work constructed or conducted under statutory authority.[190]

2.5 Conclusion

Relations between neighbours meet a mixture of regulatory and tort-based responses in English law. The traditional foundations of tort

[185] *Metropolitan Asylum District* v. *Hill* (1881) 6 App Cas 193. [186] [1914] 3 KB 772.

[187] Section 17 of the London Hydraulic Power Act 1884 read: 'Nothing in this Act shall exempt the company from any indictment, suit, action, or other proceeding at law or in equity in respect of any nuisance caused by them.'

[188] [1964] 2 QB 806 at 833–7, CA. [189] [2004] 2 AC 1.

[190] Note, in particular, the judgment of Lord Hoffmann. See, for example, Railway Act 1993, s. 122 (Statutory authority as a defence to actions in nuisance etc).

law must, in practice, be viewed in the light of the range of regulatory measures which have inevitably rendered the common law less important. Whilst the common law reflects the increasing role of fault in legal reasoning, statutory intervention is more specific and, in relation to statutory authority, the role of negligence will depend on the court's construction of the statute and the use, if any, of a nuisance clause. Statutory provisions such as Part III of the Environment Act 1990 and planning law serve to provide the public with the benefit of an accessible regime of regulation supported by procedures for enforcement. The twentieth century has, therefore, marked a movement away from common law remedies towards more centralised control. Such a development has been noted and accepted by the courts. In the words of Lord Goff in *Cambridge Water*:

> as a general rule, it is more appropriate for strict liability in respect of operations of high risk to be imposed by Parliament, than by the courts. If such liability is imposed by statute, the relevant activities can be identified, and those concerned can know where they stand. Furthermore, statute can where appropriate lay down precise criteria establishing the incidence and scope of such liability ... given that so much well-informed and carefully structured legislation is now being put in place for this purpose, there is less need for the courts to develop a common law principle to achieve the same end, and indeed it may well be undesirable that they should do so.[191]

[191] [1994] 2 AC 264 at 305.

3

Disturbances among neighbours in French law

JAMES GORDLEY

3.1 Introduction

A few provisions of the French Civil Code concern the liability of a person whose activities interfere with his neighbour's use of land. These provisions have proved to be inadequate for the task. They have been supplemented by judge-made law and legislation.

Some of these provisions recognise 'servitudes founded on the location of land' (*servitudes qui dérivent de la situation des lieux*). Others recognise 'servitudes established by law'. The provisions governing servitudes of the first type concern the duty of a lower property to receive the normal flow of rainwater and of the higher one not to aggravate it (Art. 640), as well as the right to use wells, watercourses and public water (Arts. 641–5), the right to have one's boundaries determined (Art. 646), to enclose one's land (Art. 647) and to pasture animals (Art. 648). The provisions concerning 'servitudes established by law' deal with party walls (Arts. 655–69), trees along the boundary of one's land (Art. 670) and the location of windows (Arts. 675–8). They prohibit a landowner from allowing rainwater to drip from his roof onto neighbouring land (Art. 679) and allow him, if landlocked, to claim a right of way over neighbouring property (Art. 682). Unlike the normal servitudes of private law, these servitudes are established without the parties' consent.

The only general provision that might be of use to a landowner offended by his neighbour's conduct is the very general one of Arts. 1382–3: anyone who causes another harm (*dommage*) through his own fault, intentionally or negligently, must pay compensation. No general provision of the Code says in so many words that one landowner may be liable to another without fault. No general provision imposed liability for the kinds of interferences that the English call nuisance, the Germans call *Immissionen* and the Italians call *immissioni*. French courts cured both of these omissions. In the twentieth century, their work has been supplemented by legislation establishing a scheme of public regulation of the uses that owners make of their land. We will examine in turn: (1) strict liability for harm done to neighbours; (2) liability for activities on one's own land that disturb them; and (3) the changes wrought by the regulatory system.

3.2 Strict liability

As just noted, Arts. 1382–3 of the Code imposed liability for harm done through fault. Later courts seized on the Articles that followed to impose liability without fault. The most important was Art. 1384. It held a person liable for 'the act of persons for whom one is responsible and of things which one has in one's custody (*garde*)'. It gave as examples of the persons for whom one was responsible: one's children and one's employees. Article 1385 provided that one was liable for harm done by one's animals. According to Art. 1386, one was liable for harm done if one's building collapsed due to 'lack of maintenance or a defect in construction'.

What Arts. 1384–6 meant to the drafters of the Code is unclear.[1] For a long time, however, French courts interpreted them as instances in which liability would only be imposed for fault. Their view corresponded to that of nineteenth-century French jurists who were comfortable with tort liability based on fault and much less so with strict liability.[2] In the last years of the nineteenth century, however, courts began to interpret these articles to impose liability without fault. They were influenced by the risks created by modern technology, transportation and conditions of employment. As it happened, many of the risky situations that concerned the French courts were dealt with by legislation shortly after courts imposed strict liability under the Code. Had the legislation come earlier, the courts might not have acted.

Thus, in 1896, the *Cour de cassation* held the owner of a steam tug liable to a worker injured when it exploded on the grounds that the tug was in the owner's custody.[3] Shortly thereafter, compensation for workers injured in job-related accidents was provided by the Law Concerning Liability of 9 April 1898. In 1906, the court imposed liability for damages to a railway caused when the defendant's casks of resin caught fire. Due to

[1] J. Gordley, *Foundations of Private Law* (Oxford, OUP, 2006), pp. 213–14.

[2] C. Aubry and C. Rau, *Cours de droit civil français 4*, 4th edn (Paris, Marchal & Billard, 1869–71), § 446; M. Duranton, *Cours de droit français suivant le Code civil 13*, 3rd edn (Paris, Alex-Gobelte, 1834), p. 741; M. L. Larombière, *Théorique et pratique des obligations 5* (Paris, A. Durand, 1857), pp. 738, 767; F. Laurent, *Principes de droit civil français 20* (Paris, A. Durand, 1869–78), §§ 387, 550, 589, 639.

[3] Cass., civ., 6 June 1896, D. P. 1897.1.443.

pressure from insurance companies, this result was reversed by the Law of 7 November 1922 which said that liability for the escape of fire must rest on fault. In 1919, the court held a railway liable when one of its trains exploded and injured the plaintiff's property.[4] Strict liability for railway accidents had been imposed by a special statute in Germany but there was no such statute in France. In 1930, the *Chambres réunies* – an assembly of all the judges of the *Cour de cassation* – imposed strict liability on a defendant whose truck had injured a child.[5] The following year, strict liability for automobile accidents was provided for by a special statute.[6]

Leaving the statutory changes aside, one was left with the general rule that one was liable for any harm caused by 'things' in one's 'custody'. French courts have extended that rule to harm done in the other situations described in Arts. 1384–6 such as harm done by animals or by the collapse of a house.[7] French courts have held that it does not matter if the 'thing' in question was defective or not, or abnormally dangerous or not. The thing in question need merely to have caused harm although whether it did so is not a straightforward question. Some harms are deemed to be caused by the person or property injured.[8]

Thus, a landowner can recover without proving fault if he can successfully claim that his own property was harmed by the collapse of his neighbour's house, by his neighbour's animal, or, more generally, by any 'thing' belonging to his neighbour, except in cases barred by statute, such as the escape of fire. It is hard to see in principle why this liability should not extend to any sort of harm, including emotional or economic harm, caused by the smoke, noise, vibrations and the like – that is, for the disturbances known in other legal systems as nuisances, *Immissionen* or *immissioni*. As one leading French treatise puts it, for Art. 1384 to apply 'it matters little what the dimensions [of things] are, or their character, be it inoffensive or dangerous, or their substance, be it solid, liquid or gas. Even when discord in social life results from the least material of elements and affects the most subtle of senses … the application of article 1384 is not necessarily excluded …'[9] Nevertheless, by the time strict liability under

[4] Cass. civ., 21 January 1919, D. P. 1922.1.25.

[5] Cass., ch. réun., 13 February 1930, D. P. 1930.1.57.

[6] Law no. 51–1508 of 31 November 1931.

[7] F. Terré, P. Simler and Y. Lequette, *Droit civil: Les obligations*, 8th edn (Paris, Dalloz, 2002) §§ 762, pp. 778–85.

[8] J. Gordley, *Foundations of Private Law* (Oxford, OUP, 2006), p. 215.

[9] F. Terré, P. Simler and Y. Lequette, *Droit civil: Les obligations* 8th edn (Paris: Dalloz, 2002) §768.

Arts. 1384–6 came to be recognised, French courts had already developed other bodies of case law to deal with these types of interferences. They were actionable under the judge-made law of *abus de droit* (abuse of right) and *troubles de voisinage* (disturbances among neighbours). A French court will apply these bodies of law to such disturbances rather than Art. 1384. The treatise just quoted implies that the choice does not matter: it says that Art. 1384 has 'absorbed' these bodies of law, or at least that there has been 'a partial *rapprochement* of their spheres of application'. But that certainly is not true. Article 1384, as French courts have interpreted it, imposes liability for any harm caused by any object. As we will see, the law of *abus de droit* imposes liability for conduct that is intended to aggravate or harm another. The law of *troubles de voisinage* imposes liability only for disturbances which are 'abnormal'. French courts keep these bodies of law separate, even if French commentators have difficulty explaining the separation.

3.3 *Abus de droit* and *troubles de voisinage*

3.3.1 *The Civil Code*

In modern French law, one can be liable for using one's land in a way that disturbs one's neighbour in two distinct cases: first, when one's purpose in so using the land is to disturb him, and, second, when the disturbance goes beyond what is normal for the area. These rules are not found in the Civil Code. They are creations of the courts.

Most of the provisions of the Code that govern private law were taken from the seventeenth- and eighteenth-century authors, Jean Domat and Robert Pothier. Domat had explained that one who uses his land in a way that disturbs a neighbour is liable if he does so, not for his own advantage, but in order to disturb his neighbour.[10] If the person using his land did not intend to disturb his neighbour, his liability depended on 'the character of the locality', i.e, what was normal in the area.[11] According to Pothier, the liability of one who made smoke on his own premises depended on whether the smoke 'is too thick or too much of an interference'.[12] These rules are much like those which courts apply

[10] J. Domat, *Les Loix civiles dans leur ordre naturel*, 2nd edn (Paris, 1713), at liv. 2, tit. 8, § 3.

[11] Ibid. at liv. 2, tit. 12, §§ 4, pp. 9–10.

[12] R. Pothier, *Traité du contrat de société*, at App. 2, 'Du voisinage', p. 241, in *Oeuvres de Pothier annotées et mises en correlation avec le Code civil et législation actuel*, 2nd edn by Bugnet (Paris, Marchal et Billard, 1861). See 'Introduction', this volume, p. 2 ii.

today. Yet the Code did not mention them. Presumably, the reason was an oversight by the drafters. They were working under enormous time pressure, since Bonaparte had asked them to produce a draft in a few months. There is no reason, except oversight, why they should not have borrowed the passages just mentioned from Domat and Pothier from whom they took so much else. Certainly, they did not ignore these passages because they clashed with a new theory of property according to which there should be no relief for interferences.[13]

3.3.2 The nineteenth century

Despite the silence of the Code, in the nineteenth century, French courts began to hold the defendant liable in cases like those which Domat and Pothier had described: cases in which the defendant acted in order to disturb the plaintiff, and in cases in which, as French courts put it, the interference went beyond those normal among neighbours. Although the terminology was not uniform, French commentators usually described the first case as an 'abuse of right' (*abus de droit*) and the second as an interference among neighbours (*trouble de voisinage*) although the latter expression was sometimes used to encompass cases of 'abuse of right'. As Jean Carbonnier has said, a landowner is liable if his use is either 'abusive' or 'excessive'.[14]

It is unlikely that the courts were influenced by Domat or Pothier. Nor could they have been influenced by nineteenth-century French scholars. These scholars acknowledged that they could not explain why such an action should be given. Giving relief did not sit well with their theories of property. They typically subscribed to what we now call a 'will theory'. By definition, property meant that an object was completely subject to the will of its owner. According to Aubry and Rau, 'property ... expresses the Idea [*sic*] of the most complete legal power of a person over an object and can be defined as the right by virtue of which a thing is submitted in an absolute and exclusive manner to the will and the conduct of a person'.[15] Laurent explained that a proprietor could use his thing however he wished until prohibited by law or until he injured the rights of others.[16] According

[13] J. Gordley, 'Myths of the French Civil Code', (1994) 42 Am. J. Comp. L. 459.

[14] J. Carbonnier, *Droit civil, Tome III, Les Biens*, 19th edn (Paris: PUF, 2000) §167.

[15] C. Aubry & C. Rau, *Cours de droit civil français 2*, 4th edn (Paris, Marchal & Billard, 1869–71), § 190.

[16] F. Laurent, *Principes de droit civil français 6* (Paris, A. Durand, 1869–78), § 101.

to Demolombe, 'an absolute right of property confers upon the master a sovereign power, a complete despotism over the thing'.[17]

Having defined property as a seemingly limitless right, they found it difficult to explain how the limitless rights of two adjoining landowners could be limited vis-à-vis each other. According to Aubry and Rau, the 'respective rights of [the] proprietors' of adjacent land were in a 'conflict [that] cannot be resolved except by means of certain limits imposed on the natural exercise of the powers inherent in property'.[18] Demolombe observed that if all proprietors could 'invoke their absolute right, it is clear that none would have one in reality'. What would be the result? 'It would be war! It would be anarchy!'[19] Similarly, Laurent thought that '[a]ccording to the rigour of the law, each proprietor would be able to object if one of his neighbours released on his property smoke or exhalations of any kind, because he has a right to the purity of air for his person and his goods'.[20] If that were so, he admitted, the existence of towns would be impossible.[21]

Thus, the French jurists found themselves saying that property rights were by their nature so unlimited that, if owners were allowed to exercise their rights, property would become worthless. Such a conclusion shows why, in France, the phrase used to describe using one's property for the purpose of disturbing a neighbour is *abus de droit*. If one is not allowed to use land for the purpose of disturbing one's neighbour, it would seem that one has no right to do so, and consequently one cannot be abusing a right. Yet, as the nineteenth-century commentators viewed the matter, in principle, one did have a right to use one's land as one wished. Consequently, one must be liable, because one had abused that right.

In France, as elsewhere, jurists eventually became tired of a conceptualist approach to law. By that approach, the concept of property was not defined according to the purposes of establishing and safeguarding property rights. It is defined abstractly in terms of will, and in a way that undercut these purposes. In any event, the nineteenth-century jurists failed to develop a concept of property that could explain how to resolve

[17] C. Demolombe, *Cours de Code Napoléon 9* (Paris, A. Lahre, 1854–82), § 543.

[18] C. Aubry and C. Rau, *Cours de droit civil français 2*, 4th edn (Paris, Marchal & Billard, 1869–71), § 194.

[19] Demolombe, above, n. 17. [20] Laurent, above, n. 16, 144.

[21] Ibid. In a later volume of his work, Laurent finally decided that '[t]he Code was wrong to say that the owner has the right to enjoy and to dispose of his thing in the most absolute manner ...'. 20, 417. Nevertheless, he did not suggest any other way that property could be defined.

the problem of interferences among landowners either in the case of 'abuse of rights' or in the more general case of 'disturbances among neighbours' that were not due to a desire to disturb.

3.3.3 *Today*

3.3.3.1 The general rule

French courts now give relief in much the same circumstances as they did in the nineteenth century. The owner who disturbs his neighbour is liable for an 'abuse of right' if he acts only to disturb him. Thus, the plaintiff recovered when the defendant built a false chimney to block his view[22] and when the defendant excavated with the sole purpose of cutting off his water supply.[23] The plaintiff recovered when the defendant erected a tower with spikes to prevent him from taking off and landing his dirigible[24] and when the defendant hung a manikin of 'repugnant aspect' opposite his window which represented a person who had been hanged.[25]

He is also liable if the disturbance exceeds that which is 'normal' among neighbouring properties. What is normal is judged by the character of the locality.[26] The defendant is liable if the interference is normal in kind but abnormal in degree so that the defendant is causing more of a disturbance than others engaged in the same activity.[27] He is liable, whether or not he is at fault, for causing the interference.[28] For example, if his factory emits fluorine gas, he is liable even if there is no measure he should have taken to prevent the emission. In such a case, however, a court may allow him to continue his operations but require him to pay damages for the harm they cause.[29]

Today, now that will theories of property and conceptualist approaches to law are out of fashion, commentators accept these rules without qualms.

[22] Colmar, 2 May 1855, D.P. 1856.2.9. [23] Cass. req., 16 June 1913, D.P. 1914.5.23.

[24] Cass. req., 3 August 1915, D.P. 1917.1.79.

[25] Chambéry, 21 July 1914, Gaz. trib. 19 January 1916.

[26] G. Cornu, *Droit Civil, Introduction: Les Personnes, Les Biens*, 4th edn (Paris, Montchrestien, 1990), § 1096; M. Ferid and J. J. Sonnenberger, *Das Französische Zivilrecht 2*, 2nd edn (Heidelberg: Recht und Wirtschaft, 1986), § 3 C 191; B. Starck, H. Roland and L. Boyer, *Droit civil: Obligations, Responsibité délictuelle*, 4th edn (Paris, Litec, 1985) (hereafter 'Starck, Roland and Boyer'), § 371; F. Terré and P. Simler, *Droit civil: Les biens*, 6th edn (Paris, Dalloz, 1985) (hereafter 'Terré and Simler'), § 330.

[27] Cass. 2ᵉ ch. civ., 3 January 1969, JCP 1969.II.15920 (liability for 'usage, même normale' if the 'troubles dépassent les inconvenients normaux'); Starck, Roland and Boyer, § 367.

[28] P. Malaurie and L. Aynès, *Cours de droit civil, Tome VI, Les Obligations*, 7th edn (Paris, Cujas, 1996), §123; Starck, Roland and Boyer, § 365; Terré and Simler, §§ 321, 323.

[29] Toulouse, 17 March 1970, JCP 1970.II.16534; G. Viney and P. Jourdain, *Traité de droit civil: Les Effets de la responsabilité*, 2nd edn (Paris, LGDJ, 2001), § 53.

But they have not agreed on how to explain them. Louis Josserand claimed that there is an 'abuse of right' whenever a right is not exercised in conformity with its social purpose.[30] But surely that is going too far. When a court interprets the law so as to set limits to the scope of a right, it should take into account the right's social purpose. One cannot speak of an 'abuse of right' whenever, in good faith, an individual has acted beyond the limits a court later sets to his rights. Moreover, one need not do so. One need merely speak as the Romans did and some French jurists do,[31] of an intention to harm one's neighbour. Whenever one acts solely to injure a neighbour, presumably one is going beyond the social purposes of the law in protecting one's right to act, but it does not follow that one can speak of an 'abuse of right' whenever one's action is not justified by these social purposes.

When the defendant is liable even though he is not acting in order to disturb his neighbours some French jurists have described the remedy given in this case as one for abuse of right.[32] But that seems odd since, as we have seen, the defendant may be liable even though he has not acted reprehensibly. Indeed, he may be allowed to continue provided he pays damages. In French law, however, abuse of right means that the abuser acted reprehensibly. Sometimes he was negligent. Most often he used his right to property in a manner inconsistent with its social ends.[33] But as French jurists themselves have noted, the person who interferes with his neighbours has often done nothing reprehensible. Indeed, French courts may award compensation for past and future harm and still refuse to order the defendant to stop interfering.

Louis Josserand suggested another explanation: the person who profits from an activity should pay for the harm it does.[34] Some modern French jurists have rejected his view on the ground that it does not explain why one pays only for abnormally large interferences.[35] But it is easy to answer that objection. No one can use his property without interfering with his neighbour in some way: for example, they may smell the fumes from his outdoor grill or hear the music he listens to at a normal volume in the afternoon or early evening. Since every property owner will be using his land so as to cause minor interferences, the harms cancel each other out.

[30] L. Josserand, *De l'esprit des lois et de leur relativité: Théorie dite de l'abus des droits* (Paris, Dalloz, 1927).

[31] E.g. J. Carbonnier, *Droit civil, Tome II, Les Biens* (Paris, PUF, 2004), § 829.

[32] See Starck, Roland and Boyer, §§ 379–81; Terré and Simler, § 320.

[33] See Starck, Roland and Boyer, §§ 382–91.

[34] Josserand, above, n. 30, at 18–19. In agreement are Terré and Simler, § 321.

[35] Starck, Roland and Boyer, § 393.

No one is a net gainer or loser. Elsewhere, I have defended Josserand's explanation of why, not only the French, but other legal systems give relief when an interference is grave and abnormal. The underlying principle is an ancient one: that no one should gain at another's expense.[36]

3.3.3.2 Three difficult questions

If that is so, then one can see, in principle, how to answer three difficult questions, although finding an answer that works well in practice will be more difficult.

One question is the types of interferences for which relief should be given. In France, as elsewhere, relief is given when the defendant's use of his property produces noise, smoke, smells, light, heat, or some other physical movement of mass or energy across the border of his property onto the property of the plaintiff. In German and Italian law, such interferences are called 'emissions' (*Immissionen, immissioni*). Some jurists call them 'positive interferences'. A difficult question is whether to give relief for so-called 'negative interferences', that is, when the plaintiff has aesthetic or moral objections to the defendant's use of his property: for example, the defendant has blocked his view, or created an eyesore, or is engaged in operating a brothel.

In principle, if the law wishes to protect a property owner from interferences that are grave or abnormal, it should not matter whether the interference is 'positive' or 'negative'. Yet many jurisdictions deny relief for 'negative interferences' or give it with great reluctance. The reason may be pragmatic: it is hard to determine how much of a view the plaintiff should have, or how ugly a property must be to warrant relief, or to what immoral activities the plaintiff should be able to object. In its approach to these issues, French law can be described as more principled, if less pragmatic, than other legal systems. French courts have given relief when the plaintiff objected to the height of neighbouring buildings,[37] to the 'unaesthetic character' of a wall[38] and to the presence of a brothel.[39]

[36] J. Gordley, 'Immissionsschutz, Nuisance and Troubles de Voisinage in Comparative and Historical Perspective' [1998] *ZEuP* 13.

[37] Cass., 3e ch. civ., 3 November 1977, DS 1978.434 (increasing the height of the wall along a mill blocks plaintiff's sunlight); Cass., 2e ch. civ., 3 December 1964, DS 1965.321 (height of 11-storey building makes the chimney of a three-storey building useless); Ferid and Sonnenberger, above, n. 26, § 3 C 192.

[38] Cass., 3e ch. civ., 27 November 1979, GP 1980.1.pan.146.

[39] Cass. civ., 27 Aug. 1861, S. 61.1.84; Cass. req., 5 June 1882, S. 1884.1.71. These cases are old, but Esmein claimed they still represent French law: Paul Esmein, note, DS 1965.321.

A second question is whether the plaintiff should recover if the defendant's activity only interfered with him because his own activity is abnormally sensitive: for example, the plaintiff requires an extra degree of tranquillity because he is running a clinic, or because he is sick and hypersensitive. It would seem that the plaintiff should not get relief as long as the defendant is making use of his land that is normal for the area. In that event, he is not benefiting from an abnormal use of it. The plaintiff is demanding that the defendant's activities be curtailed because of his own abnormal use or abnormal condition. Under these circumstances, some French commentators have said that the plaintiff should not have a remedy.[40] The French courts have not decided such cases consistently. For example, they have granted relief when a factory that is normal for the area interferes with a clinic[41] and denied it when the plaintiff is sick or hypersensitive.[42]

A third question is whether a plaintiff can recover even if he moved into the area in question knowing of the defendant's activity. Here again, the result that is correct in principle may not be the best one in practice. Suppose that the use to which the defendant is putting his property was not abnormal for the area at the time it began. If that use becomes abnormal, it is because people like the plaintiff have moved nearby. Since they are the ones who benefit from the change, it would seem that the defendant should not be liable. In practice, matters are more complicated. The defendant may draw far less benefit for his use of his land than the harm that use causes others. If so, it would seem that he should have to stop and that those who benefit should compensate him for the loss he will then suffer. But most often, it would be impractical to identify those who benefit and force them to pay according to the degree that they benefit. So one is left with two unpleasant alternatives: to make the defendant stop without compensating him, although nearby landowners will then benefit at his expense, or to allow the defendant to continue a use of his land that may harm others more than it benefits him.

This tension is between two imperfect solutions. For many years, the *Cour de cassation* maintained that priority in time did not matter.[43] Then

[40] G. Cornu, above, n. 26, § 1109; Starck, Roland and Boyer, § 366; Terré and Simler, § 330.

[41] Cour d'appel, Nancy, 12 April 1923, GP 1923.1.743.

[42] Trib. gr. inst., Riom, 17 March 1965, D. 1965.547.

[43] E.g. Cass., 1e ch. civ., 20 February 1968, D. 1968.350 (priority does not matter when house built near factory); Cass., 2e ch. civ., 22 October 1964, D. 1965.344 (same); Cass., 2e ch. civ., 29 June 1977, D. 1978.IR. 35 (priority does not matter when house built near sawmill). See Carbonnier, above, n. 31, § 830; Terré and Simler, § 330; Cornu, above, n. 26, § 1108; P. Malaurie and L. Aynès, *Cours de droit civil, Tome VI, Les Obligations*, 7th edn

amendments to the French Code of Building and Dwellings in 1976 and 1980 provided that those who build in an area cannot complain about interferences that existed before the building permit was issued.[44] Consequently, some French jurists claimed that priority should matter in other cases as well.[45] The problem is that neither solution is completely fair.

3.4 Public land use regulation

3.4.1 Origins

In France, public land use regulation, in its modern form, dates from a law of 14 March 1919, the so-called 'Cornudet law'. As Jacqueline Morand-Deviller notes, this law, for the first time, conferred authority to divide urban land into zones and to regulate the uses of land permissible in each zone.[46] The regulations could govern almost all aspects of land use likely to affect public or private interests. As is the case today, this authority was, for the most part, conferred on the municipalities rather than exercised centrally.

Previously, public authority had regulated land use by targeting particular activities which were deemed dangerous, unhealthy or likely to disturb others. That was the approach of an Imperial decree of 15 October 1810, which adopted a three-fold classification of activities based on the extent to which they were dangerous. These activities could only be conducted by permission of the prefect, or, in the case of the most dangerous, by permission of the Conseil d'Etat. A decree-law of 26 May 1852 imposed requirements designed to ensure a safe water supply, and was supplemented by a law of 15 February 1902 directed generally at public health.[47] These earlier laws were less comprehensive in the activities they regulated. They differed in the method of regulation since they did not provide for the establishment of zones for different uses of land.

(Paris, Cujas, 1996), § 125. But see Cass., 3^{e} ch. civ., 14 November 1985, JCP 1986.IV.42 (hotel/bar cannot complain of noise and odours from nearby restaurant because it knew of them when it moved in).

44 Law 76–1285 of 31 December 1976 and Law 80–502 of 4 July 1980, now Code of Buildings and Dwellings (Code de construction et habitation) Art. L. 122–16.

45 A. Sériaux, *Droit des obligations* (Paris, PUF, 1992), § 122.

46 J. Morand-Deviller, *Droit de l'urbanisme*, 6th edn (Paris, Dalloz, 2003) (hereinafter 'Morand-Deviller'), p. 4.

47 See ibid. p. 3.

3.4.2 *The tools*

Land use regulation today is national or local. National laws regulating land use are the core of the so-called 'national regulation of planning' (*règlement national de l'urbanisme* or *RNU*). Some of these rules are very general. For example, one national rule provides that 'a building permit should not be granted unless conditioned on compliance with special provisions if, given their location and dimensions, the buildings are such as to compromise health or public safety'.[48] Similarly, according to one of the most celebrated rules, a building permit should not be granted if 'in view of their location, architecture, size, or exterior aspect, the buildings ... are such as to adversely affect the character or interest of neighbouring properties, or sites, or natural or urban streets and passageways, or the preservation of monumental perspectives'.[49] Other national rules are precise. For example, they specify just how large a building may be in proportion to the parcel it occupies and how far back from the road it may be set.[50] They prescribe how far from a large highway a building can be built.[51]

Local authorities may make rules of their own. The local rules can make a national rule more definite or they may supplement or supersede it. Local authorities make rules in two ways: less formally by adding them to a *carte communale* which is a collage of particular rules, or more formally by a land use development plan (*plan d'occupation des sols* or *POS*) which divides the land into zones and prescribes to what uses land may be put in each zone. *Cartes communales* are common in rural areas, and land use development plans in more thickly settled communities.[52] Based on a *carte communale* or land use development plan, or on the national rules, local authorities decide when a building permit will be issued. A building permit must be obtained for any new construction or for the alteration of an existing structure when the 'effect is a change in purpose, a modification of their size or exterior appearance, or the creation of additional floors'.[53]

Land use is also regulated in France by two different types of servitudes that are imposed on land owners by statute or by administrative regulations: 'servitudes for public utility' (*servitudes d'utilité publique*) and 'planning servitudes' (*servitudes d'urbanisme*).

'Servitudes for public utility' have been created for heterogeneous purposes. Some protect national parks, forests, historic sites and

[48] Planning Code (Code d'urbanisme) Art. R. 111–2 [49] Ibid. R. 111–21
[50] Ibid. R. 111–16 – R. 111–19. [51] Ibid. R. 111–5. [52] Morand-Deviller, p. 22.
[53] Planning Code (Code de l'urbanisme) Art. L. 111–1.

defence installations.[54] Some are concerned with public health or with aesthetics.[55] Some require landowners to allow electricity, gas and water lines to pass through their property.[56] The beneficiary may be a private company.[57] It would be impossible to acquire such a right under the private law of the French Civil Code. Under the Civil Code, a servitude must burden one parcel of land for the benefit of another parcel.[58] It cannot benefit an entity such as a gas company independently of what other land it owns.[59]

Servitudes for public utility are commonly created by legislation. They are found, for example, in the Forest Code (*Code forestier*), the Rural Code (*Code rural*), the Mining Code (*Code minier*) and the portion of the Planning Code (*Code d'urbanisme*) that deals with the protection of mountain areas. French courts have held that they can be created only in the cases expressly envisioned in the legislation. For example, in 1936, and again in 1984, the *Cour de cassation* held that the operator of a ski lift could not have an enforceable servitude in the properties it crossed.[60] A 1941 statute permitted servitudes for a cable car line but a ski lift was not a cable car.[61] In 1985, the problem was solved when legislation protecting mountain areas was enacted which expressly permitted servitudes for ski lifts.[62] Presumably, that legislation would not apply to lifts crossing other terrain built for other purposes such as a scenic lift across a valley or between nearby zoos or parks.

'Planning servitudes' are a more flexible tool for land use planning. They are created by an administrative act. They are often found in a land use development plan. They may govern such matters as 'roads, health and aesthetics or for other purposes, notably, those concerning land use (*l'utilisation du sol*), the height of buildings, the proportion of the surface of each property on which one may build or not build, the prohibition of building in certain zones and along the side of certain roads, and the subdivision of property in various zones'.[63] They may limit the rights an owner would otherwise have (*servitudes passives*), for example, by limiting the height to which he can build, or they may require him to take

[54] Morand-Deviller, p. 23. [55] Terré and Simler, § 342. [56] Ibid. § 345. [57] Ibid. § 346.

[58] French Civil Code (Code civil) Art. 686 (a servitude can only be imposed 'on an estate for an "estate"').

[59] Terré and Simler, § 869.

[60] Cass. civ., 30 June 1936, D.P. 1938.1.65; Cass., 3e ch. civ., 12 December 1984, JCP 1985. II.20411.

[61] Law of 8 July 1941.

[62] Law of 9 January 1985, now Planning Code Art. L. 145–1 – Art. L. 145–3.

[63] Planning Code (Code d'urbanisme) Art. L. 160–5(1).

some action (*servitudes actives*), for example by requiring him to plant vegetation or to build in a certain way.[64] In the latter case, they establish a type of servitude which the private law of the French Civil Code does not permit. Under the Code, a servitude cannot require the owner of the burdened property to perform an affirmative act.[65]

3.4.3 Public regulation compared with the law of troubles de voisinage

The methods of land use regulation just discussed often deal with the same problem as the law of *troubles de voisinage*. They limit the extent to which a land owner's use of his own property can interfere with that of his neighbours. In dealing with that problem, they have advantages and disadvantages as compared with the law of *troubles de voisinage*.

One advantage is that rules can be more specific. As we saw, in principle, a landowner should be protected against the harm done to him by nearby buildings that are abnormally tall or unsightly. French courts try to give relief. But it is difficult for a court to determine the precise height at which a building becomes too tall or which land uses are too unsightly for a given neighbourhood. Land use regulations can do so, and thus more perfectly accomplish the goal of the law of *troubles de voisinage*: to protect against abnormal interferences.

Another advantage is that the regulatory regime makes it easier to know in advance what activities one will be allowed to carry out and what protection one's activities will receive. National and local rules are laid down prospectively. Building permits are granted and denied in advance of building. In contrast, the law of *troubles de voisinage* is normally applied retrospectively when a neighbour brings suit.

A third advantage is that those charged with the public regulation of land use will take account both of the interests of nearby landowners and of the public interest. Whether a given use of land is appropriate in a given area should depend on both of these concerns. Yet the law of *troubles de voisinage* usually takes account only of the former. Determining how the public interest is affected by a given land use is typically beyond the competence of a court.

Nevertheless, there are disadvantages that flow from the pursuit of these advantages. When the first two advantages are sought, the very

[64] Morand-Deviller, p. 24.

[65] Christian Atias, *Droit civil: Les Biens*, 4th edn (Paris, Litec, 1999), § 174; Terré and Simler, § 868.

effort to make rules more definite or more knowable in advance exacts a price. The rules may be less carefully tailored to the individual situation of the parties. When the third advantage is sought, safeguarding both public and private interests by the same rules creates a danger: it may blind one to the different ways in which the public interest and distinct private interests should be treated.

The very effort to frame definite rules may produce rules that do not correspond well with the interests which they ought to protect. For example, a national rule mentioned earlier specifies just how large a building must be in proportion to the parcel it occupies and just how far back from the road it must be set.[66] If the objective is to prevent abnormal interferences among landowners, it cannot be that one rule is right for all of France. As mentioned, local authorities can modify the rule to suit local conditions. But they will have less knowledge of the conditions of a given neighbourhood than a court looking at the situation of the parties before it.

Another way to avoid indefiniteness is to impose a flat prohibition on building whenever a land use might be objectionable, without specifying how objectionable it must be. Examples are national rules that prohibit issuing a building permit if a structure might 'compromise health or public safety'[67] or if it 'may be exposed to grave nuisances (*nuisances*), and in particular those due to noise',[68] or if it will 'adversely affect the character or interest of neighbouring properties'.[69] Once again, however, the price of definiteness is that these rules may not correspond well with the purpose of protecting land owners against abnormal interferences. Landowners are prohibited from building when they will suffer or cause any interference, abnormal or not. This ham-fisted result is avoided when such rules are relaxed or applied with discretion by local authorities. But if they relax the rules or apply them with discretion, the effect of the rules is, for that reason, less definite.

Similarly, the very effort to let people know in advance how they may use their land may lead to less accurate decisions about how they should use it. Even if the circumstances that affect how they should use their land did not change over time, there are only two ways to let people know in advance what use will be deemed to be appropriate. One is to lay down definite rules in the manner just described, which, as we have just seen, has its own disadvantages. The other is to frame general rules and to apply them in advance when the administrative authority grants

[66] Ibid. R. 111–16 – R. 111–19. [67] Planning Code (Code d'urbanisme) Art. R. 111–2.
[68] Ibid. Art. R. 111–3–1. [69] Ibid. Art. R. 111–21.

or rejects a request for a building permit. The trouble then is that an administrative authority cannot give the same consideration to each request it receives as a court can give to the cases that come before it. Indeed, in France, the administrative authorities have so little time that many requests are never actually considered. After two, three or five months of inaction, depending on the nature of the project, a request is deemed to have been granted.[70] The disadvantage is that decisions made quickly or by default will be less reliable than those made with deliberation.

Moreover, the circumstances that make a given land use appropriate in an area do change over time. As we have seen, whether the law should protect a use of land that became abnormally interfering after it was established is a difficult question. French courts will not do so. The reason may be pragmatic. In principle, while one should not indefinitely protect a person whose use of his land abnormally interferes with that of others, it seems unfair to stop him if his neighbour does not compensate him for doing so. In practice, it may not be practical to require them to pay compensation, since it is difficult, in a civil suit, to determine how much each neighbour should pay and to collect it. The least unfair outcome may be not to protect the prior user. Still, if one does not, one thwarts the goal of letting each person know in advance how he may use his land. Consequently, as mentioned earlier, laws were enacted in 1976 and 1980 which amended the French Code of Building and Dwellings. Article L. 112–16 of the Code now provides:

> The harm caused to the occupants of a building by nuisances (*nuisances*) due to agricultural, industrial or craft activities does not give rise to a right to compensation when the building permit for the building exposed to these nuisances was requested … after the existence of the activities that caused them as long as these activities were conducted in conformity with the legislative or regulatory provisions in force when they were undertaken and these activities are conducted under the same conditions.

This provision not only prevents neighbours from seeking a remedy against a land use that violates subsequently enacted laws or regulations. It prevents them from seeking compensation under the law of *troubles de voisinage*. Because it takes away a right that was theirs under private law, some French jurists think that the provision is unconstitutional.[71] In any event, the end result (that an abnormal interference continues indefinitely) is one that French civil courts would consider the greater of two

[70] Ibid. R. 421–18. [71] Carbonnier, above, n. 31, § 836.

evils. It does so in order to achieve one of the goals of land use regulation: to allow a person to know in advance how he may use his land.

The disadvantages just considered seem to be inherent in the pursuit of the corresponding advantages. If one wants to make rules more definite or more knowable in advance one must pay a price, although one can ask, as in the case just considered, whether the price is too high. The third advantage to be sought from public regulation of land use is that the interest of the public as well as private interests may be considered. The corresponding disadvantage is a danger rather than an inherent price for considering these interests at once. The danger is that one may disregard differences in the way that public interest and private interest should be treated, and in the way in which distinct private interests should be treated.

One of these differences concerns who should be able to object if a rule is violated. French law does recognise the importance of this difference. As we have seen, some so-called rules of public law merely give definiteness to the standards that should be applied in principle to protect a landowner against abnormal interference by a neighbour. Examples are rules limiting the height of buildings or specifying the activities permissible in a neighbourhood. Because they are more definite, these rules can more perfectly protect a landowner against abnormal interferences, which is the goal of the law of *troubles de voisinage*. Since the goal is the same, a landowner should have a remedy when such a rule is violated. He should not, in contrast, if the rule was not meant to protect his interests but happens to be advantageous to him. Suppose, for example, a rule prevents his neighbour from erecting a building which is not abnormally high for the neighbourhood but which would interfere with the view the public would otherwise have of an historic monument. A building erected in violation of that rule may disadvantage a neighbour, but no more so than other buildings which are appropriate for the area but do not happen to block the public's view. French law recognises this difference. A private landowner can only complain about the violation of a land use regulation or the issue of a building permit if the harm to himself is 'direct' and 'personal'. 'Personal' means that the rule in question must be intended to protect his interests, not those of the general public. A textbook example is the one just given: a private person can complain about a rule governing the height of buildings which was designed to protect him but not one designed to preserve a panoramic view for the public.[72]

[72] Morand-Deviller, p. 153.

In contrast, French law has blurred the distinction between public and private interests and between different private interests in its treatment of so-called servitudes for public utility and planning servitudes.

Sometimes these servitudes are established to protect the interest of the public in general. For example, as we have seen, servitudes for public utility may protect national parks, forests, historic sites and defence installations. Both they and some planning servitudes may protect 'health' and 'aesthetics'. The accepted view is that because the end sought in creating these servitudes is to protect the public interest, no compensation can be demanded by the landowner on whom the servitude is imposed except where provided by statute. That may be unfair. It might be better to distinguish between cases in which a person is required to make a sacrifice for the public interest which is not demanded of landowners similarly situated, and cases in which he is prohibited from harming the public interest by using his land to obtain a benefit not obtained by landowners similarly situated.[73]

In any event, the purpose of some of these servitudes is to protect the same interests as the rules of private law. French law fails to distinguish these servitudes from those which merely protect the general interest. It also fails to distinguish two different ways in which these servitudes modify the rules of private law to protect private interests. One has already been discussed: a servitude, like a planning regulation, can give definiteness to the standard of abnormal interference of the law of *troubles de voisinage*. That is likely to be the case with planning servitudes which govern 'land use (*l'utilisation du sol*), the height of buildings, the proportion of the surface of each property on which one may build or not build, [and] the prohibition of building in certain zones …'. In that case, the landowner on whom the servitude is imposed should have no more right to compensation than he does under the law of *troubles de voisinage*.

In other situations, the rules that govern servitudes of public utility and of planning are meant to give flexibility to the rules of private law that prescribe how a servitude is established and what servitudes will be enforced. Private law servitudes are established by agreement of the parties. Servitudes of public utility and planning may require a party's consent but most often are imposed whether he consents or not.[74] The advantage is that a party can neither refuse to create a servitude which is desperately needed by others nor exact an extortionate price for doing so. Moreover, as we have

[73] J. Gordley, 'Takings: What Does Matter?' (2004) 31 Environmental LQ 291.

[74] Terré and Simler, § 348.

seen, private law servitudes must burden one parcel of land for the benefit of another parcel, and cannot require the owner of the burdened parcel to perform an affirmative act. In contrast, servitudes for public utility allow an electric, gas or water company to run wires or pipes over a landowner's property. Therefore, the company does not need to repurchase this right whenever the land is sold. Planning servitudes can require a landowner to plant or to clean up. The benefits to others of requiring him to do so can often outweigh the costs. There are occasions, then, when it is advantageous to dispense with the severity of the rules of private law that govern servitudes.

Still, if a burden is being imposed on one person to further the private interests of others, it is only fair to compensate the person who is burdened. He can demand compensation when a private law servitude is created. There is no reason why he should not be able to do so when the burden is imposed on him by a servitude for public utility or planning.

But that is not French law. Since 1857, French courts have held that the person on whom a servitude for public utility is imposed has no right to compensation unless the statute so provides.[75] Some French jurists defend this result, arguing that because a landowner often benefits from public work without paying, he should not be compensated when work undertaken in the public interest burdens him.[76] That argument may or may not be valid when servitudes are actually imposed in the public interest. It is not valid when a so-called servitude for public interest is established in the private interest to serve the same purposes as the law of private servitudes but with a gain in flexibility. French courts have actually allowed compensation without statutory authority in one case: when the servitude is for power lines.[77] If to deny compensation is unfair in that case, however, it must be unfair in others as well.

Similarly, when a planning servitude is opposed, compensation is due only by way of exception. Article L. 160–5, para. 1 of the Planning Code (*Code d'urbanisme*) provides:

> No indemnity shall be required in the case of servitudes imposed by application of this Code as matters of roads, health and aesthetics or for other purposes, notably, those concerning: land use (*l'utilisation du sol*), the height of buildings, the proportion of the surface of each property on which one may build or not build, the prohibition of building in certain

[75] CE, 5 February 1857, D. 1857.3.74. [76] Terré and Simler, § 348.

[77] Cass., 3e ch. civ., 12 December 1984, JCP 1985.II.20411; Cass. civ. 6 January 1930, S. 1930.1.337.

zones and along the side of certain roads, the subdivision of property in various zones.

By way of exception, para. 2 provides that 'an indemnity is due if these servitudes cause an infringement on a right which has already been acquired (*droit acquis*) or an alteration of the prior state of premises which results in harm which is direct, material and certain ...'. Without agreement by the parties, the amount of the indemnity is to be set by an administrative tribunal.[78] Nevertheless, when this exception applies, the defendant in a civil action may be ordered to pay damages or to comply with the servitude,[79] even if it means demolishing what he has built.[80] That is so even though, supposedly, such servitudes are imposed in the public interest and not for the benefit of a dominant estate as in private law.[81] But unless the exception applies, no compensation is due.

This provision is so drastic that some think that it violates the European Convention on Human Rights.[82] Some French jurists claim it is justified since planning servitudes are imposed in the 'general interest' which should prevail over 'private interests'.[83] But, as we have seen, often such servitudes are not established to serve the public interest or even the private interests that are protected by the law of *troubles de voisinage*. They are established to give flexibility to the private law rules that govern servitudes. In such a case, a party should be compensated whether or not the servitude infringes 'a right that has already been acquired' or 'results in a harm which is direct, material and certain'.

3.5 Conclusion

Interferences among neighbours are now governed chiefly by three bodies of law which were not envisioned by the drafters of the French Civil Code. Articles 1384–6 have been interpreted to impose strict liability on anyone who is injured by animals, by the collapse of a house and, more generally, by any 'thing' in another's 'custody'. A land owner can sue when a neighbour's animal, house or 'thing' harms him or his property without the need to prove fault. In contrast, interferences caused by noise, smoke, vibration and the like are governed by the law of *abus de droit* and *troubles*

78 Planning code Art. L. 160–5(2).

79 Cass., 1e civ., 9 June 1959, Bull. civ. I, no. 291, p. 242.

80 Cass., 3e civ., 2 July 1974, Bull. civ. III, no. 282, p. 214; Cass., 1e civ., 1 March 1965, Bull. civ. I, no. 158, p. 121.

81 Cass., 1e civ., 8 May 1963, Bull. civ. I, no. 254, p. 215.

82 See Morand-Deviller, p. 25.

83 Ibid. p. 24.

de voisinage. The defendant is liable for *abus de droit* when he intends to harm or disturb another, and under the doctrine of *troubles de voisinage* when his use of land is abnormally offensive. Although similar rules were endorsed by Domat and Pothier, the writers who most influenced the drafters of the Civil Code, the drafters seem to have left them out of the Code by oversight. Courts had to rediscover them. Finally, in the twentieth century, French legislation has adopted a systematic regulatory scheme in which land use is governed by national and local rules and by the imposition of servitudes on often unwilling proprietors.

As we have seen, French law as to strict liability is confused. French jurists have not clearly explained what should count as the 'act of a thing' or when liability under this doctrine should end and liability for *abus de droit* and *troubles de voisinage* should begin.

The French have been relatively successful in developing the second of these bodies of law. The law governing *troubles de voisinage* should give relief only when one person's use of his land interferes abnormally with that of another. That is true, at least, if the French jurist Josserand is correct as to the rationale of the doctrine: that he who profits from an activity should pay for the harm it does. While any use of land may harm another to some extent, it seems fair that one who uses his land to get a benefit that his neighbour does not receive, and consequently disturbs his neighbour in a way in which his neighbour does not disturb him, should pay for the interference. If that is the rationale, then it would seem that the French courts are correct in giving relief when the defendant uses his land in a way that is aesthetically or morally offensive. They are also correct to deny recovery to one who is only disturbed because he, for his own advantage, is conducting an activity that is abnormally sensitive. It would also seem that, in principle, people who change the character of a neighbourhood for their own advantage, so that the defendant's activity becomes abnormally offensive, should not be able to make the defendant stop without paying compensation. Under French law, they can stop him without paying, but the reason may be that it is not practical to identify and impose liability on all those who will benefit if the defendant stops.

The third body of law, the regulatory scheme, has advantages that the second does not. It can bring definiteness to the concept of abnormal interferences. It can better enable a person to know in advance how he can use his land. Moreover, those in charge of regulating land use can take account of both the public and the private interests. Yet, a price has to be paid for the first two of these advantages: rules that make the law definite and knowable in advance are often less suitable than decisions about land use than those made by courts who have more time for reflection and can examine the particular situation of the parties concerned. Moreover, in considering both public and private interests at once, one may ignore the differences between how the public interest and private interests should be protected. Thus sometimes a person has been denied relief even when burdens are imposed on him to further the private interests of others.

One can learn both from what the French have done successfully and from what they could have avoided. One can also learn how unreliable national stereotypes can be. One imagines French law as the product of rational design and English law as the fruit of experience. In fact, these three bodies of French law grew independently and pragmatically over the course of time. The absence of an overall design explains why it has been difficult to relate each one to the other. The success of a pragmatic approach explains why, on the whole, the French have dealt with a variety of problems so well.

4

Disturbances between neighbours in Germany 1850–2000

ANDREAS THIER

4.1 Introduction

The modern German law of neighbour relations is mainly based on a concept of coordinated property rights:[1] §§ 903, 906 and 1004 BGB[2] form a complex framework of rules which limit the use of property and create a duty to tolerate certain forms of neighbourly land use and the nuisance caused by that use. § 906 sect. 2 BGB provides compensation claims for this duty.[3] These compensation claims come close to strict liability. There are also, however, provisions of neighbourhood law which regulate the relations between neighbouring property owners using tortious obligations and therefore presupposing fault: § 909 BGB prohibits digging on someone's own land, if such an act could be dangerous for the situation of the adjoining land. § 907 BGB provides the right to prohibit facilities on the neighbour's land which could effect unlawful intrusion onto the land of the property owner. Even though §§ 907 and 909 BGB are part of the property rights section of the German Civil Code, they constitute delictual obligations at the same time. A culpable violation of these obligations results in a claim for compensation.[4] Besides these provisions, the delict law in general, established first and foremost in § 823 BGB, is also applicable to the legal relations between neighbours.[5] Moreover, the compensation

[1] J. Neuner, 'Das nachbarrechtliche Haftungssystem', Juristische Schulung (2005), 385–7.

[2] The rules about the protection of possession, §§ 858, 862, 869 BGB, will not be discussed here, as they are of limited relevance for the perspectives of this paper; for a survey on these rulings see Neuner, 'Haftungssystem', p. 488.

[3] For the provisions in § 912 sect. 2 (superstructure) and § 917 sect. 2 BGB (way of necessity), which establish claims for an annuity see as a survey O. Jauernig, *Kommentar zum BGB*, 11th edn (Munich, Beck, 2004), § 912, n. 9 and § 917, n. 5. These claims can be described as a type of denial damage, cf. Neuner, 'Haftungssystem', above, n. 1, p. 490.

[4] For a first survey see H. Westermann, *Sachenrecht. Ein Lehrbuch*, 7th edn by Westermann, Gursky & Eickmann (Heidelberg, Müller Verlag, 1998), pp. 517–18.

[5] For a short survey see R.-J. Haag, *Öffentliches und privates Nachbarrecht* (Munich, VVF, 1996), pp. 28–30.

rules in § 906 BGB are – in principle – subsidiary to delict law.[6] Beyond those property-based rules, the civil law protection of other goods – particularly health and privacy – is based, in principle, on delict law.

This summary could give the impression that property-based neighbourhood law and fault-based delict law are clearly distinguishable from each other. There is, however, a close connection between both normative spheres: so it is argued that the compensation rules in § 906 BGB are also to be applied to health damages and to mere land users.[7] At the same time, the provisions of property-based neighbourhood law are often used to shape standards for delictual liability: a person acting within the limits of property-based neighbourhood law cannot be liable by delict law.[8] On the other hand, the culpable violation of obligations, established in §§ 907, 909 and 1004 BGB, results in liability for damages to the neighbour's land caused by such actions.[9] But beyond these provisions of delict law, damages are, under certain conditions, also compensated by denial damages.[10] There is an even stronger link between these civil law provisions and administrative law. Administrative rules have had an increasing impact on the legal ruling of neighbour relations, especially as the provisions of administrative law are linked to the rulings both of delict law and of property law by legislators and judges.[11] Moreover, administrative rules are often also used as binding standards for fault liability, even though most authors argue for the autonomy of civil law liability standards as a basic principle.[12]

This chapter will describe the developments outlined above in further detail. In the first section, the function of the *actio negatoria* as limitation for the use of property rights and the rise of the concept of denial damage as essential legal remedies for the legal settlement of neighbour conflicts

[6] BGH 26 October 1978, NJW 1979, 164, 165; BGH 20 November 1992, BGHZ 120, 239, 249. *Germany*; summarising: J. Fritzsche, *Beck'scher Online-Kommentar zum BGB* (1 August 2006) § 906, n. 82.

[7] See as a first short survey T. J. Möllers, *Rechtsgüterschutz im Umwelt und Haftungsrecht. Präventive Verkehrspflichten und Beweiserleichterungen in Risikolagen* (Tübingen, Mohr, 1996), p. 49.

[8] BGH 18 September 1984, BGHZ 92, 143, 148–9. As a survey see G. Wagner, *Münchner Bürgerlichen Gesetzbuch*, 4th edn (Munich, Beck, 2004), § 823, n. 306.

[9] See for a survey P. Bassenge, in *Bürgerliches Gesetzbuch*, founded by O. Palandt, 66th edn (Munich, Beck, 2007), § 907, n. 3, § 909, n. 12 and § 1004, n. 49.

[10] H. Roth, *J. von Staudingers Kommentar zum Bürgerlichen Gesetzbuch mit Einführungsgesetz und Nebengesetzen*, 12th edn (Berlin, Schweitzer de Gruyter, 2002), vol. 3, § 907, nn. 51, 53.

[11] As a survey see K. H. Schwab and H. Prütting, *Sachenrecht*, 32nd edn (Munich, Beck, 2006), nn. 352–4.

[12] For a survey on this debate see Wagner, *Münchner Kommentar*, above, n. 8, § 823, nn. 267–70.

will be discussed (at 4.2). In the second section, the tight connections between those property-based rules and the provisions of delict law will be addressed (at 4.3). The third section will deal with the delictual protection of privacy and health in neighbour relations (at 4.4).

4.2 *Actio negatoria* and denial damage

In conflicts between neighbours about the use of land, the *actio negatoria* was an important legal remedy in the tradition of the *ius commune*:[13] by the *actio negatoria*, the property owner could protect himself, especially against emissions caused by his neighbours. This action was based on his property right and figured as a 'replevin for the freedom of our real estate resulting from the right of property',[14] as Glück stated. The intruder could be ordered to stop all emissions and even to dispose of factories or other buildings causing the emissions. It was also possible to make a claim for compensation and to prevent future emissions.[15] But not every act was seen as unlawful: in the tradition of the *ius commune*, established especially by Bartolus, the right of property granted its owner the power to dispose of his assets at his own free will.[16] Hence, the crucial question arose of where to draw the line between this entitlement and the entitlement of the neighbour to defend himself against nuisance by the *actio negatoria*. Since the period of ancient Roman law, the property owner of a real estate could use his land only as long as he did not disturb his neighbour. As the Roman jurist Aristo said, '*in suo ... alii hactenus facere licet, quatenus nihil in alienum immittat*'.[17] Since about the time of Bartolus, the limits

[13] For a survey on the Roman tradition: M. Kaser and R. Knütel, *Römisches Privatrecht*, 18th edn (Munich, Beck, 2005), § 27/nn. 23–24; M. Kaser, *Das römische Privatrecht I*, 2nd edn (Munich, Beck, 1971), § 98 III 5; M. Kaser, *Das römische Privatrecht II*, 2nd edn (Munich, Beck, 1975), § 245 IV.

[14] Ch. F. Glück, *Ausführliche Erläuterung der Pandecten nach Hellfeld. Ein Commentar X/1* (Erlangen, Palm, 1808), §685, p. 241: 'eine aus dem Eigentumsrechte entspringende Vindication der Freyheit unsers Grundstücks'.

[15] See Glück, *Erläuterung*, above, n. 14, § 685, p. 239.

[16] Bartolus de Sassoferrato, *Commentaria in primam digesti novi partem*, Note 4 to D. 41,2,17 (= lex *Si quis vi*), edn Lyon 1550, fol. 91vb: *Dominium est ius de re corporali perfecte disponendi nisi lege prohibeatur.* For Bartolus and his doctrine of property see H. Coing, 'Zur Eigentumslehre des Bartolus', ZRG RA 70 (1953), 348–71. For a short survey on the history of property in early modern times see A. Thier, 'Eigentum – rechtlich', *Enzyklopädie der Neuzeit III* (Stuttgart/Weimar, Metzler, 2006), cols. 98–103.

[17] D. 8.5.8.5 (Ulpian); for a discussion of this statement see especially A. Rodger, *Owners and Neighbours in Roman Law* (Oxford, Clarendon Press, 1972) pp. 164–5, A. Watson, *The Law of Property in the Later Roman Republic* (Oxford, Clarendon Press, 1968), pp. 179–80.

for a forbidden *facere* were set, where the property owner acted *animo iniuriandi*, a category derived from the *actio iniuriarum*.[18] Bartholomaeo Caepolla, whose book on the law of servitudes was one of the best-known jurisprudential works in early modern times,[19] granted in such cases this type of legal action against the emitting property owner.[20] In this doctrinal perspective, the protection against nuisance was, to a certain extent, linked to the general prohibition of chicanery.[21] But, besides these cases, the extended commercial use of land was also judged inadmissible: *facere tabernam vel hostiarium, ubi continue fieret ignis et fumus magnus* was, as Bartolus stated,[22] a violation of the property limitations between neighbours.[23]

This tradition had a strong influence on the development of neighbourhood law in the early nineteenth century. As will be shown in the first subsection, the German courts originally set strict limits on the industrial use of land especially; before then, the Reichsgericht, the supreme court of the second German Empire, changed the general structure of the *actio negatoria* in favour of industrial interests (see 4.2.1). At the same time, administrative law exerted more and more influence on the settlement of conflicts between neighbours. The state started to intervene in relations between neighbours. This development has continued until now (see 4.2.2). As a consequence, the structure of compensation changed. The traditional form of damage compensation lost ground and was increasingly substituted by a sort of denial damage. A concept of

[18] For a deeper discussion see R. Zimmermann, *Law of Obligations. Roman Foundations of the Civilian Tradition* (Oxford, Clarendon Press, 1990), pp. 1059–61.

[19] For the widespread reception of Caepolla in Europe see P. Liver, 'Die vom 15. bis 19. Jahrhundert meistgedruckte juristische Monographie: Bart. Caepollae Veronensis I. C. clarissimi Tractatus de servitutibus, tam urbanorum, quam rusticorum praediorum 1473–1859', ZRG RA 99 (1982), 326–41.

[20] Bartholomaeus Caepolla, *Tractatus de servitutibus, tam urbanorum, quam rusticorum praediorum* (1473/1477), edn Cologne 1759, 1.31, qu. 4 and 1.53, qu. 1, pp. 95 and 166.

[21] For this linkage see H. P. Haferkamp, in: *Historisch-kritischer Kommentar zum BGB, Bd. 1: Allgemeiner Teil, §§ 1-240* (Tübingen, Mohr Siebeck, 2003), §§ 226–31, n. 7; as an example of the legal provision for this type of ruling see I 8 § 27 Allgemeines Landrecht für die preussischen Staaten, which prohibited the 'misuse' of someone's property in order to offend or to damage other persons.

[22] Bartolus de Sassoferrato, *Commentaria* , above, n. 16, N. 2 for D. 8.5.8.5, fol. 210va-[vb]; for a discussion of this concept see J. Gordley, 'Immissionsschutz, Nuisance and Troubles de Voisinage in Comparative and Historical Perspective', *ZEuP* 1998, 14.

[23] For this tendency in the jurisprudential doctrine of the usus modernus pandectarum see P. C. Klemm, *Eigentum und Eigentumsbeschränkungen in der Doktrin des usus modernus pandectarum* (Basel/Frankfurt a. M., Helbing & Lichtenhahn, 1984), pp. 154–6.

compensation created in the field of public law was transferred to the area of civil law (see 4.2.3).

4.2.1 Actio negatoria *and the (un)usual use of land*

In the period around 1850, German courts were quite hostile towards the use of land for industrial purposes.[24] In their view, probably influenced in particular by Ernst Peter Johann Spangenberg, judge at the court in Celle,[25] the use of land was unlawful and could therefore be forbidden by the *actio negatoria*, if it figured as a *permanent unusual form of use*.[26] In such cases, the property owner had to pay damage compensation and to cease running his factory; sometimes he was sentenced only to reduce emissions.[27] In this sense, a factory was the near typical form of an impermissible use of land, because, as the court of Wolfenbüttel stated, the 'running of a factory … is to be seen as an unusual use [of land]'.[28] Even though the courts sometimes emphasised the fact that the plaintiff would have to indicate a serious interest, based on damage or nuisance,[29] the owner of industrially used land was continually handicapped in conflicts with his neighbour. So Rudolf Ihering, one of the most influential German jurists of his time, recommended that the business should move to a remote

[24] For the following see R. Ogorek, 'Actio negatoria und industrielle Beeinträchtigung des Grundeigentums', *Wissenschaft und Kodifikation des Privatrechts im 19. Jahrhundert IV: Eigentum und industrielle Entwicklung, Wettbewerbsordnung und Wettbewerbsrecht*, ed. Coing and Wilhelm (Frankfurt a. M., Klostermann, 1974), p. 40, at 49–56; A. Thier, 'Zwischen actio negatoria und Aufopferungsanspruch: Nachbarliche Nutzungskonflikte in der Rechtsprechung des 19. und 20. Jahrhunderts', *Das Bürgerliche Gesetzbuch und seine Richter. Zur Reaktion der Rechtsprechung auf die Kodifikation des deutschen Privatrechts (1896–1914)*, ed. Falk and Mohnhaupt (Frankfurt, Klostermann, 2000), p. 407, pp. 415–24, both with further references.

[25] [E. P. J.] Spangenberg, 'Einige Bemerkungen über das Nachbarrecht', Archiv für die civilistische Praxis a. F. 9 (1826), 265, 270–2. For a discussion in further detail see Thier, 'Zwischen actio negatoria und Aufopferungsanspruch', above, n. 24, p. 417.

[26] OAG Lübeck 25 November 1858, Seufferts Archiv 15 (1862), Nr. 2, p. 3 *Lübeck*; see also AG Dresden 17 December 1843, OAG Dresden 11 May 1844, Seufferts Archiv 3 (1851), Nr. 7, S. 8–14 (for a gas plant). *Saxony.*

[27] OAG Munich 16 April 1861, Seufferts Archiv 14 (1861), Nr. 208, p. 354. *Bavaria*; summarising OLG Braunschweig 22 October 1890, Seufferts Archiv a. F. 46 (1891) = n. F. 16 (1891), Nr. 249, p. 391. *Braunschweig.*

[28] OG Wolfenbüttel 26 May 1876, Seufferts Archiv a. F. 32 = n. F. 2 (1877), Nr. 18, p. 26 f., 27. *Braunschweig*; see also OT Berlin 12 October 1875, Seufferts Archiv 31 a. F. (1876) = n. F. 1 (1876), Nr. 116, p. 148, 150 (*Prussia*) and OLG Jena 2 November 1882, Seufferts Archiv 39 a. F. (1884) = n. F. 9 (1884), Nr. 194, p. 280 *Saxony-Weimar-Eisenach.*

[29] OG Wolfenbüttel 28 May 1878, Seufferts Archiv a. F. 34 (1879) = n. F. 4 (1879), Nr. 181, p. 269, pp. 270–1 (*Braunschweig*) with further reference to jurisdictional practice.

location, if it wished to continue the production process of its factory.[30] This situation changed when the Reichsgericht set new standards for the *actio negatoria*. Up to this time, the German courts had judged the quality of the use of land and the intensity of the emissions in abstract.[31] The situation of the surrounding land, e.g. the presence of industrial plants on neighbouring land, had not been taken into account. In 1882, however, the Reichsgericht shifted to a more concrete standard by also including surrounding land. The judges ruled, therefore, that the property owner had to tolerate emissions which were usual for the time and place.[32] Emissions were allowed as long as they were in accordance with the *local circumstances*.[33] Maybe this new approach was influenced by Pothier's concept of a 'quasi-contrat, qui forme des obligations réciproques entre les voisins'[34] in French law: at least in theory, the idea of an 'obligation' not only of the emitting property owner, but also of his neighbour, laid the ground for an obligation to tolerate industrial emissions.[35] Actually, in the case law of the Rhenish law area,[36] from about 1860 there emerged a tendency towards a widened obligation to tolerate nuisance, which appeared to have also influenced the case law of the Reichsgericht.[37] There are two other

[30] R. v. Jhering, 'Zur Lehre von den Beschränkungen des Grundeigenthümers im Interesse der Nachbarn', *Jahrbücher für die Dogmatik des heutigen römischen und deutschen Privatrechts* 6 (1862), 81, newly published in R. von Jhering, *Gesammelte Aufsätze aus den Jahrbüchern für die Dogmatik des heutigen römischen und deutschen Privatrechts, vol. 2: Abhandlungen aus Band 5–15 der Jahrbücher* (Jena, Fischer, 1882, repr. Aalen, Scientia, 1969), pp. 22, 64.

[31] Thier, 'Zwischen actio negatoria und Aufopferungsanspruch', above, n. 24, pp. 423–4 for the situation around 1880.

[32] RG (3. Senate) 23 May 1882, Seufferts Archiv a. F. 38 (1883) = n. F. 8 (1883), Nr. 8, p. 13 f., 13.

[33] As summarising judgement see RG (3. Senate) 15.5.1896, Seufferts Archiv a. F. 52 (1897) = n. F. 22 (1897), Nr. 146, p. 269 f., 270.

[34] R.-J. Pothier, *Traité du contrat de société*, ch. 9, appendix II, *Oeuvres de R.-J. Pothier, contenant les traités du droit francais: augmenteée d'une dissertation sur la vie et les ouvrages de ce célébre jurisconsulte, et d'une table alphabétique, analytique et raisonnée des matières du droit civil français contenues dans les oeuvres de Pothier par le même* III, ed. A. M. J. J. Dupin, 2nd edn (Paris, Charles Béchet, 1835), p. 443, pp. 549–60.

[35] Similar judgement with A. Bürge, *Das französische Privatrecht im 19. Jahrhundert. Zwischen Tradition und Pandektenwissenschaft, Liberalismus und Etatismus*, 2nd edn (Frankfurt a. M., Klostermann, 1995), p. 405.

[36] W. Schubert, *Französisches Recht in Deutschland zu Beginn des 19. Jahrhunderts. Zivilrecht, Gerichtsverfassungsrecht und Zivilprozeßrecht* (Cologne/Vienna, Böhlau, 1977); R. Schulze (ed.), *Rheinisches Recht und europäische Rechtsgeschichte* (Berlin, Duncker & Humblot, 1998).

[37] A. Thier, 'Actio negatoria, Nachbarrecht und Industrialisierung der deutschen Rechtsprechung zum Code civil', *Richterliche Anwendung des Code Civil in seinen europäischen Geltungsbereichen ausserhalb Frankreichs*, Dölemeyer, Mohnhaupt,

reasons which might explain the change of the jurisdictional line: Rudolf Jhering's concepts of liability and also of the *actio negatoria* appeared to have had a strong influence on the Reichsgericht.[38] Even though Jhering had argued against industrial emissions, he advocated a balancing of the interests of both the emitting property owner and his neighbour.[39] Similar to the doctrine in Rhenish law, this concept made it possible to give the interest of industrial land use more weight than before. As a second point, industrial interests in general grew in importance from about the late 1880s.[40] Apparently, the 5th senate of the Reichsgericht, especially, was not insensitive to industrial emission interests.[41] This becomes clear if one looks at the interpretation of § 906 sect. 1 BGB (1900), wherein the concept of the Reichsgericht had been adopted.[42] According to this rule, the property owner had to tolerate emissions from neighbouring land which were 'usual for the local circumstances'. So the limits of permissible emissions depended on the situation of the surrounding land. One of the essential points for the application of this rule was the question of where the boundaries for the reference area were to be drawn. At least two judgments of the Reichsgericht make clear that judges supported the emission interests of big producers. In both cases, the judges compared the situation of the disputed land with the situation in other cities; 'local circumstances' could mean, in this interpretation of § 906 BGB, 'different municipalities of one area'[43] – and not the situation in the nearby

Somma (ed.) (Frankfurt a. M., Klostermann, 2006), p. 217, pp. 224–33. A similar opinion in Bürge, *Das französische Privatrecht im 19. Jahrhundert*, above, n. 35, pp. 230–3.

38 See for example the adoption of the concept of fault liability by the Reichsgericht, 29.3.1882, RGZ 6,217, 220–221; R. v. Jhering, *Das Schuldmoment im römischen Privatrecht* (Giessen, Roth, 1867), reprinted in: R. v. Jhering, *Vermischte Schriften juristischen Inhalts* (Leipzig, Breitkopf & Härtel, 1879, repr. Aalen, Scientia, 1968), pp. 155–240. For Jhering's doctrine on the *actio negatoria* see RG 23.5.1882, Seufferts Archiv a. F. 38 = n. F. 8 (1883), Nr. 8, p. 13, 14

39 Jhering, 'Lehre', above, n. 30, p. 48.

40 For this development in general see H. P. Ullmann, *Politik im Deutschen Kaiserreich 1871–1918* (Munich, Oldenbourg, 1999), pp. 21, 69, 78–9.

41 The underlying reason for this case law appeared to be the link between the 'advantages granted to someone (i.e. the property owner affected by emissions) (higher prices of sale and lease)' and the 'disadvantages', quoted from RG 15.10.1887, Bolze, *Die Praxis des Reichsgerichts in Zivilsachen III* (Leipzig, Brockhaus, 1887), Nr. 89, p. 2. Same perspective with Roth on the legislative conception, *Kommentar*, above, n. 10, § 906, n. 206.

42 For the influence of the jurisdictional concept on the drafting of § 906 BGB see Thier, 'Zwischen actio negatoria und Aufopferungsanspruch', above, n. 24, pp. 429–33; for the question of the influence of Jhering's doctrine see *ibid.*, p. 430 n. 102 on the one hand and Gordley, 'Nuisance', above, n. 22, p. 15 n. 17 on the other.

43 RG 5 April 1911, Das Recht 1911, Nr. 2733.

surroundings of the emitting land. Even though this standard was also applied in favour of great agricultural plants,[44] judges stressed that § 906 BGB would demand an 'equitable (*billige*) attentiveness for the industry and its need to make emissions'.[45] In principle, the concept of § 906 BGB (1900) is still in force, even though it was slightly modified in 1959: a non-essential (*unwesentliche*) nuisance has to be tolerated, § 906 sect. 1 BGB. A (1) substantial (*wesentliche*) nuisance has to be tolerated if it is (2) customary in a place (*ortsüblich*) and (3) cannot be prevented by means which are economically reasonable (*zumutbar*) for the user of the emitting land.[46] At the time of its emergence, the new conception favoured most notably, but not solely, the industrial use of land. Significantly for this aspect, in numerous judgments, industrial use of land appeared to be the central issue.[47] During the course of time, agricultural forms of land use such as piggeries also came to be supported by this standard.[48] In modern times, the interpretation of § 906 sect. 1 BGB by the courts has not changed, if compared to the case law of the Reichsgericht.[49] The reference area, for example, can still be widened beyond the boundary of a township.[50] Nevertheless, this rule appears to have lost a little of its importance. This is because of the increasing importance of administrative law for the settlement of neighbour conflicts, which is now to be addressed.

4.2.2 *Administrative rules and the obligations of neighbours*

Until the middle of the nineteenth century, the regimes of public and civil law were strictly separate. Therefore the administrative permit for an industrial plant, a mill or a workshop had no consequences for relations between neighbours in civil law.[51] This situation changed fundamentally

[44] RG 27 December 1909, JW 1910, p. 149.

[45] RG 6 July 1910, Gruchots Beiträge 52 (1911), Nr. 6, p. 105, 107.

[46] BGBl. 1959 I 781 (22 December 1959); for the history of this provision see H. Hagen, 'Der nachbarrechtliche Aufopferungsanspruch nach § 906 Abs. 2 Satz 2 BGB als Musterlösung und Lösungsmuster – Rechtsfortbildung in mehreren Etappen', *FS Hermann Lange*, ed. Medicus, Mertens, Nörr, Zöllner (Stuttgart/Berlin/Cologne, Kohlhammer, 1992), pp. 483, 493.

[47] See e.g. RG 27 December 1909, JW 1910, 149–150 (Nr. 14); 10 March 1937, RGZ 154, 161; BGH 6 July 2001, NJW 2001, 3119, 3120–311.

[48] See for example BGH 30 October 1998, NJW 1999, 356, 357.

[49] For a vast survey see Roth, *Kommentar*, above, n. 10, § 906, nn. 205–36.

[50] BGH 23 March 1990, NJW 1990, 2465, 2467.

[51] Prussian higher tribunal (Preussisches Obertribunal) 7 June 1852, Entscheidungen des Königlichen Obertribunals 23, pp. 252, 262 (*Prussia*). For more details see Thier, 'Zwischen actio negatoria und Aufopferungsanspruch', above, n. 24, pp. 435–8.

in 1869, when the Industrial Code for the North German Federation (*Gewerbeordnung für den Norddeutschen Bund*) was issued.[52] Paragraph 26 of this law protected the owner of a factory, licensed by an administrative permission, against his neighbour: the property owner of land in the neighbourhood of such a factory could not claim the *actio negatoria* in order to stop it. He could only claim measures preventing nuisance or, if these measures would be too expensive, compensation for his damages. As a consequence, § 26 of the Law transferred decisions about the permission of nuisance from the civil courts to the administration.[53] Even though this rule was only applicable for quite a small number of factories, the Reichsgericht transferred this legislative concept step by step to all sorts of factories with an administrative permission. The beginning of this process was marked by the Reichsgericht decision on an action brought by the neighbour of a railway in 1882. The plaintiff had suffered damages by flying sparks from the trains, as they travelled near his land. As the permit for the railway did not regulate the duties of the railway entrepreneur based on civil law, the plaintiff claimed the prohibition of the railway by the *actio negatoria*. The Reichsgericht, however, stated that 'the permission for the railway includes the general order from the state authority that the adjoining property owner has to tolerate this nuisance, without which the business would not be feasible'.[54] In the following years, the Reichsgericht extended this concept to nearly all public permitted factories and similar facilities.[55] Since then, not only facilities covered by § 26 GewO, but also facilities 'being important for the public good' (*gemeinwichtige Betriebe*), such as police stations,[56] post facilities,[57] motorways,[58] power lines[59] or, in the present day, a care centre for drug addicts,[60] were protected against the *actio negatoria*[61] and also against claims based on delict law.[62] Meanwhile, this jurisdictional case law *praeter legem* is

52 *Bundesgesetzblatt für den Norddeutschen Bund* 1869, 245 (21 June 1869); for the history of the industrial code see K. Pollmann, *Parlamentarismus im Norddeutschen Bund 1867–1870* (Düsseldorf, Droste, 1985), pp. 475–80.

53 Thier, 'Zwischen actio negatoria und Aufopferungsanspruch', above, n. 24, pp. 438–9.

54 RG 20 September 1882, RGZ 7, 265, 267.

55 For further detail see Thier, 'Zwischen actio negatoria und Aufopferungsanspruch', above, n. 24, pp. 439–43.

56 RG 25 March 1908, *Warneyers Jahrbuch der Entscheidungen*, supplementary volume 1 (1908), Nr. 380, pp. 285, 286.

57 RG 16 October.1910, RGZ 73, 270, 271.

58 RG 9 January 1939, RGZ 159, 129, 137–41; BGH 15 June 1967, NJW 1967, 1857, 1858.

59 BGH 25 January 1973, NJW 1973, 508.

60 BGH 7 April 2000, NJW 2000, 2901, 2902.

61 For a survey see Roth, *Kommentar*, above, n. 10, § 906, nn. 29, 42–6, 58.

62 Clearly expressed in BGH 7 April 2000, NJW 2000, 2901, 2902.

strongly (and rightly) criticised,[63] as it leads to a limitation of property without any legislative legitimation and therefore violates § 14 sect. 1, 2 GG. From a historical perspective, the continuity of this case law highlights once more the intense state intervention in neighbour relations.

The development towards an administration-dominated settlement of neighbour disputes in the field of industrial and agricultural emissions continued in the twentieth century: in 1974, the 'Federal law for the pro tection against emissions' (BImSchG, *Bundesimmissionsschutzgesetz*) took up the concept of §26 of the Industrial Code.[64] § 14 BImSchG excludes an *actio negatoria* against every factory licensed by the rules and procedures established in that law; the neighbour is limited to a claim for precautions against nuisance or compensation for his damages.[65] This ruling has been adopted in legislative rulings on nuclear power plants,[66] in the law concerning air traffic (*Luftverkehrsgesetz*),[67] in some essential parts of the law concerning gene technology (*Gentechnikgesetz*)[68] and in some provisions of the neighbourhood law relating to traffic corporations issued by the individual German states.[69] As a consequence, in a wide range of cases, the administration-issued licence legalises the use of land and the production of emissions, granting the neighbour denial damage at the same time. The question of liability is, in these situations, irrelevant.[70]

[63] F. Peine, 'Privatrechtsgestaltung durch Anlagengenehmigung', NJW 1990, 2442, 2443 with n. 22 and further reference.

[64] BGBl I 721 (21 March 1974). For a list of the legislative changes since 1974 see H. D. Jarass, *Bundesimmissionsschutzgesetz, Kommentar unter Berücksichtigung der Bundes-Immissionsschutzverordnungen, der TA Luft sowie der TA Lärm*, 6th edn (Munich, Beck, 2005), Einleitung, n. 2.

[65] 65 As a survey see Roth, *Kommentar*, above, n. 10, § 906, nn. 20–6; in further detail see Jarass, *Bundesimmissionsschutzgesetz* , above, n. 64, § 14, n. 2–11 with further reference.

[66] Gesetz über die friedliche Verwendung der Kernenergie und den Schutz gegen ihre Gefahren (Atomgesetz), first issued in BGBl. I S. 814 (23 December 1959), current version BGBl. I S. 1565 (15 July 1985, last change 31 October 2006). For the reference to § 14 BImSchG see § 7 sect. 6 AtomG.

[67] Luftverkehrsgesetz, originally issued 1 August 1922 (RGBl I 681), current version BGBl I 1999, 550, last change 9 December 2006. For the reference to § 14 BImSchG see § 11 LuftVG.

[68] Gentechnikgesetz, originally issued 20 June 1990 (BGBl. I 1990, 1080), current version BGBl. I S. 2066, last change 17 March 2006; § 23 GenTG excludes the claim for a suspension of production, but grants the neighbour the right to claim such means against nuisance as are possible by the state of technology; economic reasonableness is not demanded.

[69] See, for a survey, Säcker, *Müncher Kommentar zum Bürgerlichen Gesetzbuch*, 4th edn (Munich, Beck, 2006), Art. 125 EGBGB, n. 3.

[70] G. Wagner, *Öffentlich-rechtliche Genehmigung und zivilrechtliche Rechts widrigkeit* (Cologne/Berlin/Bonn/Munich, Heymann, 1989), pp. 7–116 and *pass.*; Peine, 'Privatrechtsgestaltung', above, n. 63, 2445–8.

The strong influence of administrative law on civil neighbourhood law also becomes clear if one looks at another provision of § 906 BGB, issued in 1994: according to § 906 sect. 1, cl. 2, 3 BGB, the essentiality of nuisance is indicated by the data issued in administrative rulings such as the *TA-Luft* or *TA Lärm*.[71] By this clause, a sort of limited legislative accessory character between civil law and administrative law has been established.[72] In the settled case law of the German Federal Court, the Bundesgerichtshof, this has been widened. In 1998, the court ruled that emissions caused by a facility not licensed by the administration could not be judged as customary in a place (§906 sect. 2, cl. 1 BGB).[73] Again, administrative law sets the conditions for the lawfulness of emissions in civil law too.

But also beyond the field of environmental law there are tendencies for a dominance of administrative law-based rulings in neighbour relations: since the late nineteenth century, first on the level of the individual states[74] and in 1960 at the federal level, the planned use of space came to be an issue of legislative ruling and municipal statutory law.[75] In the field of neighbour relations, the federal law about building (*Bundesbaugesetz*),[76] since 1987 the building code (*Baugesetzbuch*),[77] is – beside the state laws on building regulations – essential for the coordination of neighbour interests in

[71] BGBl I 2457 (21 September 1994). For the history of the drafting of this rule see K. Fritz, 'Das Verhältnis von privatem und öffentlichem Immissionsschutzrecht nach der Ergänzung von § 906 I BGB', NJW 1996, 573. In further detail for the application of these provisions see Roth, *Kommentar*, above, n. 10, § 906, nn. 188–91.

[72] For the term 'limited accessory character of civil law in relation to administrative law' (*limitierte Verwaltungsrechtsakzessorietät*) see J. Petersen, *Duldungspflicht und Umwelthaftung. Das Verhältnis von §906 BGB zum Umwelthaftungsgesetz* (Munich, Beck, 1996), p. 77.

[73] BGH 30 October 1998, BGHZ 140, 1, 6. *Germany.*

[74] For the history of the early zoning see B. Ladd, *Urban Planning and Civic Order in Germany, 1860–1914* (Cambridge, Mass./London, Harvard University Press, 1990), pp. 187–95. For the roots of this remedy in the late Middle Ages see M. Stercken, 'Gebaute Ordnung. Stadtvorstellungen und Planung im Mittelalter', *Städteplanung – Planungsstädte*, ed. Fritzsche, Gilomen and Stercken (Zürich, Chronos, 2006), p. 15.

[75] For a short survey see W. Berg, 'Wirtschaftsverwaltung einschliesslich Bauwesen', *Deutsche Verwaltungsgeschichte IV*, ed. Jeserich, Pohl and von Unruh (Stuttgart, Deutsche Verl.-Anst., 1985), p. 421, pp. 431–4; H. J. v. d. Heide, J.-D. Kühne, 'Die sozialstaatliche Entwicklung des Boden-, Bau- und Wohnungswesens zwischen Wiederaufbau und umfassender Planung', *Deutsche Verwaltungsgeschichte V*, ed. Jeserich, Pohl and von Unruh (Stuttgart, Deutsche Verl.-Anst., 1987), pp. 874, 881–5.

[76] 29 June 1960 (BGBl. I 341). For a short survey on its history see M. Krautzberger, *Baugesetzbuch*, 5th edn (Münich, Beck, 2005), Einleitung, nn. 11–14.

[77] 8 December 1986 (BGBl. I 2253). See for a survey on the history of this law Krautzberger, *Baugesetzbuch*, above, n. 76, nn. 20–2.

building cases: the constitutionally authorised power of municipalities to plan building developments in the area under their jurisdiction is set in concrete. In building plans, issued by municipal councils, zones of specific types of land use (e.g. *housing construction*) are established; the 'Decree about the use of buildings' (*Baunutzungsverordnung*)[78] supplements the provisions of building plans or can even substitute some of them. These regulations set out quite precisely the form, and to a certain extent also the dimensions, of the use of building land. Such provisions are also intended to settle conflicts between different land use interests of neighbours and grant neighbours administrative law-based subjective rights.[79] If the municipality does not issue a building plan, legislative planning provisions, set by the *Baugesetzbuch* directly, are applicable. These rulings grant neighbours individual rights based on administrative law as well.[80] There are, however, no legislative rulings on the effects of these norms to civil law. Against this background, the relationship between the administrative law of neighbourhood and the civil law of neighbourhood has been strongly debated, particularly in the last third of the twentieth century.[81] This seems to be the effect of another legal development which first emerged in the case law of some administrative courts of the late nineteenth century[82] and gained full strength from 1960. Since then, neighbours have been granted the right to sue the administration in order to enforce individual administrative rights against the administratively unlawful land use of a neighbour.[83] As a consequence, the legal settlement of neighbour conflicts became even deeper embedded in administrative law. Both administration and administrative courts were responsible for the cooperation of conflicting land use interests of neighbours in the situation of buildings and, related to this, emissions. As a consequence, a debate arose: if and to

[78] 26 June 1962 (BGBl. I 429); last change 22 April 1993.

[79] For an introduction see W. Krebs, 'Baurecht', *Besonderes Verwaltungsrecht*, E. Schmidt-Aßmann (ed.) (Berlin, de Gruyter, 2003), p. 367, pp. 496–504, nn. 232–45; for a detailed discussion see R.-P. Löhr, *Baugesetzbuch*, 5th edn (Munich, Beck, 2005), §31, nn. 62–74.

[80] Löhr, *Baugesetzbuch*, above, n. 79, §31, nn. 77–80.

[81] For a survey see Haag, *Öffentliches und privates Nachbarrecht*, above, n. 5, pp. 34–42, 106–17.

[82] In 1877 the Prussian Higher Administrative Court denied such an action, PrOVG 30 April 1877, PrOVGE 14, 378, 382 (*Prussia*). In 1902, however, the Saxonian Higher Administrative Court granted the neighbour action, SächsOVG 26 March 1902, SächsOVGE 2, 77 (*Saxony*). For the history of this development see P. Preu, *Die historische Genese der öffentlichrechtlichen Bau- und Gewerbenachbarklagen (ca. 1800–1970)* (Berlin, Duncker & Humblot, 1990), pp. 54–72.

[83] BVerwG 18 August 1960, BVerwGE 11, 95; 25 February 1977, BVerwGE 52, 122. For further detail see Preu, *Die historische Genese*, above, n. 82, pp. 73–90.

what extent the provisions of administrative law would substitute for the remedies of civil neighbourhood law. Since then it has been argued that this legal framework is exclusive in a sense, that civil law-based remedies such as the *actio negatoria* or the provisions of delict law are excluded.[84] As a consequence, it is also sometimes argued that the building licence granted by the administration is therefore exclusive.[85] Other authors favour a slightly modified effect of zoning law rules on civil law. According to them, the provisions of building plans in particular contain mandatory declaratory statements on the essential character of a nuisance or at least on its traditional nature in that locality.[86] But, at least for the time being, the interference of administrative law in neighbour relations appears to encounter resistance at this point. Even though the dominant opinion in the literature on public law argues in favour of the effects of building plans previously mentioned,[87] the Bundesgerichtshof and the dominant opinion in civil law literature favour a complementary function of administrative zoning law and civil law.[88] Hence a building plan is judged only as one indicator among others for the appropriate use in a locality[89] and an administrative building licence does not exclude civil claims.[90] Even though the 56th German Assembly of Jurists (*Deutscher Juristentag*) voted plainly for this solution,[91] the debate does not appear to be settled. The increasing importance of environmental protection and the resultant

[84] K. Kleinlein, *Das System des Nachbarrechts. Eine Darstellung anhand des BBauG, des privaten Nachbarrechts und des BImSchG* (Düsseldorf, Werner, 1987), pp. 123–5, 132–3, 138–1; K. Kleinlein, 'Neues zum Verhältnis von öffentlichem und privatem Nachbarrecht', NVwZ 1982, 668.

[85] J. Schapp, *Das Verhältnis von privatem und öffentlichem Nachbarrecht* (Berlin, Duncker & Humblot, 1978), passim.

[86] K. Gaentzsch, 'Ausbau des Individualschutzes gegen Umweltbelastungen als Aufgabe des bürgerlichen und des öffentlichen Rechts', NVwZ 1986, 601, 603–4; see also BVerwG 29 April 1988 NJW 1988, 2396, 2397.

[87] See H.-J. Birk, 'Umwelteinwirkungen durch Sportanlagen', NVwZ 1985, 689, 697; M. Dolderer, 'Das Verhältnis des öffentlichen zum privaten Nachbarrecht', DVBl 1998, 19, 23–6 with further reference.

[88] See for example Haag, *Öffentliches und privates Nachbarrecht*, above, n. 5, pp. 87–94 with further reference; H. Hagen (presiding judge for the 5th senate at the Bundesgerichtshof, which judges on civil neighbour law), 'Privates Immissionsschutzrecht und öffentliches Baurecht', NVwZ 1991, 817, 819–23 (who argues towards a harmonisation of public and civil law).

[89] BGH 17 December 1982 NJW 1983, 751, 752 (*Germany*); Roth, *Kommentar*, above, n. 10, § 906, n. 218 with further reference.

[90] Wagner, *Öffentlich-rechtliche Genehmigung und zivilrechtliche Rechtswidrigkeit*, above, n. 70, pp. 90–116.

[91] '56sten Deutscher Juristentag: Die Beschlüsse', n. 52, NJW 1986, 3069, 3072, Nr. 52.

development towards a strengthening of administrative power to enforce it could strengthen the impact of administrative law in the area of neighbour conflicts too. As civil law does not provide effective legal remedies for the prevention or even compensation of environmental damages,[92] a development towards an administration-based neighbourhood law is not unlikely. As a consequence, it could happen that the concept of fault liability loses more ground against the concept of denial damage.

4.2.3 *The concept of denial damage*

As shown above, since the middle of the nineteenth century, legislators and courts have tended to limit the property right-based legal remedies of property owners against nuisance. As compensation for this limitation of property, the property owner was granted a reimbursement. The core of this concept is part of the European legal tradition and had its legal definition, most especially, in the great codifications of the late eighteenth and early nineteenth centuries, such as the Prussian General Land Law (cf. §§ 73, 74 Introduction), strongly linked with the concept of expropriation compensation.[93] Against this background, it becomes clear that a claim for compensation such as the one granted in § 26 GewO was independent from fault liability. The property owner lost his claim to prohibit nuisance and was given a claim for money instead. This ruling was later adopted in § 14 cl. 2 BImSchG. The Reichsgericht transferred the concept of denial damage in § 26 GewO in two steps for all situations in which the neighbour had to tolerate nuisance. First, in 1904, the neighbour of a factory licensed by the administration and thus not regulated by the provisions of the industrial code was granted this denial damage.[94] In a second step, the neighbour who had to tolerate nuisance because of the local circumstances was granted the same compensation.[95] In 1959, the legislator adopted this concept in § 906 sect. 2, cl. 2 BGB: since then, the property owner who has to tolerate nuisance as a consequence of a land use customary in a locality and who cannot use his own land customary in a locality or whose yield is

[92] Wagner, *Münchner Kommentar*, above, n. 8, § 823, nn. 167–8 with further reference; for this lack of regulating power in civil law in general see Roth, *Kommentar*, above, n. 10, § 906, nn. 6–7.

[93] For a short survey see A. Thier, 'Enteignung', *Enzyklopädie der Neuzeit III* (Stuttgart, Metzler, 2006) coll. 336–8 with further reference.

[94] RG 11 May 1904, RGZ 58,120, 132–6.

[95] RG 10 March 1937, RGZ 154, 161. For the development of the case law established by this judgment see D. Deneke, *Das nachbarschaftliche Gemeinschaftsverhältnis* (Cologne/Berlin/Bonn/Munich, Heymann, 1987), pp. 10–19.

limited beyond 'a tolerable degree' can claim an 'appropriate' (*angemessene*) compensation in money.[96] This compensation is to be paid not only for damage to the property, but also for health impairments caused by land-related nuisance;[97] it is sometimes even argued that privacy is also covered by § 906 BGB, in so far as land-related nuisance interferes with this right.[98] The same principle is applied to the question of whether movable assets are also protected by § 906 sect. 2 BGB, e.g. the cars of workers which were damaged by the emissions from a factory in the neighbourhood: the Bundesgerichtshof did not grant the workers' compensation claims, as they were only visitors to the protected land and their linkage to the land was not close enough;[99] otherwise the liability according to § 906 sect. 2 BGB would be almost without limit.[100] At this point, the strong connection between liability in neighbour relations and landed estates, and also its problems,[101] becomes especially clear.

In some ways, this is also proved by the judicial extension of § 906 BGB which is strictly related to the use of landed estate. The Bundesgerichtshof has even begun to grant compensation claims in cases where § 906 BGB is not applicable by its wording. If it was impossible for the property owner to defend himself against emissions, because he was inhibited from doing so (1) by legal provisions; or (2) by factual causes, and if (3) this nuisance is essential, he can claim compensation[102] by analogy of § 906 BGB. Typical

[96] For a detailed discussion see Roth, *Kommentar*, above, n. 10, §06, nn. 249–67.

[97] K. Larenz, C.-W. Canaris, *Schuldrecht II/2*, 13th edn (Munich, Beck, 1994), p. 663.

[98] Roth, *Kommentar*, above, n. 10, § 906, n. 111.

[99] For this case see BGH 18 September 1984 BGHZ 92, 142, *Germany*, denying claims of the workers; for support of this judgment see Fritzsche,*Beck'scher Online-Kommentar*, above, n. 6, § 906, n. 79 with further reference. For a similar case see OLG Düsseldorf 17 August 2001 NJW-RR 2001, 26.

[100] For this argument see P. Marburger, H. Herrmann, 'Zur Verteilung der Darlegungs und Beweislast bei der Haftung für Umweltschäden – BGHZ 92, 143', *Juristische Schulung* 1986, 354, 356.

[101] In this case, judged by the Bundesgerichtshof, the workers were forced to return every day to the same place; hence their situation was similar to the situation of the property owner, but nevertheless they were not granted the same legal protection; for the same view as the dominant opinion in the literature, see e.g. Larenz, Canaris, *Schuldrecht II/2*, above, n. 97, p. 663, Wagner, *Öffentlich-rechtliche Genehmigung und zivilrechtliche Rechtswidrigkeit*, above, n. 70, p. 267 n. 96.

[102] As a survey see Säcker, *Münchner Kommentar*, above, n. 69, § 906, n. 141; for further detail see Roth, *Kommentar*, above, n. 10, § 906, n. 66–75 and as a report from the side of the judges at the Bundesgerichtshof H. Hagen, 'Der nachbarrechtliche Aufopferungsanspruch nach § 906 Abs. 2 Satz 2 BGB als Musterlösung und Lösungsmuster – Rechtsfortbildung in mehreren Etappen', *Festschrift for H. Lange*, ed. Medicus, Mertens, Nörr and Zöllner (Stuttgart/Berlin/Cologne, Kohlhammer, 1992), p. 483.

for the first sort of case are the facilities that are important for the common good and run by private persons, such as the care centre for drug addicts mentioned above.[103] Here, the neighbour has to tolerate the limited access to his property, even though this means an essential burden for him and lowers the yield of his real estate.[104] Therefore, he is granted compensation. An example of the other sort of case can be found where compensation was granted for damages caused by insecticide that had been (illegally) sprayed on a neighbour's land and was then washed into the plaintiff's ground by the rain.[105] Here, it had been impossible for the claimant to act against his neighbour, because he had had no notice of his neighbour's actions. On the other hand, a claim based on delictual liability, i.e. fault liability, could not be granted, as the neighbour had acted without fault in relation to the intrusion of the insecticide. This constellation of facts marks a characteristic type of case: an unlawful land use or a similar action which would result in delictual claims if the defendant had acted with fault, results in damage on the neighbour's land.[106] Here, a gap in legal protection emerges for the property owner. The Bundesgerichtshof closes this gap by an analogy with § 906 BGB. In this way, the court has created a sort of strict liability for these types of neighbour conflicts. This sort of case law *praeter legem* has been strongly criticised in part,[107] as it blurs the boundaries between fault liability and strict liability. The court tried, however, to draw the following boundary for fault liability in the field of legal consequences: it granted only compensation, but not full damages. This means that the property owner is entitled to claim as a maximum the current market value of his land, while higher losses are not covered by § 906 sect. 2 BGB and therefore neither by this judicially created *nachbarlicher Ausgleichsanspruch*.[108] This approach has been criticised by some authors as well. They argue for an entitlement to damages, as § 906 sect.

[103] See above, n. 60 (BGH 7 April 2000, NJW 2000, 2901).

[104] Actually the visitors to the care centre not only crossed the property of the claimant, but used to stay there; the judges also reported contaminations to the disputed real estate by 'mainline paraphernalia, blood and excrements' (NJW 2000, 2901, 2902).

[105] BGH 2 March 1984 BGHZ 90, 255, 262.

[106] Neuner, 'Das nachbarrechtliche Haftungssystem', above, n. 1, p. 491.

[107] P. Schlechtriem, 'Nachbarrechtliche Ausgleichsansprüche und Schaden ersatzhaftung', *Festschrift für J. Gernhuber zum 70. Geburtstag*, ed. Lange, Nörr and Westermann (Tübingen, Mohr, 1993), p. 407, pp. 413–19; see also H. Roth, 'Vortrag', *Der bürgerlich-rechtliche Aufopferungsanspruch* (Heidelberg, Müller, 2001), pp. 1, 23–31, 45 and *passim*.

[108] See the summary of the established case law concerning this point in BGH 7 April 2000, NJW 2000, 2902; Roth, *Kommentar*, above, n. 10, § 906, n. 73 with further reference.

2 BGB would cover not only the substance of the property, but also the potential yield gained by the use of the property.[109]

4.3 Property law and delict law

Paragraph 823 sect. 1 BGB protects, inter alia, the legal rights of life, body, property and health. In principle, an unlawful, culpable violation of these rights results in a claim for damages. That means that the damage caused by a delictual act has to be removed. If this is not possible, the losses of the claimant have to be compensated by money (§§ 249–53 BGB). Contributory negligence reduces the compensation for damages (§ 254 BGB). Para. 823 sect. 2 BGB extends these provisions for the protection of legal rights. Hereafter, a culpable violation of a so-called protective law (*Schutzgesetz*) also results in compensatory damages. Even though these provisions are also applicable to neighbours, the legal framework, described above, modifies their effects in this area: the question of unlawfulness is assessed against the background of the rule laid down in § 906 BGB.[110] Hence, an emission which is lawful by the rulings of § 906 BGB cannot result in compensatory damages by §823 BGB. In this sense, § 906 BGB is a legal justification for nuisance.[111] Moreover, the Bundesgerichtshof has judged that even damages to movable assets, caused by emissions within the limits set by § 906 BGB, are justified and that the owner of these assets could claim no compensatory damages according to § 823 BGB.[112] Again, the court argued that the limits for nuisance are set only by § 906 BGB. This ruling has effected a strong reduction of property protection, because the owner of movable assets cannot claim compensation under the rule of § 906 sect. 2 BGB.[113] The

[109] Säcker, *Münchner Kommentar*, above, n. 69, § 906, n. 137; Roth, *Kommentar*, above, n. 10, § 906, n. 73; supporting the case law of the BGH by arguing that § 906 only contains the provision for *Entschädigung*, not for *Schadensersatz* (as provided in §§ 249–54 BGB), Fritzsche, *Beck'scher Online-Kommentar*, above, n. 6, § 906, n. 77.

[110] Wagner, *Münchner Kommentar*, above, n. 8, § 823, n. 306.

[111] BGH 13 July 1965 BGHZ 15, 146, 148; BGH 2 March 1984 BGHZ 90, 255, 257–8; BGH 24 January 1992 BGHZ 117, 110, 111 (for the situation of a special delictual rule ordering tortious liability for livestock owners, whose animals cause damage, § 833 BGB. In the case, judged by the Bundesgerichtshof, bees of the defendant had fertilised the flowers on the land of the plaintiff. The plaintiff claimed compensatory damages, because he could not sell the fertilised flowers any more).

[112] BGH 18 September 1984, BGHZ 92, 143, 148–9.

[113] See above, at n. 99. For a critical analysis of this judgment see Wagner, *Öffentlich-rechtliche Genehmigung und zivilrechtliche Rechtswidrigkeit*, above n. 70, pp. 267–8.

same concept is applied in cases of emitting factories licensed by the provisions of emission law and protected by § 14 BImSchG.[114] Even in the area of environmental strict liability, there is a tendency in literature to justify emissions resulting in compensatory damages by the application of § 906 BGB: the 'Law about the liability for environmental damages' (*Umwelthaftungsgesetz*), issued in 1990, provides strict liability for damages to life and body, health and property, caused by certain types of factories, specified in the law.[115] But, as previously mentioned, it is argued that those claims for compensatory damages would be excluded if the emissions in question were covered by § 906 BGB.[116]

On the other hand, administrative orders on the limits of emissions provide the basis for compensatory claims: if the rules of an administrative licence for factories are violated, the neighbour can claim compensatory damages for losses caused by this violation. The problem here is, however, that the neighbour has to prove the linkage between this illegal act and the damage.[117] But German courts have ruled that a shift of the burden of proof takes place if the claimant can prove that emissions have exceeded the maximum permissible values of emissions. In that case, the plaintiff has to prove that the damages have not been caused by the emissions of his factory.[118]

The concept of denial damage, developed in the emission cases, has also influenced the application of other legal provisions which were originally intended to protect property in neighbour relations: the provisions in §§ 907 and 909 BGB can result in fault liability if the violation of those rules has caused damage.[119] But even in this area the courts have granted claims for denial damage if the property owner could not act against such intrusions for factual or legal reasons.[120] Once more, the impact of the denial damage concept becomes clear.

[114] Wagner, *Münchner Kommentar*, above, n. 8, § 823, n. 626.

[115] 10.12.1990 (BGBl. I 2634), §1. For a detailled analysis see P. Salje and J. Peter, *Umwelthaftungsgesetz. Kommentar*, 2nd edn (Munich, Beck, 2005).

[116] Petersen, *Duldungspflicht und Umwelthaftung*, above, n. 72, pp. 11–40; J. Petersen, 'Beweislast bei Gesundheitsbeeinträchtigungen durch Emissionen und nachbarliche Duldungspflicht', NJW 1998, 2099, 2100.

[117] Wagner, *Münchner Kommentar*, above, n. 8, § 823, n. 628.

[118] BGH 18 September 1984, BGHZ 92, 143, 147–8.

[119] See above at n. 9 and Roth, *Kommentar*, above, n. 10, § 907, n. 53, § 909, n. 45.

[120] For cases related to §909 BGB see BGH 26 October 1978 BGHZ 72, 289, 292; 26 November 1982 BGHZ 85, 375, 384; 23 February 2001 NJW 2001, 865, 866.

4.4 Protection of health and privacy

Life, body and health are protected, as mentioned above, in principle only by the provisions of delict law. Beside these fault liability-based provisions, a strict liability for industrially caused damages has been established by the *Umwelthaftungsgesetz*.[121] Nevertheless, the rise of denial damage and administrative law has resulted in a new approach to these provisions: it has been argued that the duty to tolerate administration-licensed emissions, issued in § 14 cl. 1 BImSchG, is to be applied to health too.[122] The same argument is brought forward for the provisions in § 1 UmweltHG, as far as emissions are concerned, which would be (at least in the case of impairments to health, such as headaches) justified by § 906 BGB.[123] In these cases, compensation according to § 14 cl. 2 BImSchG, § 906 sect. 2 BGB is to be paid.

The protection of privacy appears to be influenced by administrative law too. The case law in this field is discussed under the name 'ideal emissions'.[124] It covers situations such as the running of a brothel[125] or the video surveillance of a neighbour's grounds.[126] Even though the courts sometimes grant a claim for forbearance by §§ 823 and 1004 BGB,[127] the solution of such conflicts is more and more seen as a specific task for administrative law.[128]

4.5 Conclusion

Nowadays, legal conflicts between neighbours are often marked by a triangular structure: the state acts – at least in an ideal perspective – as moderator. The strong impact of administrative law mirrors this trend. As a consequence, neighbourhood law is marked by a double-tracked legal structure of administrative law and civil law provisions. This development has become part of a discussion about its further consequences for

121 See above at n. 115.

122 Wagner, *Münchner Kommentar*, above, n. 8, § 823, n. 307, 626 with further reference.

123 Petersen, *Duldungspflicht und Umwelthaftung*, above, n. 72, pp. 6–10, 109; Petersen, 'Beweislast', above, n. 116, p. 2100.

124 For a survey see Fritzsche, *Beck'scher Online-Kommentar*, above, n. 6, §903, nn. 26–7.

125 BGH 12 July 1985 BGHZ 95, 307.

126 LG Bonn 16 November 2004 NJW-RR 2005, 1067. For those cases see H. R. Horst, 'Der Nachbar als "Big Brother" – Grenzen zulässiger Videoüberwachung', NZM 2000, 939.

127 Roth, *Kommentar*, above, n. 10, § 906, n. 131–2 with further reference.

128 Fritzsche, *Beck'scher Online-Kommentar*, above, n. 6, § 903, n. 28.

the unity of the legal order.[129] Actually, there is a strong tendency for the dominance of public law in neighbourhood law. One of the main reasons for this development is the fundamental economic change and its consequences for the situation of neighbour relations: the Roman jurist Aristo took a cheese shop as an example of unlawful emissions.[130] Since the Industrial Revolution, however, emissions have, in many cases, affected not only a single neighbour, but whole regional areas. As a consequence, the law of emissions has grown from a small-scale context[131] to become a matter of public interest.

From a historical viewpoint, this situation could be described as a development from civil property law, based primarily on the rules of the *actio negatoria*, to a complex framework of administrative and civil law provisions ruling neighbour relations. In this legal order there is comparatively little space left for the concept of fault liability. This also becomes clear by looking at the rise of new legal remedies for environmental damages which are based on the concept of strict liability. Resulting especially from the economic change caused by the Industrial Revolution, the regulation of nuisance has increasingly become an issue of public regulation by legislation, statutory law and administration-issued provisions.

[129] D. Felix, *Einheit der Rechtsordnung. Zur verfassungsrechtlichen Relevanz einer juristischen Argumentationsfigur* (Tübingen, Mohr Siebeck, 1998), pp. 83–109; Ch. Bumke, *Relative Rechtswidrigkeit. Systembildung und Binnendifferenzierungen im öffentlichen Recht* (Tübingen, Mohr Siebeck, 2004), pp. 60–5.

[130] D. 8.5.8.5. see above, n. 17.

[131] For a similar approach see Roth, *Kommentar*, above, n. 10, § 906, n. 5.

5

Fault liability between neighbours in the Netherlands 1850–2000

A. J. VERHEIJ*

5.1 Introduction

This chapter will consider the role of fault liability between neighbours in the period 1850–2000. Although the tort of negligence and therefore the fault principle was present during this entire period, it took some time before it became the dominant approach in nuisance cases. Furthermore, it will be seen that the importance of negligence has been reduced by the growth of administrative law. This is the case with regard to industrial activities that can potentially cause damage to neighbours. An entrepreneur needs to obtain a licence in order to engage in an activity that can cause nuisance to his neighbours. This means that, in practice, there has been a shift from judge to (local) government. Instead of judges deciding *ex post facto* whether a certain activity was negligent, (local) government will decide this *ex ante* when deciding upon the (terms and conditions of the) licence. Between private individuals the tort of negligence remains more important.

The structure of this chapter is as follows:

- sections 5.2 and 5.3 provide some general information about the tort of negligence and the law of neighbours;
- sections 5.4–5.12 describe changes that have taken place in the private law regime governing nuisance;
- sections 5.13 and 5.14 give an overview of developments in public law;
- section 5.15 investigates whether the industrialisation process in the Netherlands influenced the law regime of nuisance in any way;
- section 5.16 attempts to identify some causes of legal developments and draws some tentative conclusions

* When working on this article, the author was Associate Professor at the Centre for Liability Law of the University of Tilburg in the Netherlands. He now works as an attorney in the law firm *Stibbe* in Amsterdam. Further, he is Extraordinary Professor at the North-West University in South Africa, Honorary Associate Professor at the University of Utrecht in the Netherlands and Research Fellow at Intervict, University of Tilburg in the Netherlands.

5.2 Tort of negligence: from the Civil Code of 1838 to the Civil Code of 1992[1]

In the Civil Code of 1838, the tort of negligence was contained in Art. 1401, which was a translation into Dutch of Art. 1382 of the French *Code Civil*. It was feared, however, that the French formulation was too broad in scope and could thus lead to many misunderstandings and prolific litigation. The formulation '*Tout fait quelconque de l'homme, qui cause à autrui un dommage, oblige celui par la faute duquel il est arrivé, à le réparer*' could give the impression that *every* behaviour that causes damages obliges the payment of compensation. The requirement of *faute* was deemed not clear enough. In order to make clear that this was not the case, the word 'unlawful' was inserted before the word 'behaviour'. The elements of Art. 1401 were therefore: unlawfulness, damage, causal link and fault. The relationship between unlawfulness and fault became a matter of discussion. It was resolved by saying that unlawfulness appertained to the *behaviour* of the person who caused the damage, while fault regarded the *person*. Simply stated, someone who displays unlawful behaviour cannot necessarily be blamed for it (because of age or lack of mental capacity).

The meaning of unlawfulness became a matter of intense debate. Roughly speaking, there were two conflicting approaches. According to the first, unlawfulness meant that the behaviour in question was forbidden by a statute. According to the second, behaviour could also be regarded as unlawful if it violated a rule of unwritten law pertaining to proper social conduct (hereafter 'the proper social conduct test').[2] The second approach was adopted by the Dutch Supreme Court (*Hoge Raad*) in 1919 in its famous decision in *Lindenbaum/Cohen*.[3] In the Civil Code of 1992, Art. 1401 was succeeded by Art. 6:162.[4] The tort of negligence that had been developed by the courts on the basis of Art. 1401 remained essentially intact.

It should be stressed that, according to Dutch law, there is no specific tort of nuisance in the sense of a specific Article that deals with it. Whether

[1] See with references C. C. van Dam, *Zorgvuldigheidsnorm en aansprakelijkheid* (Deventer, Kluwer, 1989), ch. 5.

[2] The Dutch term is *maatschappelijke zorgvuldigheid*.

[3] HR 31 January 1919, NJ 1919, 161, note EMM (*Lindenbaum* v. *Cohen*).

[4] Section 2 of Art. 6:162 BW reads as follows: 'Except where there are grounds for justification, the following are deemed unlawful: the violation of a right and an act or omission breaching a duty imposed by law or rule of unwritten law pertaining to proper social conduct.'

or not nuisance is actionable is to be decided on the basis of Art. 1401 old BW and Art. 6:162 BW.

5.3 Law of neighbours: from the Civil Code of 1838 to the Civil Code of 1992

The Civil Code of 1838 contained some specific clauses that defined the rights of neighbours vis-à-vis each other.[5] In the present Civil Code, the law of neighbours is codified in Art. 5:37–59. Despite the increase in the population density since 1838 and despite the introduction of many technical innovations, the law of neighbours has remained essentially the same.[6] This means that there are no special provisions for electricity and telephone cables, gas pipes, aerials, and pets in city areas, and no special provisions for new draining methods and the use of insecticide and fertiliser in rural areas.

Article 5:37 BW contains a general provision to the effect that the owner of land is not allowed to cause nuisance to his neighbour that amounts to negligence in the sense of Art. 6:162 BW. The reference to the tort of negligence (Art. 6:162 BW) illustrates that the law of neighbours does not provide an exhaustive set of rules that governs relations between neighbours.[7]

Article 5:37 BW does not come up with a definition of nuisance but gives some illustrations: noise, disgusting smell, smoke, deprivation of air, light or support. The last two examples are new compared to the notion of nuisance under the old Civil Code.

Article 5:37 BW is a general clause; the subsequent Articles contain more specific rules for all kinds of issues that might arise between neighbours, e.g. water-related problems (Arts. 5:38, 5:39, 5:52, 5:53, 5:58 and 5:59 BW), vegetation that hangs above adjacent land (Art. 5:44, s. 1 BW), roots originating from adjacent land (Art. 5:44, s. 2 BW), the ownership of fruits that fall into the garden of a neighbour (Art. 5:45 BW) and a procedure for establishing the border between two adjacent plots of land in case of uncertainty (Art. 5:47 BW). The powers that are laid down in the

[5] The 4th title of Book 2 of the Civil Code of 1838. It contained 48 articles.

[6] C. J. J. C. van Nispen, 'Het burenrecht in het NBW', in H. Drion (ed.) *Rechtsgeleerde opstellen vervaardigd door leden van het Leids Juridisch Dispuut 'Juri Sacrum', ter gelegenheid van het honderdjarig bestaan van het Dispuut* (Deventer, Kluwer, 1982), pp. 101 and 107, and W. J. M. Davids, F. J. H. Mijnssen and P. de Haan, *C. Asser's Handleiding tot de beoefening van het Nederlands burgerlijk recht.* Deel 3. *Zakenrecht* (14th edn, Zwolle, Tjeenk Willink, 2001).

[7] W. J. M. Davids, ibid., p. 6.

law of neighbours should not be abused; like other powers, their exercise is limited by the doctrine of abuse of powers (Art. 3:13 BW).

5.4 From property to tort

5.4.1 Introduction

Nuisance can be approached from two angles: property and tort.[8] The first approach prevailed in the nineteenth century; the latter gains momentum in the twentieth century. In the first approach, the emphasis is on the abuse of rights doctrine, whereas in the second the emphasis is on the proper social conduct test for unlawfulness. The history of this development is not easy to sketch since decisions are not always clear and scholars disagreed a lot on the questions involved. The following paragraphs try to present a coherent overview.

5.4.2 Article 625 or Art. 1401 old BW?

The first question that arose regarded the right legal framework in which to solve the nuisance issue. There are some decisions in which judges tried to answer the question of whether nuisance was allowed or not by means of Art. 625 old BW. This Article determined that an owner is not allowed to use his property in such a way that he 'causes nuisance to the rights of others'. In this approach, the focus was not on the *conduct of the person who caused the nuisance* (the defendant) but on the scope of the *rights of the victim* (the plaintiff). The question to be answered was whether there was nuisance to the rights of the plaintiff. In practice, this meant in most cases that a plaintiff, in order to succeed, had to prove that his ownership (property right) had been infringed.

Although there was nothing inherently wrong with this approach, it caused confusion on a systematic level. The problem was that it could give rise to the idea that Art. 625 BW constituted a specific course of action besides the law of delict. The Supreme Court at first seemed to sanction the fact that plaintiffs based themselves on Art. 625 BW, but later on it made clear that relations between neighbours were governed by the law of delict.[9]

[8] Ibid., p. 18.

[9] HR 14 May 1886, W. 5288; HR 10 December 1909, W. 8944; HR 23 November 1917, W. 10210. For an overview, see A. van Oven, 'Behoort de burgerlijke wet de rechten, voortvloeiende uit eigendom, te omschrijven of te beperken in verband met hinder, overlast of schade, en zo ja, op welke wijze?', *Preadvies NJV* (Zwolle, Tjeenk Willink, 1958), pp. 66–9.

It pointed out that (in Art. 625 BW) the words 'that owners are not entitled to cause nuisance to the rights of others' only mean that someone who is sued because of nuisance cannot successfully defend himself by arguing that the nuisance was caused in the exercise of his property right.

5.4.3 Legal change but the substantial question remains the same

Until the decision of the Supreme Court in 1919[10] there were only two recognised categories of unlawfulness: violation of a statutory duty and violation of a subjective right. In the absence of much regulation, the second category was the more important in practice. This meant in most cases that a plaintiff had to prove that his ownership had been infringed. Although the issue had been transferred from Art. 625 BW to Art. 1401 BW, there was no substantial change. The focus remained on the scope of the concept of ownership. That damage to someone's property constituted a violation of his property right had been established before,[11] but whether 'immaterial' violations (e.g. noise, smoke) could also violate the right to property was still an open question. Against the opinion of the most authoritative writers,[12] the Supreme Court decided in 1914 in *Krul/Joosstens* that noise and drilling that prevented someone from using his property in a normal way indeed amounted to a violation of his property right and thus could incur liability under Art. 1401 old BW.[13]

5.4.4 What should be the test under Art. 1401 BW?

The next step and the climax in the development of nuisance law was a clash between the two different approaches. In the first approach, the question of whether or not there was unlawfulness had to be solved by establishing the respective scope of the property rights of the people involved. This was deemed to be an objective question which meant that notions of

[10] HR 31 January 1919, above, n. 3. [11] HR 14 May 1886, W. 5288.

[12] C. W. Opzoomer, *Het Burgerlijk Wetboek verklaard III* (Amsterdam, Gebhard, 1876), p. 235 footnote 1, G. Diephuis, *Het Nederlandsch Burgerlijk Regt VI* (Groningen, Wolters, 1880), p. 163 and N. K. F. Land, *Verklaring van het Burgerlijk Wetboek II* (Haarlem, Bohn, 1901), p. 117.

[13] HR 30 January 1914, NJ 1914, 497, note EMM. See also A. van Oven, above, n. 9, p. 79 and S. J. F. M. Jurgens, *Industriële hinder. Privaatrechtelijke beschouwingen* (Deventer, Kluwer, 1975), p. 1.

fault and foreseeability should not play any role in the determination of unlawfulness.[14]

In the second approach, it was argued that foreseeability on the part of the person that caused the nuisance did indeed play a role. After the Supreme Court had adopted the proper social conduct test for unlawfulness in 1919,[15] it was argued that the proper social conduct test should exclusively decide whether the nuisance was unlawful and thus negligent in the sense of Art. 1401 old BW. The proponent of this approach was Meijers.[16] Famous is his description of the differences between the two approaches: whereas in the first approach the unlawfulness of nuisance depends on the scope of the property right of the victim, in the second approach the scope of his property right is determined by the unlawfulness of the nuisance.[17]

In the first approach, the doctrine of abuse of rights plays a vital role. It prevents a deadlock in the situation where someone violates the property right of his neighbour by causing nuisance while exercising his property right. Thanks to the abuse of rights doctrine, the right of the owner who suffered the nuisance could prevail under certain circumstances. It was therefore important to establish what those circumstances were.

In the second approach, the unwritten rules of proper social conduct are the only standard by which to decide whether nuisance is unlawful. There is no need for the abuse of rights doctrine in this context.

5.4.5 The Supreme Court and the abuse of powers doctrine

In three famous cases, the Supreme Court analysed nuisance in terms of the abuse of rights doctrine. The first two cases, which are called the *Water Tower I and II* case, deal with Van Stolk who hates his neighbour Squire Van der Goes. In order to annoy Van der Goes, Van Stolk first puts certain poles with pieces of cloth on his land to destroy the view of Van der Goes.

[14] Advocated by W. H. Drucker, 'Een en ander over burenrecht', *Rechtsgeleerd Magazijn* 1919, pp. 210–67; Asser-Scholten, *Zakenrecht* (Zwolle: Tjeenk Willink 1945), pp. 125–7; P. H. Smits, 'Aantasting en uitoefening van subjectieve rechten in hare beteekenis voor de onrechtmatige daad', WPNR 3688–90 (1940), pp. 373–9, 385–9 and 397–402.

[15] HR 31 January 1919, above, n. 3.

[16] E. M. Meijers, 'Misbruik van recht en wetsontduiking', *Verzamelde Privaatrechtelijke Opstellen I* (Leiden, Universitaire Pers Leiden, 1954), pp. 62 ff.

[17] In his case comment under HR 31 December 1937, NJ 1938, 517 (*Nobel* v. *Unitas*).

Van der Goes goes to court and obtains an injunction. Van Stolk was not discouraged by this and built a water tower in his backyard, allegedly to water his land. He put this tower in exactly the same spot as the poles and so destroys the view of Van der Goes again. The question of whether this constituted abuse of his property right was the object of two Supreme Court decisions. The Court of Appeals, in the procedure that would lead to Water Tower I, decided that Van Stolk had abused his right of property because he could have easily built the tower in a location that would not have destroyed the view of Van der Goes. The Supreme Court did not agree; this is not enough for abuse of right.[18] It was key whether Van Stolk had the sole intent to cause nuisance to his neighbour and whether Van Stolk had a reasonable interest in building the water tower in that specific location. After referral, the Court of Appeals was of the opinion that there is evidence that Van Stolk had the sole purpose to destroy the view of his neighbour and this decision is upheld by the Supreme Court in the Water Tower II decision.[19]

This interpretation of the abuse of rights doctrine is confirmed in a later case in which Driessen had placed a three-metre-high fence in between his garden and the garden of his neighbour Teunissen. Teunissen claimed that this fence took away sunlight and went to court to have it removed. Driessen convinced the Court of Appeals that his purpose was to put an end to successive confrontations between his wife and the wife of Teunissen. The Court of Appeals decided therefore that Driessen did not have the sole purpose to annoy Teunissen and ruled in favour of Driessen. The Supreme Court upheld this decision.[20]

It is clear from the above case law that abuse of rights is not easy to establish. The difference between the two approaches, therefore, assumes practical significance.[21] The approach in which the unlawfulness of nuisance has to be decided by the proper social conduct test seems to put the victim of nuisance in a stronger position than the approach that takes the property right of the person that causes the nuisance as a point of departure.[22] There is no immediate justification for this difference and it has,

[18] HR 13 March 1936, NJ 1936, 415 (*Watertoren I*).

[19] HR 2 April 1937, NJ 1937, 639 (*Watertoren II*).

[20] HR 2 December 1938, NJ 1938, 353, note PS.

[21] This is denied by G. H. A. Schut, 'Rechterlijke verantwoordelijkheid en wettelijke aansprakelijkheid' (dissertatie VU, Amsterdam 1963), p. 145 and S. J. F. M. Jurgens, *Industriële hinder. Privaatrechtelijke beschouwingen* (Deventer, Kluwer, 1975), pp. 12–14.

[22] W. J. M. Davids, above, n. 6, p. 24.

therefore, been argued that the abuse of rights doctrine should play no role in this context whatsoever.[23]

It should be noted that the Supreme Court only seemed to favour the abuse of rights approach in a special category of cases. In the cases described above, the person who causes the nuisance (A) does not interfere directly with the use his neighbour, (B), wants to make of his own property. But he (A) frustrates the enjoyment his neighbour, (B), has of the property of the person who causes the nuisance (A). It has been argued by Scholten that the justification for this is that neighbour B has no right to enjoy certain features of the property of A.[24] He (B) does not have a right to a pleasant view or to a certain amount of sunlight. Therefore the threshold for unlawfulness should be higher than in other cases.

Despite criticism in the literature,[25] the Supreme Court only relaxed the test for abuse of rights in 1970[26] by allowing for a more equal balancing of interests between the parties involved.

5.4.6 *Present Civil Code*

In the present Civil Code, the approach of Meijers seems to be adopted, which is not strange given the fact that he wrote it. Article 5:37 BW first of all extends the definition of nuisance by stating specifically that deprivation of light and air and withdrawal of support are examples of nuisance. Subsequently, Art. 5:37 BW only refers to the tort of negligence (Art. 6:162 BW) as the principle that governs relations between neighbours. There is no reference whatsoever to the doctrine of abuse of rights that has been laid down in the form of abuse of powers in Art. 3:13 BW. With regard to forms of nuisance that are not mentioned in Art. 5:37 BW, there can be doubt as to whether the doctrine of abuse of powers should play a role. However, there is a clear tendency to minimise the role of this doctrine and to embrace the proper social conduct test as the only approach.[27] A reason for this tendency may be found in the fact that the limits of property

[23] A. van Oven, above, n. 9, pp. 89–90. W. J. M. Davids, above, n. 6, p. 24 is of the opinion that the doctrine of abuse of rights should still play a role but he does not specify which one.

[24] Asser-Scholten, *Zakenrecht* (Zwolle, Tjeenk Willink, 1945), pp. 127–8.

[25] Apart from Van Oven and Meijers, this distinction has been criticised by Wolfsbergen, *Onrechtmatige daad* (Leiden, Universitaire Pers Leiden, 1946), pp. 81–9.

[26] HR 17 April 1970, NJ 1971, 89, note PhAN (*Grensoverschrijdende garage*).

[27] W. J. M. Davids, above, n. 6, p. 25.

rights are not very well defined.[28] Abuse of rights or abuse of powers is a correction mechanism that seems out of place here.

5.5 Evolution of the proper social conduct test for unlawfulness

In 1965, the Dutch Supreme Court adopted a new approach regarding the element of unlawfulness in Art. 1401 old BW.[29] It provided a list of factors that judges should take into account in order to decide whether a certain type of behaviour was unlawful or not. The enumeration of a list of relevant factors to be weighed by judges represents a 'factual turn' in Dutch private law. A list of factors, of course, cannot be equated to a definition or a rule. Instead of trying to give a hard and fast rule, the Supreme Court allowed lower courts to take into account the specific circumstances of the case at hand. The role of the Supreme Court became to provide the lower courts with some guidelines in the form of lists of factors and to check whether these factors figured in the motivation of the lower courts. Since lists of factors formulated by the Supreme Court were hardly limitative, they allowed lower courts to come up with new relevant factors and add them to the list of the Supreme Court which in turn could decide whether or not the new factor was relevant. The interplay between lower courts and Supreme Court led over the course of many years to lists of factors in many areas of private law.[30]

The list of factors to be taken into account when deciding upon the unlawfulness of a certain type of behaviour was the following: (1) the chance that others would not pay attention; (2) the chance that as a result damage would ensue; (3) the seriousness of that damage; and (4) the extent to which precautionary measures are burdensome.[31] In the course of time, the first two factors merged into one factor: the probability that the behaviour would result in damage. Later on, the nature of the activity that caused the damage was also regarded as relevant.

[28] This was advanced as an argument by A. van Oven, above, n. 9, p. 95 but from the present point in time it might explain the demise of the abuse of rights doctrine in this field.

[29] HR 5 November 1965, NJ 1966, 136, note GJS (*Coca-Cola Company* v. *Duchateau*).

[30] Scholars have sometimes criticised the 'list of factors approach', since it provided little certainty. What factors are relevant may be more or less clear but the relative weight of each factor remains a mystery. See among others J. M. Barendrecht, *Recht als model van rechtvaardigheid* (Deventer, Kluwer, 1992).

[31] There is a clear similarity with the Learned Hand Formula in *United States* v. *Carroll Towing Co.* (1947) 159 F. (2d) 169.

For the question of whether or not a certain behaviour constituted a nuisance or not, the list of factors provided by the Supreme Court has grown over the years. In the beginning, only the seriousness of the nuisance and the circumstances under which it took place were listed.[32] Later on, it became more specific. Relevant were the nature, the seriousness and the duration of the nuisance.[33] In a later decision, it was said that whether or not a nuisance was unlawful depended on the nature, the seriousness and the duration of the nuisance and the damage caused by it. Such an assessment had to take account of the specific circumstances of the case, including the locality.[34] This formulation seems to be standard now, although the Supreme Court is not always consistent. Sometimes added to this are the costs of and willingness to take precautionary measures.[35]

It should be noted that the distinction between the elements of unlawfulness and damage in the tort of negligence seems to have disappeared in the enumeration of the Supreme Court. Whether the behaviour that causes the nuisance is unlawful or not seems to depend entirely on the consequences of that behaviour.

5.6 Tortfeasors: when tenants make their neighbours suffer

Imagine the following situation. A causes nuisance to his neighbour B. Both A and B rent their house from one and the same person, landlord C. Of course B can sue A, but does he also have an action against his landlord C? The line of reasoning would then be that landlord C has a contractual obligation to B to make sure that B can enjoy the rented property. Therefore, landlord C should make sure that A will stop being a nuisance to B. We can even go one step further. Assume that B is not the tenant of C. Does B in that situation have an action for negligence against C when the latter does nothing to constrain his tenant A?

The Dutch Supreme Court decided in 1960 that in the above situations B had no action against the landlord (C) of the person who caused the

[32] HR 10 March 1972, NJ 1972, 278 (*Vermeulen* v. *Lekkerkerker*).

[33] HR 23 September 1988, NJ 1989, 743 (*Kalimijnen*).

[34] HR 3 May 1991, NJ 1991, 476 (*De Jong* v. *Van Tol*).

[35] This factor was listed in HR 15 February 1991, NJ 1992, 639, note CJHB (*Staat* v. *OVB*), but were, for example, not listed in HR 18 September 1998, NJ 1999, 69, note ARB (*Luykx* v. *Bastiaansen*).

nuisance (A).[36] The reason for that was found in Art. 1592 old BW that prescribed that the landlord is not under an obligation to protect his tenant against intrusions and trespasses (in general, interferences) of third parties that deprived the tenant of the quiet enjoyment of the rented house. According to the Supreme Court, other tenants were also regarded as third persons as meant by Art. 1592 old BW. Later on, however, in 1992, the Supreme Court changed its position.[37] It decided that a landlord is under an obligation to prevent one of his tenants from causing nuisance to other persons. This is a general rule; there is no distinction between the situation in which the person who suffered the damage is a tenant and the situation in which he is not. The fact that the basis of the action is not the same (contract or tort) is of no practical importance.

The reason why landlords have been burdened with an extra obligation is that they can evict the tenant who causes the nuisance.[38] This is of course an *ultimum remedium*, but if all other things failed the landlord can and even should evict the tenant. This result cannot be achieved by the person who suffered the damage on the basis of traditional tort law. In a tort action against the tenant that causes the nuisance he can only claim damages and request an injunction plus recognisance.

5.7 Who can recover for harm?

The law of neighbours in principle applies only to owners but judges are allowed to make exceptions in appropriate circumstances.[39] Article 5:37 BW determines that the owner of a plot of land is not allowed to cause nuisance to the owner of other plots of land when that would be unlawful according to Art. 6:162 BW. The purpose of Art. 5:37 BW is to provide the yardstick by which to determine unlawful nuisance. It ends the debate between Scholten and Meijers in favour of the latter. The theory of abuse of powers plays no role; the decision is solely left to the tort of negligence.

Because the proper social conduct test of Art. 6:162 BW is decisive, there seems to be no clear limit to the people who can sue for nuisance.[40] This is confirmed by case law after the Supreme Court adopted this test in 1919.[41] The fact that Art. 5:37 BW only speaks of owners does not therefore mean that family members of owners or tenants cannot sue for damages

[36] HR 24 June 1960, NJ 1960, 495. [37] HR 16 October 1992, NJ 1993, 167.

[38] See Attorney-General Asser in his advice (para. 2.7) to the Supreme Court for HR 5 October 1990, NJ 1991, 295 (*Sloots* v. *Lazaroski*).

[39] See with references W. J. M. Davids, above, n. 6, p. 10.

[40] A. van Oven, above, n. 9, p. 82. [41] HR 31 January 1919, above, n. 3.

on the basis of Art. 6:162 BW. In practice, the question of whether owners or also other persons are entitled to damages depends on who suffers damage. As will be shown in the next section (5.8), this is not always easy to determine.

5.8 Kinds of loss: financial or emotional?

What kinds of losses does nuisance cause? Financial losses or more personal, that is to say emotional, losses? It largely depends on the nature of the nuisance. There are differences between more 'physical' violations as a result of which property is damaged or destroyed and violation of a less tangible nature such as noise and smell.

In a case of *property damage*, it is clear that there is at least a financial loss, but, depending on the circumstances, it might be argued that there is also an emotional loss, e.g. in the event that someone's house is flooded as a result of the negligence of his neighbour. No doubt the furniture that is damaged by the water represents a financial loss. It is also clear that the flooding caused considerable physical discomfort and emotional distress. Legally, however, it is not so easy to say whether the victim is entitled to a (relatively small) sum of money by way of compensation for his emotional distress. Article 6:95 BW distinguishes between financial losses and emotional losses/emotional distress and determines that compensation is available for emotional losses[42] if the law explicitly provides for that. Article 6:106 BW subsequently only allows for compensation of emotional distress in a limited number of instances: physical injury, defamation and other violations of the person(ality). The question to be answered, according to Dutch law, is, therefore, whether physical discomfort and emotional distress caused by a flooding can be regarded as an interference with the person of the victim. This is not entirely clear since the Supreme Court has never taken a definitive decision in this respect. Some authors argue that, in order to qualify as a violation of the person, the violation itself or the resultant damage must be of a serious nature.[43] The threshold for compensation on that view is high and mere discomfort is probably not enough for compensation of emotional distress. A competing view is that the flooding can be regarded as an invasion of privacy and

[42] Art. 6:95 BW in fact does not speak of emotional distress but only contains a negative formulation by speaking of 'other losses'. Generally it is held, however, that 'other losses' should be understood as emotional distress.

[43] S. D. Lindenbergh, *Smartengeld* (Deventer, Kluwer, 1998), p. 88.

should therefore be compensated.[44] The idea that nuisance can constitute a violation of privacy has not been recognised by judges either.[45]

In a case where there is *no property damage*, the question as to the nature of the damage becomes more problematic. On the one hand, it is possible that the victim suffered a financial loss. This is the case when the owner of a house wants to sell it but sees the value diminished by noise. What is the answer when the owner of a house does not want to sell it? The fact that his house has decreased in value will not materialise. He suffers no concrete financial loss; there are no out-of-pocket expenses or lost profits. He only suffers a financial loss on paper. In some cases, an owner might even have a tax advantage as a result of the decrease in value. Since financial and emotional losses are mutually exclusive categories, it has been argued in the past that in this situation the loss should be regarded as an emotional one.[46] This viewpoint has been criticised, however.[47] It has been argued with some force that, although the victim did not suffer a *concrete* financial loss, he did suffer an *abstract* financial loss. In order to determine the amount of damages, judges should not take into account the fact that the owner will not sell his house. He is entitled to a sum of money that corresponds with the decrease of value of his house.

An important reason for wanting to abstract from the concrete circumstances of the case is that the market provides a yardstick for determining damages. This makes the task of judges easier. The standpoint that the loss should be regarded as a financial one is therefore motivated by practical considerations. Several arguments have been advanced against this approach.[48] The first is that in this approach there is no distinction between a house owner who lives alone and a house owner who lives together with his family. As long as the decrease in value is the same, the same amount of damages is awarded, although the number of people who suffer as a result of the noise or smell is not the same. This has been one reason to argue that fairness should dictate that the loss be regarded as an emotional one. A second argument against the 'abstract financial loss theory' is that it works in favour of rich people and to the disadvantage of

44 A. J. Verheij, *Vergoeding van immateriële schade wegens aantasting in de persoon* (Nijmegen, Ars Aequi, 2002), no. 282.

45 See below, p. 119.

46 Meijers in his comment on HR 29 January 1937, NJ 1937, 570 (*Voortse Stroom III*).

47 A. R. Bloembergen, *Schadevergoeding bij onrechtmatige daad* (Deventer, Kluwer, 1965), nos. 56–7.

48 A. J. Verheij, *Vergoeding van immateriële schade wegens aantasting in de persoon* (Nijmegen, Ars Aequi, 2002), no. 282.

people who are less well off. People in cheaper neighbourhoods get less compensation than people in more expensive ones. From both a fairness and a deterrence perspective, this seems difficult to accept. It should finally not be forgotten that in many cases the 'abstract financial loss theory' does not provide a clear yardstick to determine damages. When there is only noise for relatively short periods, as opposed to structural noise, the market does not provide a clear answer.

5.9 Calculation of the loss in cases of property damage

In a case of damage to property, the damage is defined as the loss in value. However, the owner is entitled to *restitutio in integrum* in the sense that he can claim the cost of repair unless that is not reasonable (e.g. in a case of a total loss). This rule was formulated by the Supreme Court in 1961[49] and was applied in a case of nuisance in the form of drilling resulting in property damage in 1995.[50] The consequence of this rule is that the owner can claim the costs of repair even though he does not want to repair or sell his property and the damage does not interfere with the use he makes of his property. It should be added that he is entitled to the objective costs of repair. The fact that he repairs the damage himself at a minimum of costs does not preclude him from claiming the costs of repair that a professional would have charged. Proof by the defendant that the plaintiff will not have to contract a professional is not admissible. What happens here is that, in order to calculate the damages, a judge abstracts from the particular fact of the case. The reason for this procedure is that it is simple to do and therefore efficient. There is no room for proof and counterproof, which makes the processing of property damage claims more speedy. These benefits outweigh the fact that sometimes owners whose property has been damaged are in fact enriched.[51]

However, in 1998, the Supreme Court ruled in a case of nuisance that the costs of repair should not exceed the loss of profit. The loss of profit, therefore, constitutes the maximum amount of damages to which the owner whose property is damaged is entitled.[52] The Supreme Court gives no motivation for this rule. The reason for departure from the standard

49 HR 16 June 1961, NJ 1961, 444, note GJS (*Telefoonkabel*).

50 HR 1 July 1995, NJ 1995, 43, note CJHB (*Den Haag* v. *Van Schravendijk*).

51 Some scholars remain critical, however. See, for example, Asser-Hartkamp, *De verbintenis in het algemeen, 4-1* (Deventer, Kluwer, 2004), no. 418.

52 HR 18 September 1998, NJ 1999, 69, note ARB (*Luykx* v. *Bastiaansen*).

rule is not clear and has been criticised by Bloembergen in his comment published under the case.

5.10 Nuisance as a violation of privacy?

The idea that nuisance can constitute a violation of privacy is not very well accepted in Dutch law. Even a physical destruction of the home is not as such regarded as a violation of privacy that entitles the victim to compensation. In *Eillert* v. *De Groot*, the defendant had deliberately destroyed the wall of the bedroom in the house of the plaintiff but this was not labelled by the plaintiff's attorney or by any of the courts as a gross violation of privacy.[53] A plane crash on a block of flats only gave rise to a claim for damage to the person because the victim could establish that he suffered from a post-traumatic stress disorder.[54] Several attacks by an angry mob on a house, however, were regarded as a violation of the safety of the home, which is closely related to privacy.[55] Only the members of the family who were present during the ordeal were entitled to damages. The son who was warned not to come home did not obtain compensation. The position of Dutch law is, therefore, that destruction of the home in most cases can only lead to compensation for damaged property. Inhabitants are only entitled to damages in the rather exceptional event that they suffered acute fear or a psychiatrically recognised disease. Privacy, as such, is not protected by tort law in these cases.[56]

5.11 Introduction of strict liabilities

Animals such as cocks, donkeys and dogs can make a lot of noise. In 1980, the Supreme Court created a strict liability for damage caused by animals.[57] This decision has been codified subsequently in Art. 6:179 BW: possessors are strictly liable for damage caused by their animals. No distinction is made between pets and animals that are used by professionals in the context of a business (e.g. farmers and their bulls). However, strict liability

[53] HR 23 January 1987, NJ 1987, 555, note G.

[54] Rb Amsterdam 19 July 2000, NJkort 2000, 78.

[55] HR 9 July 2004, NJ 2005, 391, note JBMV, although in this case the emphasis seemed to be mainly on the fear of the inhabitants.

[56] Despite the extensive interpretation of the European Court of Human Rights of Art. 8 ECHR (family life). See, for example, ECtHR 19 February 1998, *Guerra* v. *Italy*, ECtHR Reports 1998–I, 210.

[57] HR 7 March 1980, NJ 353 (*Stierkalf*), note GJS.

does not make the position of the victim of nuisance much stronger. Although he does not have to prove that the possessor is accountable for the behaviour of his animal, he will still have to prove that the nature, etc (see above at 5.5) of the noise is such that it is unlawful.[58] In this respect, the test under the tort of negligence is the same as the test under Art. 6:179 BW. For this reason, the additional value of a strict liability in this realm is practically non-existent. The fault liability of the tort of negligence continues to be the main cause of action.[59]

The present Civil Code of 1992 introduced strict liability for immovables (Art. 6:174 BW). This can be helpful when a person suffers damage (either physical or property damage) when the house of his neighbour (partly) collapses. However, the Supreme Court refused to apply this strict liability in the event of the roof of a building containing asbestos catching fire, causing small particles of asbestos to land on the premises of neighbours and in the rest of the city.[60] Liability can only be based on the tort of negligence.

5.12 Other remedies than damages

Apart from damages, a plaintiff who bases himself on a tort can also demand an injunction plus recognisance.[61] Usually, damages for the past and an injunction for the future go hand in hand, but this is not always the case. Art. 6:168 BW determines that, if a certain activity or a certain conduct should be accepted because of weighty societal interests,[62] a judge can refuse to grant an injunction. This possibility was not introduced by the present Civil Code of 1992 but was created by the Supreme Court in a series of cases starting from the 1920s.[63] The plaintiff remains entitled to damages, otherwise his interest would be entirely sacrificed for the common good.

[58] HR 28 April 1995, NJ 1995, 513 (*Sweep* v. *MLTS*).

[59] See case law mentioned by Lindenbergh (looseleaf), title 5.4, annotation 17.

[60] HR 15 June 2001, NJ 2002, 336, note CJHB (*Almelo* v. *Wessels*).

[61] Asser-Hartkamp, *De verbintenis uit de wet, 4-III* (Deventer, Kluwer, 2002) chapter IV. Other possibilities are less relevant in the context of nuisance. A plaintiff can, for example, also request that a situation or conduct is unlawful and instead of money damages he can request that the plaintiff undoes the damages by other means (e.g. in the case of libel by publicly announcing that information about someone was incorrect).

[62] The term general interest that was used in the original draft was avoided on purpose in order to make clear that the general interest is the sum total of different interests that might collide, such as employment and a clean environment. See further Asser-Hartkamp, *De verbintenis uit de wet, 4-III* (Deventer, Kluwer, 2002), no. 119.

[63] See for an overview A. van Oven, above, n. 9, pp. 96–111.

The history of Art. 6:168 BW shows that it is especially relevant for nuisance. The original version of this Article was written specifically for nuisance and was to be placed directly after Art. 5:1 BW which defines ownership. Later, the rule of this Article was deemed of general importance and, therefore, it was transferred from Book 5 of the Civil Code (property law) to Book 6 (law of obligations).[64] The present Art. 6:168 BW is not confined to cases of nuisance.

Conversely, it is also possible that an injunction will be granted although the plaintiff is not entitled to damages. This is the result of Art. 6:106 BW which limits the right to compensation for emotional distress to – briefly summarised – more serious violations of the person. A violation of the person can be so insignificant that the plaintiff is not entitled to compensation for emotional distress but this does not stand in the way of granting an injunction. It is suggested that this might be the case in relation to certain types of nuisance.[65]

The most far-reaching and innovative change that took place was the introduction of a collective action that gave standing to organisations that are defending a collective or even general interest. The point of departure is, and has traditionally always been, that a personal interest is required for admissibility (Art. 3:303 BW). In the 1980s, judges allowed for collective actions if certain conditions were met.[66] Admissible were associations or foundations that according to the articles of association advanced certain collective interests and that were representative enough. Furthermore, the interests at stake had to be of such a nature that a collectivisation was possible. Damages cannot be obtained in a collective action. The advantage of a collective action is first of all that an unnecessary proliferation of claims is avoided. Tens or hundreds of cases are replaced by one. Second, it is also advantageous for individual claimants because it relieves them of the burden of taking legal action. Finally, it is in the interest of law enforcement. Cases that would otherwise not have gone to court (too costly, too time-consuming for individuals) will now be put before a judge. The legislator followed the case law and created many collective actions which culminated in the law of 1994[67] that inserted a general collective action in the Civil Code (Arts. 3:305a and 3:305b BW).[68]

[64] Asser-Hartkamp, *De verbintenis uit de wet*, 4-III (Deventer, Kluwer, 2002), no. 119.

[65] S. D. Lindenbergh, *Smartengeld* (Deventer, Kluwer, 1998), p. 291.

[66] Asser-Hartkamp, *De verbintenis uit de wet, 4-III* (Deventer, Kluwer, 2002), no. 118c–118d.

[67] Law of 6 April 1994, Stb. 1994, 269.

[68] Asser-Hartkamp, *De verbintenis uit de wet, 4-III* (Deventer, Kluwer, 2002), no. 118e.

5.13 Public law – regulation of nuisance caused by industry

5.13.1 Overview[69]

Activities that were likely to cause nuisance were subjected to administrative control. Before 1798, this control was exercised at a local level and the guilds played an important role. In the Constitution of 1798 (Art. 53), the guilds were abolished and every citizen was granted the right to engage in business or found a factory. Article 53 also determined that the legislator guaranteed order and comfort which implied that the right to engage in business or to found a factory could be subjected to regulation in the interest of others. The first general law to do this was the Imperial Decree[70] of 15 October 1810. This Decree remained in force long after the end of French occupation. It was replaced by the Royal Decree of 31 January 1824 which in turn was replaced by the Industrial Nuisance Act (*Hinderwet*) of 1875.[71] This Act was changed many, many times before it was finally absorbed by the Environmental Management Act of 1993 (*Wet Milieubeheer*).[72] The focus of this section is on the system that was introduced by the Industrial Nuisance Act of 1875 which has essentially remained unchanged until today.

5.13.2 From the Royal Decree 31 January 1824 to the Industrial Nuisance Act 1875

The Royal Decree of 31 January 1824 (like its predecessor) distinguished between three classes of (industrial) activities that could not be engaged in without previous permission by the national, provincial and local government: activities that should not be carried out close to living areas (permission by Royal Decree), activities that should not cause nuisance to neighbours (permission by provincial decree) and activities that could be carried out close to living areas (permission by local government).

The desire to create the Industrial Nuisance Act arose because the subject was deemed too important to be dealt with by a Royal Decree[73] which

[69] For an overview of developments in the nineteenth century see H. van der Weerd, *De practijk der hinderwet* (Utrecht, Buijs, 1914), pp. XI–XII and M. M. van Praag, *De Hinderwet* (Zwolle, Tjeenk Willink, 1928), ch. I.

[70] The Netherlands was still part of the Napoleonic Empire.

[71] Law of 2 June 1875, Stb. 95.

[72] See for this Act F.C.M.A. Michiels, *De wet milieubeheer* (Deventer, Kluwer, 2003). Licences required by various other laws were integrated in the Environmental Management Act as well: see Lindenbergh (looseleaf), title 5.4, annotation 14.

[73] The legality of the Royal Decree of 31 January 1824 had been doubted but was upheld by the Supreme Court (HR 24 February 1846 [v.d. Honert, *Gemengde zaken*, deel IV, p. 59]).

was not wholly satisfactory, as time had shown. The immediate reason[74] was a decision by the Supreme Court in 1855 which made it necessary for every butcher to obtain permission by the local government before establishing himself as a butcher.[75] In its decision, the Supreme Court annulled a municipal regulation that provided that slaughtering animals was legal provided that it was done in the municipal slaughterhouse. The extra administrative obstacles for people to establish themselves as butchers were deemed undesirable. Although this decision is regarded as the immediate reason, it was only after ten years, in 1865, that a bill was presented to Parliament and only after twenty years, in 1875, that the Industrial Nuisance Act would come into force.

The first question that was raised regarded the amount of discretionary power that the government should have in issuing or refusing to issue a licence. The first bill was, according to a majority in Parliament, too vague in this respect, leaving too much discretionary power to the government. In later bills this was changed. The most important article was what later was to become Art. 11 of the Industrial Nuisance Act. This article provided the limitative grounds for refusing to issue a licence. These were: (1) danger; (2) damage to property, businesses and health; and (3) serious nuisance, e.g. nuisance that makes a house partially or entirely impossible to live in and spreading of waste or disgusting smells.

This article was hotly debated in Parliament. It was argued that a licence should only be refused when the *public interest* required that.[76] *Private* interests should be dealt with by judges under the private law. The background of this discussion was the nineteenth-century conviction that rights should be sharply distinguished from mere interests. Rights were interests that were deemed of such importance that they had been transformed into rights that deserved legal protection. Mere interests that had not been transformed into rights should not be equally protected. Nuisance that did not cause immediate damage to property or health was therefore eyed with suspicion. As described above (5.4.3), it was only in 1914 that the Supreme Court settled this issue in the sense that 'immaterial' nuisance was actionable as well. However, Art. 11 as described above makes clear that this narrow view was rejected. A rather extensive view

[74] According to M. M. van Praag, *De Hinderwet* (Zwolle, Tjeenk Willink, 1928), p. 5.

[75] HR 15 May 1885, M. M. van Praag, *De Hinderwet* (Zwolle, Tjeenk Willink, 1928), pp. 5–6.

[76] H. van der Weerd, *De practijk der hinderwet* (Utrecht, Buijs, 1914), pp. 96–101; M. M. van Praag, *De Hinderwet* (Zwolle, Tjeenk Willink, 1928,) pp. 115–17.

of nuisance was adopted, since serious nuisance of an 'immaterial' nature was also grounds for refusal of a licence.

All in all, the Industrial Nuisance Act and its successors created a preventive system. Activities that could cause nuisance had to apply for a licence. When deciding upon the request for a licence, neighbours of the applicant could voice their opinion.

5.14 A licence to cause nuisance?

An important question is whether a licence insulates against an action in tort. On the one hand, it seems unfair that the licensee who incurs costs to obtain a licence and who complies with the conditions of the licence could still be held liable in tort. It has been argued that this would mean that certain people and companies have to pay twice[77] – once for the administrative system and the second time through the law of delict. On the other hand, it would also be hard to accept that a governmental authority can dispose of the rights of its citizens simply by issuing a licence.

The situation in the Netherlands is as follows. Article 6:162 BW (and also its predecessor Art. 1401 old BW) has three categories of unlawfulness: violation of a subjective right; violation of a statutory duty; and violation of the unwritten rules of proper social conduct. A licence protects against liability on account of the violation of a statutory duty but it does not exclude the possibility of liability on account of the other two categories. Whether liability exists on either of those two grounds depends on the circumstances, which makes it impossible to say in general whether conduct in accordance with the terms of the licence is sufficient to escape liability or not.

The first time that the Dutch Supreme Court adopted this approach was in 1914 in the earlier mentioned[78] decision in *Krul* v. *Joosstens*.[79] The Supreme Court ruled that a licence on the basis of the *Hinderwet* (Industrial Nuisance Act) does not protect the licensee against an action in tort.[80] Significantly, the Supreme Court added that this is also the case in

[77] L. Bergkamp, *De vervuiler betaalt dubbel* (Antwerp/Groningen 1998), pp. 69–70.

[78] See above, p. 111.

[79] HR 30 January 1914, NJ 1914, 497, note EMM. Later confirmed by HR 10 March 1972, NJ 1972, 279 (*Vermeulen* v. *Lekkerkerker*).

[80] G. Diephuis, *Het Nederlandsch Burgerlijk Recht II* (Groningen, Wolters, 1888), pp. 116–17 had argued differently.

the event that the person who sues in tort had previously tried to prevent the issue of a licence in an administrative procedure.

It is self-evident that there is a clash here between private law and administrative law and between judges and public authorities that issue licences. The way the conditions of the licence are formulated determines to an important extent the room judges have to hold the licensee liable. In a case where the licence allows for a maximum number of decibels to be produced by a factory, it seems unlikely that a judge will hold the licensee liable as long as he keeps below this maximum set by the licence. If, on the contrary, a licence only prescribes a minimum, the chance that a judge will regard conduct in accordance with the licence as a violation of the standard of proper social conduct increases. If a licence prescribes that a café should have at least one emergency exit, it is very possible that the particular circumstances of the case should have induced the owner to create a second emergency exit.[81]

Conversely, the absence of a licence does not automatically lead to liability if the nuisance does not constitute a violation of a subjective right or a violation of the unwritten rules of proper social conduct. The judge has to answer the question of whether a licence would have been given if the defendant had applied for it. If it is likely that a licence would indeed have been given by the relevant authority, the sheer absence of a licence is not enough for liability on the basis of negligence (Art. 6:162 BW).[82]

5.15 In search of an industrial revolution

It has proved difficult to find data on industrialisation in the Netherlands that could be compared easily with data in other countries. In order to determine the extent to which nineteenth-century Dutch society was industrialised, historians have used different data: the number of workers in the industrial sector compared to the number of workers in other sectors, the number of limited companies and the number and capacity of stationary steam engines.[83] A 'guestimate' reveals that the steam engine capacity in the United Kingdom around 1850 was in the order of 500,000

[81] E. Brans, De vergunning vrijwaart niet van aansprakelijkheid, ed. A. Akkermans and E. Brans, *Aansprakelijkheid en schadeverhaal bij rampen* (Nijmegen, Ars Aequi, 2002), p. 253.

[82] HR 3 November 2000, NJ 2001, 108, note ARB (*GEM/Tuinders*).

[83] R. T. Griffiths, 'Industrial retardation' in *The Netherlands 1830–1850* (Den Haag, Martinus Nijhoff, 1979), pp. 4 and 36.

h.p. compared to 6,537 h.p. in the Netherlands.[84] In short, the general picture emerges that the industrial era hardly touched the Netherlands in the first half of the nineteenth century. This is confirmed by the fact that the construction of railways took off seriously only after 1860.[85] The 'pathetic performance' at the Great London Exhibition in 1851 is also quoted as an example of the relative backwardness of the Netherlands.[86]

Against this background, the question that puzzled Dutch historians was: when did *the* industrial revolution take place? At first, the period after 1890 was regarded as the moment of industrialisation,[87] but almost all decades in the second half of the nineteenth century have been regarded as such by subsequent historians.[88] Therefore, the modern view is that the initial question was wrong and that Dutch historians, given what had happened in the United Kingdom, mistakenly assumed that somewhere in the nineteenth century there must have been *a single* industrial revolution that formed a watershed between the previous period and the period that followed. It is now believed that no such thing happened. Instead of *one* industrial revolution, there was a more gradual transformation from 'commercial capitalism' to 'modern industrial capitalism'.[89] From the fact that the Netherlands was relatively slow to industrialise, one should not conclude, however, that the economy stagnated or that there was no economic growth whatsoever. It has been estimated that in 1830 the Netherlands was one of the richest countries in the world.[90]

Three periods of industrial growth can be distinguished.[91] During the first period (1825–50), industrial growth was the result of the invention of the 'Cultivation System' in the Dutch Indies (now Indonesia)

84 Ibid., pp. 5–6.

85 J. L. van Zanden, 'Industrialisation in The Netherlands', in ed. M. Teich, R. Porter, *The Industrial Revolution in national context. Europe and the USA* (Cambridge, Cambridge University Press, 1996), p. 86. Although the first train dated from 1839, in 1880 the Netherlands still had a smaller rail network than Belgium.

86 H. Baudet, 'De dadels van Hassan en de start der Nederlandse industrialisatie' in I. J. Brugmans and W. J. Wieringa, *Bedrijf en Samenleving: economisch-historische studies over Nederland in de negentiende en twintigste eeuw, aangeboden aan prof. dr. I. J. Brugmans bij zijn aftreden als hoogleraar aan de Universiteit van Amsterdam* (Alphen aan de Rijn, Samson, 1967), pp. 1–15.

87 J. A. de Jonge, *De industrialisatie in Nederland tussen 1850 en 1914* (Amsterdam, Scheltema & Holkema, 1968).

88 J. L. van Zanden, above, n. 85, p. 78.

89 Ibid. For an analysis of the factors that prevent industrialisation see especially R.T. Griffiths, above, n. 83, ch. 3.

90 R. T. Griffiths, above, n. 83, pp. 37–8. This estimation is based on a comparative analysis of the average income per head of population.

91 J. L. van Zanden, above n. 85, pp. 78–94.

that forced local peasants to cultivate certain products for export by the colonial government. In this period, the domestic market did not grow, however, because of a decrease in the standard of living between 1830 and 1855. In the second period (1850–80) industry working for the domestic market developed as a result of increased use of steam engines, increased construction of railways and liberalisation of the economy through reduction of import and export tariffs and abolition of various local and national taxes. The development of heavy industry had to wait until the third period (1880–1914), however. It only gained momentum after 1890.

5.16 Concluding remarks

There are several conclusions to be drawn from the above description of developments over the past 150 years. In order to draw these conclusions, the most important changes have to be reiterated:

(1) In the nineteenth century, lawyers distinguish between rights and mere interests.[92] The first category is protected; the latter is not. Given this distinction, it is doubtful whether nuisance that does not lead to physical injury (injury to health) or property damage is actionable. However, the Supreme Court decides in *Krul* v. *Joosstens* in 1914[93] that 'immaterial' forms of nuisance can also be regarded as the violation of a property right.

(2) In order to rely on the tort of negligence, a victim of nuisance had to establish that one of his rights was violated.[94] Since *Lindenbaum* v. *Cohen*,[95] however, the plaintiff can also argue that the nuisance went against the unwritten rules of proper social conduct. This shifted the focus from the limits of the right of ownership of the plaintiff to the harm done to his interests.[96]

(3) The proper social conduct test became the dominant one; the abuse of powers doctrine has been discarded by the present Civil Code, since Art. 5:37 BW only refers to the tort of negligence.[97]

(4) It seems plausible that the victory of the proper social conduct test has paved the way for the next important development: the introduction of collective actions.[98]

[92] See section 5.13.2. [93] HR 30 January 1914, NJ 1914, 497, note EMM.
[94] See section 5.2. [95] HR 31 January 1919, above n. 3. [96] See section 5.5.
[97] See section 5.6. [98] See above, p. 123.

(5) Although one could argue that in theory the tort of negligence and the proper social conduct test have achieved an overall victory, it should be stressed that a parallel development in administrative law has reduced the practical importance of the tort of negligence to a significant degree in relation to industrial nuisances.[99]

Who brought these changes about and why did they take place? The triumph of the tort of negligence and the proper social conduct test was brought about by judges. They even introduced collective actions. Only in the field of administrative law has the legislator been the force behind change.

The fact that over a long period judges have brought about all the important changes in the field of private law makes it difficult to identify the exact causes for change. Although that might be unsatisfactory, it seems only possible to come up with a rather general explanation.

The victory of the proper social conduct test and the tort of negligence at the expense of alternative approaches can be regarded as a shift from a rights-based approach to an approach in which the particular facts of the case determine the outcome. In this approach, judges more or less openly engage in a balancing of the different interests at stake. This approach has been adopted by judges in other areas as well. Neither the system of private law nor the intention of the legislator is regarded as most important. The goal is to arrive at a just decision in every specific case (*Einzelfallgerechtigkeit*). In the Netherlands it has been said in this context that the law had a service role.[100] From a slightly different angle this could also be regarded as evidence of the growing dominance of an instrumental view of laws and rules. They do not exist for their own sake but are designed to realise certain goals. This different approach has also taken place in other Western countries.[101]

Although the most important changes in public law were brought about by the legislator, identifying the causes of these changes is not very easy either. The reasons the government advanced for presenting a bill to Parliament in 1865 were very general indeed.[102] The most specific reason given was a decision by the Supreme Court, but since that decision was then already ten years old it cannot be regarded as the true reason.

[99] See sections 5.13 and 5.14.

[100] A. Pitlo, *Evolutie in het privaatrecht* (Groningen, Tjeenk Willink, 1972), ch. II.

[101] See for an interesting analysis B. Z. Tamanah, 'The perils of pervasive legal instrumentalism', *Tilburg Law Lectures Series, Montesquieu Seminars vol. 1* (Nijmegen, Wolf Legal Publishers, 2006).

[102] See section 5.13.2.

In this context as well, the question as to the causes of change seems to escape specific answers. It seems reasonable to suggest that the process of industrialisation, that in the Netherlands only took off in the second half of the nineteenth century,[103] played a role here. The liberals in government who started to break down local taxes and tariffs might have viewed the Royal Decree of 1824, as interpreted by the Supreme Court, as just another example of regulation that hampered commercial activity. One clear system at a national level might have seemed a good idea. Abolishing all regulation in this respect and leaving it to the law of delict was never seriously considered.[104]

What tentative conclusions can be drawn from these developments?

(1) The proper social conduct test has been triumphant because it made it possible to weigh all the circumstances of the case at hand.
(2) The strength of the proper social conduct test is, at the same time, its weakness. It creates uncertainty which is burdensome for both entrepreneurs and private individuals. It is burdensome for the former because they have to decide in advance on investment; it is burdensome for the latter because it is difficult to predict the outcome of legal proceedings.
(3) It might be argued that the developments as described above have more or less turned the notion of 'neighbour' into an empty concept. The proper social conduct test, in combination with collective actions, makes it possible (under certain circumstances) for a sufficiently representative association that promotes nature to prevent a certain area from being polluted. It has been suggested that the shrinking environment in the Netherlands has caused people to identify more with what is left.[105] Emotionally, people experience 'nuisance' when they learn about pollution of a certain area even though they do not go there frequently. Whereas in the past individuals only went to court if the view they entertained from their own premises was destroyed by their neighbour, nowadays they might bring an action if a view or an area is destroyed that they cannot see from their house.

[103] See section 5.15.
[104] A reason might have been that a preventive system is more efficient than the law of delict in which judges only decide after the harm has been done. Entrepreneurs naturally want to be as certain as possible that the investments they are making while setting up a factory will not be undone by judges. However, all this is pure speculation.
[105] F. W. Grosheide, 'Stank, stof en lawaai en verstoord woongenot', TMA 1992, p. 13.

6

Neighbourhood liability in Scotland 1850–2000

GORDON D. L. CAMERON*

6.1 Introduction

This chapter is concerned primarily with the development of fault liability between neighbours in Scotland. The discussion is focused on common law nuisance. The basis in fault of liability for property harm or personal injury caused through means other than nuisance was, in Scots law, established well before the commencement of the period researched, although this position was challenged in a small number of cases from which emerged a nascent doctrine of inferred fault that became associated with nuisance. The relation between nuisance and fault liability was unclear or debatable and remained so until towards the end of the twentieth century. Since nuisance was relatively novel in nineteenth-century Scotland, it has been thought appropriate to consider the doctrine from the time it emerged in the mid-eighteenth century.

While the common law provided protection to individual proprietors against wrongful interferences with enjoyment of property, a more pressing need arose during the nineteenth century to improve sanitary conditions for the sake of public health. Nuisance, in this context, was viewed in terms of things that might lead to contagion. The legislative response required municipal regulation of nuisances which, in turn, required the development of regulatory bodies. Thus, control of nuisance or nuisances became bound up with the evolution of local government. This chapter will consider in outline only the development of municipal regulation during the nineteenth century leading on to the later development of modern planning and environmental regimes.

6.2 Origins of nuisance

Scotland does not share with England a long history of nuisance. The first case grounded on nuisance and described as such was *Fleming* v.

* University of Dundee

Ure[1] in 1750. The Dean of Guild in Edinburgh exercised his jurisdiction to interdict the use of premises as a fencing school, because the noise inhibited the prospects of the petitioner letting the property beneath.

The powers exercised by the Dean of Guild were not new. It was within the competence of municipal officials in burghs to interdict noxious trades and regulate fire hazards.[2] For example, three years previously a petition had been brought before Aberdeen magistrates in an attempt to interdict a proposed soap manufactory on grounds of 'the nauseousness of the smell and the danger of fire'.[3] The innovation of 1750 is the use of the term 'nuisance' to describe an objectionable state of affairs. The decision in *Fleming* anticipates rather than completes the inception of nuisance in Scots law. Probably the term was used in its everyday sense. Over the succeeding half century, nuisance developed into a doctrine of the common law of Scotland and English authority was of some significance in the process.

Clearly, the need was felt for a doctrine such as nuisance. It may be assumed that this need was driven by the twin processes of industrialisation and urbanisation. There may be some doubt, however, concerning the relative extent to which industrialisation operated as a driving factor. While the emergence of nuisance is broadly contemporary with the earliest stages of industrialisation, its origin in burghs precedes the textile boom that indicated the first phase of the industrial revolution in Scotland.[4] Moreover, the subject matter of complaint in the earlier cases tended not to be new or large-scale industrial operations, but traditional crafts: blacksmithing, bleaching and dying, tanning, skinning, glue-making, boiling of tripe or whale blubber and so on.

By the time Scotland acquired the heavy industry that characterised the later nineteenth-century Scottish economy, the doctrine of nuisance

[1] (1750) Mor 13159.

[2] Deans of Guild were separate from Burgh courts. Historically, they had jurisdiction over causes between merchants, APS 1583 c. 184, and jurisdiction over buildings. 'It belongs to the Dean of Guild to take care that buildings within boroughburgh be agreeable to law, neither encroaching on private property, not on the public streets or passages; and that houses in danger of falling be thrown down.' Erskine, *Institute* (Edinburgh, John Bell, 9th edn, 1871) I, iv 4, 105. On origins and nature of the Dean of Guild's jurisdiction see: J. Campbell-Irons, *The Law and Practice of the Dean of Guild Court* (Edinburgh, Green, 1895) pp. 33–57.

[3] *Leith & Lesley* v. *Aberdeen Magistrates* (1748) Elchies Decisions sv 'Public Police' No. 9.

[4] While precise dates have been set for the Industrial Revolution this is considered by some historians to be problematic. Industrialisation may be better seen in terms of a lengthy process. See Whatley etc. The first cotton spinning mills in Scotland were opened in 1783.

had been fully established in the law for half a century or longer. Actions were brought against chemical works, railway companies and iron foundries, but the volume of litigation appears never to have been very great. Neither is there much evidence of any significant change in the common law doctrine consequent upon heavier and more seriously polluting industry.

The development of nuisance in the latter half of the eighteenth century may be seen in the context of social and legal change. This was a period that saw a general transformation of Scottish society and economy.[5] It was also a time of dramatic expansion of towns and of the urban population. The enlightenment led to new thinking on law which is evident in the work of the two earliest commentators on nuisance, Lord Kames and Baron Hume. Law was no longer seen purely as a product of reason, but as tied to social and economic circumstances.

It has been observed of Lord Kames that 'his underlying purpose was to develop the law more rapidly in accordance with the needs of the times'.[6] This concern may be seen in a note appended to the report on *Kinloch* v *Robertson* in 1756[7] in which the Dean of Guild had been petitioned for the removal of a blacksmith's workshop on the second floor of a building separated from the petitioner's home by a mutual gable. Lord Kames noted that the close proximity of neighbours gave rise to a need for a legal rule that would protect the comfortable habitation of property against extraordinary disturbances.[8]

Having considered the absolute right of proprietors to use corporeal property as they wish, Baron David Hume went on to consider the 'somewhat more delicate' issue of rights over heritable property.

> But it is quite otherwise in the case of landed possessions of which every man's portion is bounded immediately, and on all sides, by that of others. Hence there results an interference of interest in a variety of particulars, each claiming a preferable regard to himself; and this situation issues naturally at length from a sense of common interest, in a certain limitation of a proprietor's right of enjoyment, in certain reciprocal concessions, by each heritor to another, for the sake of peace and general convenience and accommodation. Every individual comes to see, that, if he were to

[5] See e.g. R. B. Sher, 'Scotland Transformed: The Eighteenth Century' in J. Wormald (ed.), *Scotland: a History* (Oxford, OUP, 2005).

[6] P. Stein, 'Law and Society in Scottish Thought' in N.T. Phillipson and R. Mitchison (eds.), *Scotland in the Age of Improvement* (Edinburgh, Edinburgh University Press, 1970) p. 158.

[7] (1756) Mor 13164.

[8] See quote given at p. 150; see below, text at note 130.

> insist on the absolute disposal of his own, he might indeed incommode his neighbours, but that he would be liable to be equally molested by them in return. He contracts too in time some degree of regard for them.[9]

The need for nuisance or an equivalent doctrine was seen to arise from increasingly congested living or 'close neighbourhood' rather than an increase in or new forms of economic activity. The appropriate response was seen by both Kames and Hume in terms of a need to limit absolute rights of ownership. In the case of Hume, the influence of his uncle, the philosopher David Hume, is evident in the way in which the argument for limitation of rights is presented by reference to self interest.

The doctrine of nuisance was seen as a legal element appropriate to a society aspiring to an advanced state of civilised refinement. Whitty reports advice given by clerks to the Glasgow Dean of Guild in *Charity* v *Riddell*:[10] 'in a comparatively rude and uncultivated state of society, direct damage to persons or property appears to have been necessary to constitute a nuisance; but in the progress of society to a higher degree of civilisation, the general comfort of individuals has come to be considered of greater importance; and to this general comfort, the power of the individual in the use of his property has been postponed'.[11]

While Hume discussed limitations on absolute rights of land use with reference to civilian doctrines such as *aemulatio* and *immissio* before moving on to consider nuisance, it has been observed that these aspects of Scots law were not well developed. Johnston has noted that no consistent view on limitations on absolute rights is found in institutional writing except as regards restrictions imposed by servitude.[12] While Scots law appears to have recognised both *aemulatio* and *immissio*, the former did not receive full discussion in court before 1808[13] and, although the latter was cited in a number of eighteenth- and early nineteenth-century cases, its relevance to the decision is clear in very few of these.[14] While *aemulatio*

9 *Baron David Hume's Lectures*, 1786–1822 (Edinburgh, Stair Society, 1952) vol. III, p. 207.

10 5 July 1805 FC, Mor 'Public Police ' App. No. 6.

11 This passage is not in the case reports. N. Whitty quotes it in 'Nuisance', *Stair Memorial Encyclopaedia of the Laws of Scotland* (Edinburgh, Butterworths, 2001) Reissue, para. 11 note 4 giving the source as: Hume Session Papers vol. cxviii No. 8, App. 2; Signet Library, Old Session Papers, vol. 480, 4, App. 2.

12 D. Johnston, 'Owners and Neighbours: From Rome to Scotland' in R. Evans-Jones (ed.), *The Civil Law Tradition in Scotland* (Edinburgh, Stair Society, 1995), p. 184.

13 *Glassford* v. *Astley* (1808) Mor 'Property', App. No. 7.

14 E.g. *Hall* v. *Corbet* (1698) Mor 12775; *Brodie* v. *Cadel* (1707) 4 Brown's Supp 660.

served as a restriction on absolute rights of property use, its basis in malice meant that claims could be easily defended.

The failure of the Scottish courts to derive from existing civilian principle a doctrine equivalent to nuisance is exemplified in the case of *Dewar* v. *Fraser* in 1767.[15] This was not a Dean of Guild case: it appears to have been initiated in the Court of Session. The petitioner sought to interdict the respondent from operating a lime kiln, the smoke from which caused serious discomfort in the petitioner's home. Since it was found that the kiln was situated for the convenience of the respondent and not maliciously, to spite his neighbour, the claim based on *aemulatio* was successfully defended. The Court refused to apply the *immissio* principle on the basis that the smoke was not directed at the neighbour, but blew as the wind took it.

Dewar v. *Fraser* demonstrates not only a lack of judicial creativity, but also the fact that the earliest developments in nuisance by Deans of Guild did not automatically lead to recognition of nuisance as a legal doctrine by the Court of Session. The Court had appellate jurisdiction over decisions of the Dean of Guild and had affirmed the jurisdiction of the municipal authorities over 'nuisances',[16] but it took time for nuisance to become fully integrated as a doctrine of the common law.

In the following year, the petitioner in *Ralston* v. *Pettigrew*[17] was successful in circumstances similar to those in *Dewar.* The distinction with *Dewar* turns on the fact that in *Ralston* material damage to property was proved. *Ralston* may be regarded as the first nuisance case in the common law, but in truth the grounds for the decision are obscure.

Until almost the end of the eighteenth century, nuisance remained within the province of Deans of Guild, albeit with appeals to the Court of Session. The nuisance case law of the eighteenth century involved pleas, mostly by individuals, but in some cases by groups of neighbours, to interdict or remove noxious, noisy or otherwise harmful operations and fire hazards. No distinction, equivalent to that found in England between public and private nuisance, was drawn. Complaints of inconvenience or disturbance to individuals were sometimes combined with pleas of nuisance to the wider neighbourhood.[18] There were no claims for

[15] (1767) Mor 12803.

[16] E.g. in *Carrubbers Close Proprietors* v. *Reoch* (1762) Mor 13175 it was the Court of Session that approved the jurisdiction of the Dean of Guild and held that the issue resolved into a regulation for preventing fire.

[17] (1768) Mor 12808.

[18] E.g. *Kinloch* v. *Robertson* (1756) Mor 13163; *Carrubber's Close Proprietors* v. *Reoch* and *Wood* v. *Sandeman* (1762) Mor 13175; *Vary* v. *Thomson* 2 July 1805 FC, Mor 'Public Police' App. No. 4.

damages; indeed Deans of Guild had no jurisdiction to hear actions for reparation.

By the end of the eighteenth century, sheriffs and justices of the peace had assumed jurisdiction over nuisance cases although the sheriffs' jurisdiction was based on no clear footing until an Act of 1838.[19] From 1816, nuisance cases were submitted to the Jury Court and in 1825 nuisance became an enumerated cause for jury trial.[20] Deans of Guild were abolished in all burghs except Edinburgh, Glasgow, Aberdeen, Dundee and Perth in 1833[21] and remaining Deans of Guild had their jurisdiction reduced by the Court of Session in 1834.[22] As jurisdiction was assumed by the superior courts, nuisance passed from a subject for municipal regulation to a fully-fledged element of the common law. Dean of Guild courts were re-established in all burghs in 1892[23] and continued to exercise jurisdiction over 'architectural nuisances' until their abolition in 1975.[24]

The development of the doctrine of nuisance was facilitated by the citation and acceptance of English authority. The English public nuisance case, *R* v. *White and Ward,*[25] was cited for the first time in a Scottish court in *Dewar* v. *Fraser* although no mention of nuisance was made in the report. Citations of Blackstone and the *sic utere tuo ut alienum non laedas* maxim followed thereafter.[26] To the extent that the English tort of nuisance provided a proposition: to constitute nuisance it is not necessary that the source of complaint should damage health, but it is sufficient if it causes substantial discomfort, English law was significant in the development of Scots nuisance. This proposition is taken from *R* v. *White and Ward* and its acceptance in Scotland can be seen in case law.[27]

There was, however, no lock, stock and barrel importation of English nuisance. When Blackstone's treatment of nuisance is compared with

[19] Sheriff Courts (Scotland) Act 1838 (c. 119), s. 15.

[20] Court of Session Act 1825 (c. 120), s. 28. [21] Royal Burgh Reform Act 1833, c. 76.

[22] *Donaldson* v. *Pattison* (1834) 13 S 27. Jurisdiction was reduced to 'architectural nuisances', conventional nuisances and noxious trades 'ticketed by law' as nuisances. See Whitty, *Nuisance*, above, n. 11. para. 14.

[23] Burgh Police (Scotland) Act 1892.

[24] Local Government (Scotland) Act 1975 (c. 65), s. 227. [25] (1757) 1 Burr 333.

[26] The first citation of the maxim is found in *Cuming* v. *Robertson* 1781 (unreported); see Whitty, above, n. 11, para 16, note 7. However, in *Gray* v. *Maxwell* (1762) Mor 12800, 12801 'No man is entitled to use his property so as to hurt another' is found in English. While the maxim may indeed have been derived from civilian sources (see J. Gordley, '*Immissionschutz*, nuisance and *troubles de voisinage* in comparative and historical perspective', *ZEuP*, 1998 13) it came to Scotland, not through the *ius commune*, but via Blackstone.

[27] E.g. *Inverness Magistrates* v. *Skinners of Inverness*, 20 January 1804 FC, Mor 13191; *Hart* v. *Taylor* (1827) 4 Murr, 307.

contemporary Scottish authorities, it can be seen that nuisance in England embraced a far broader range of circumstances than was ever the case in Scotland.[28] In comparison with England, nuisance in Scotland is relatively narrow in scope. This remains the case in the modern law.[29] *Aemulationem vicini* has survived in Scots law, but it has been marginalised by nuisance. References to the *immissio* principle simply ceased in the early nineteenth century.

6.3 Establishing nuisance

Nuisance may be regarded as a wrongful invasion of property rights. Early Scottish definitive statements are descriptive, but provide no absolute standard indicating when a state of affairs amounts in law to nuisance.[30]

Although the commission of nuisance has been described as 'illegal',[31] the better view may be that nuisance arises from activities that are not unlawful per se, but become so only because of their effects on the interests of others.[32] The consistent approach has been to view nuisance as a relative concept: '[E]very case depends on its own circumstances; and that is a nuisance which a jury of intelligent gentlemen think so in the circumstances of each case.'[33]

[28] See further G. D. L. Cameron, 'Scots and English Nuisance...Much the Same Thing?', (2005) 9 Edin LR, 98, pp. 111–15.

[29] *Hunter* v. *Canary Wharf Ltd* [1997] AC 655 per Lord Hope of Craighead, p. 723.

[30] Bell, *Principles* (Edinburgh, Clark, 1899) para. 241: '... [W]hatever is noxious, or renders life uncomfortable, to the King's subjects generally, or to the neighbourhood, is a nuisance. Whatever is offensive to individuals in their dwelling houses, or inconsistent with the comfort of life, whether by stench, noise, indecency...is a nuisance.' Lord Chief Commissioner Murray in *Hart* v. *Taylor* (1827) 4 Murr pp. 307, 313–14: 'In a question of nuisance, the first point is, whether the product of the work is noxious or unwholesome; but though it may not be absolutely noxious, still if it renders the enjoyment of life substantially uncomfortable, either in the pursuer's house or grounds, it is a nuisance.'

[31] See e.g. A. T. Glegg, *Reparation* (Edinburgh, Green, 1892) p. 281; W. Mitchell, 'Nuisance and Non-Natural Use of Property' in *Green's Encyclopaedia of the Law of Scotland* (Edinburgh, Green, 1930) vol. x, para. 692.

[32] H. Burn-Murdoch, *Interdict* (Edinburgh, Hodge, 1933) p. 209: '[N]uisance consists in an impermissible degree of harm, resulting from conduct that is not in itself otherwise unlawful.' Note however that reference has been made at times to 'nuisances ticketed by law' meaning things that cannot be carried out without amounting to nuisance. See Whitty, above, n. 11, para. 6.

[33] Per Lord Gillies in *Arrott* v. *Whyte* (1826) 4 Murr 149, 158. See also J. C. C. Broun, *Law of Nuisance* (Edinburgh, Green, 1891) p. 4: '[A] question of nuisance is very much a question of fact, to be determined according to the circumstances of each particular case.'

The standard that has emerged is that of reasonable tolerability.[34] This was formalised in 1954 by Lord President Cooper in the case of *Watt* v *Jamieson*.[35] Lord Cooper's dictum in that case provides what is now regarded as the modern definitive statement of nuisance in Scots law:

> I deduce that the proper angle of approach to a case of alleged nuisance is rather from the standpoint of the victim of the loss or inconvenience than from the standpoint of the alleged offender: and that if any person so uses his property as to occasion serious disturbance or substantial inconvenience to his neighbour or material damage to his neighbour's property, it is in the general case irrelevant to plead merely that he was making a normal and familiar use of his own property. The balance in all such cases has to be held between the freedom of a proprietor to use his property as he pleases and the duty on a proprietor not to inflict material loss or inconvenience on adjoining[36] proprietors or adjoining property; and in every case the answer depends on considerations of fact and degree…The critical question is whether what he was exposed to was *plus quam tolerabile* when due weight has been given to all the surrounding circumstances of the offensive conduct and its effects.[37]

The *plus quam tolerabile* requirement introduced into the law a mechanism by which the competing interests of the parties may be balanced.[38] The defender's interest in the free use of his land yields to the pursuer's interest in the comfortable enjoyment of hers at the point at which the interference becomes more than reasonably tolerable, having regard to the circumstances. The test of tolerability is objective inasmuch as reasonable tolerability is considered from the point of view of the reasonable occupier in the locality of the pursuer.

The relevant circumstances that may be considered are: the nature and extent of the alleged harm or interference; the sensitivity to harm of the pursuer or the pursuer's property; the character of the locality; the purpose of

[34] See: *Robertson* v. *Stewarts & Livingstone* (1872) 11 M 189 per Lord Ardmillan, 198; *Maguire* v. *Charles McNeill Ltd* 1922 SC 174 per Lord Skerrington, p. 190.

[35] 1954 SC 56.

[36] 'Neighbouring' might have been a better word than 'adjoining' since there is no requirement that properties be adjoining.

[37] 1954 SC 56, 57–8. See also *Maguire* v. *Charles McNeil Ltd* 1922 SC 174 per Lord Skerrington at 190.

[38] The view that nuisance proceeds on a balance of interests has been a consistent theme in writing on nuisance in Scotland. See e.g. Hume, *Lectures 1786–1822* (Edinburgh, Stair Society, 1939) vol. III p. 207, text at note 9 above; H. Burn-Murdoch, *Interdict* (Edinburgh, Hodge,1933), pp. 206–7; J. Rankine, *The Law of Landownership in Scotland*, 4th edn (Edinburgh, Green, 1909), p. 368; T. B. Smith, *Short Commentary on the Law of Scotland* (Edinburgh, Green, 1961), p. 530.

the respective parties' land use; the ability of the pursuer to effect protective measures; and the ability of the defender to abate the nuisance.[39]

In order to establish nuisance, it is incumbent on the pursuer to establish a prima facie case. In order to do this, it is necessary to establish materiality. Disturbance must be serious, inconvenience must be substantial and damage to property material in order to amount to nuisance. Evidence must be led on the extent and nature of the harm in every case. Where the pursuer establishes a prima facie case, the onus then shifts to the defender to provide sufficient justification or excuse.[40] The defender may, of course, dispute the extent of harm and may answer the pursuer's case, for example by pleading that the pursuer is unduly sensitive, that the defender has taken all practicable measures to minimise the degree of disturbance and that what remains is immaterial or that the pursuer himself could take simple measures to obviate the disturbance.

Thus, issues such as reasonableness of the defender's conduct or the locality are relevant factors that may be weighed in the balance when determining whether the harm is *plus quam tolerabile* and therefore amounts to nuisance, but such factors must be distinguished from defences properly so called. A defence, if established, will negate any finding of nuisance.[41]

It is necessary to establish nuisance irrespective of the remedy sought. The primary remedy for nuisance in Scots law is interdict rather than damages. Orders *ad factum praestandum* are also available and the Court of Session has statutory powers to make other orders, for example for removal.[42] The pursuer may seek declarator, particularly where title is disputed or defences of acquiescence or prescription are anticipated. For remedies other than damages there is no requirement to prove fault in addition to establishing nuisance. Where nuisance is established, interdict is available by right and the Court has no power to make an award of damages in lieu. If, on the other hand, the harm or disturbance is complete or abatement is impossible, damages will be the only remedy available.[43]

It has been described as an invalid defence: '[t]hat the manufacture or other operations creating the nuisance are for the public convenience, or for the good of the country or mankind in general'.[44] In practice, while

[39] See Whitty, *Nuisance*, paras. 44ff. [40] See Whitty, *Nuisance*, para. 107.

[41] The defences to nuisance are: acquiescence, prescription and statutory authority.

[42] Court of Session Act 1988 ss. 46, 47.

[43] *Chalmers* v. *William Dixon Ltd* (1876) 3 R 461.

[44] J. C. C. Broun, above, n. 33, p. 110 founding upon *Arrott* v. *Whyte* (1826) 4 Murr 158; and *Duke of Buccleuch* v. *Cowan* (1866) 5 M 229. See also *Ben Nevis Distilleries Ltd* v. *British*

the public interest in the continuation of an activity cannot override the private interest in its abatement, there are devices whereby the harmful activity can be allowed to continue, at least pending the implementation of remedial measures.

The terms of interdict must be framed no more widely than is necessary to obviate the harm or disturbance. Since nuisance does not involve conduct that is wrongful per se, it follows that the activity wherever possible should be allowed to continue, but not in such a way as to give rise to nuisance. For example, in *Inglis* v. *Shotts Iron Co* the Court of Session interdicted the defenders from calcining iron within a mile of the pursuer's boundary. Anticipating that improved methods of calcining might yet be developed, the House of Lords added the following terms to the interdict: 'in the manner hitherto practised by them, or in any other manner whereby noxious vapours may be caused to pass over the pursuer's lands, or any part thereof, to the damage or injury of the pursuer's plantations or estate'.[45]

Interim interdict may be awarded at the discretion of the Court which will base its decision on the balance of convenience giving due weight to the public interest. Such an award can be postponed pending submission by the defender of proposals for remedial measures. Once granted, interim interdict can be continued while the effectiveness of remedial measures is assessed.

An award of perpetual interdict may also be postponed where the defender offers to implement remedial measures. This power is exercised where either: 'the granting of immediate interdict would be attended with consequences to the rights of the respondents as injurious as, or possibly more so, than the wrong that was complained of, or ... because the effect of an immediate interdict would be to cause some great and immediate public inconvenience'.[46] A good example of a case in which interdict was postponed on the second of these grounds is *Webster* v. *Lord Advocate*,[47] in which a local resident established that noise made during the preparations for the Edinburgh Military Tattoo constituted nuisance.

Aluminium Co Ltd 1948 SC 592 in which the defenders, whose manufacturing output constituted seventy-two per cent of UK aluminium production at the time, failed to have overturned on appeal an interlocutor allowing proof before answer.

45 (1882) 9 R (HL) 78.

46 Per Lord McLaren, *Clippens Oil Co* v. *Edinburgh & District Water Trustees* (1897) 25 R 370, 383.

47 1985 SLT 361.

Although nuisance is fairly described as a wrong against property, Scots law is relatively flexible in recognising a range of types of harm that may be actionable. In addition to typical complaints of nuisance where harm takes the form of disturbance or physical damage to property, actions are competent in respect of injury to health[48] or damage to economic interests.[49]

Scots law is similarly flexible on questions of title. Title to sue follows from an interest in the property affected. The interest will differ according to whether the pursuer is a landlord, tenant or a feudal superior. A landlord has title to sue in respect of any nuisance affecting his interest as landlord, for example where there is a diminution in the value of the property affected or physical harm. Tenants can sue where their tenancy is affected, for example where there is physical harm or disturbance. Where a tenant is responsible for nuisance the landlord may sue on the lease. Historically, superiors were entitled to sue on the feu charter. Since the abolition of feudal tenure, the ability of remaining superiors to enforce burdens is severely restricted and both title and interest require to be proved.[50]

There is no ruling in Scots law that denies title to an occupier in possession without rights of ownership. Broun noted that the issue whether a property qualification was required was raised, but not determined in *Gardner* v. *Fraser.*[51] In *Shanlin* v. *Collins,*[52] a husband and wife sued in respect of noise nuisance. The husband was the property owner, but the wife obtained an award of damages in respect of nervous debility brought about by the barking of her neighbour's dogs. Mrs Shanlin's title was not challenged. As Whitty states: '[p]ossibly any possessor may sue'.[53]

6.4 Fault

The issue of whether fault required to be proved in nuisance was determined in the context of an action for declarator and interdict in 1866.

48 *Chalmers* v. *William Dixon Ltd* (1876) 3 R 461; *Shanlin* v. *Collins* 1973 SLT (Sh Ct) 21.

49 Economic interests may take the form of diminution in property value or letting value: see *Fleming* v. *Ure* (1750) Mor 13175; *Pentland* v. *Henderson* (1855) 17 D 552; *McKay* v. *Greenhill* (1858) 20 D 1251; or diminution in business: see *Adam* v. *Alloa Police Commissioners* (1874) 2 R 143; *Central Motors (St Andrews) Ltd* v. *St Andrews Magistrates* 1961 SLT 290; *The Globe* v. *North of Scotland Water Authority* 2000 SC 392; or both: see *Swinton* v. *Peddie* (1837) 15 S 775, (1839) Macl & R 1018.

50 Abolition of Feudal Tenure (Scotland) Act 2000 s. 24; Title Conditions (Scotland) Act 2003 s. 8.

51 (1860) 22D 1501. See Broun, above, n. 33, p. 82. 52 1973 SLT (Sh Ct) 21.

53 Above, n. 11 para. 134.

It was held, in *Duke of Buccleuch* v. *Cowan*, that since nuisance was 'a wrong', provided the pursuer established nuisance, there was no further requirement for proof of wrongfulness since this would be tautological.[54] Where nuisance is established and remedies other than damages are sought, it remains the case that there is no requirement to prove fault.[55] Such remedies are only relevant in the context of a prospective or continuing state of affairs. Once he or she has been made aware of the harm or discomfort anticipated or caused, the defender is culpable for allowing such circumstances to persist in the knowledge that they give rise to nuisance:[56] '[f]or nuisance is a use of property causing continuing damage, and the persistence of an occupier in so using his property to the known detriment of his neighbour, supplies a presumption of negligence which renders proof of it unnecessary'.[57]

Since the need to prove fault in the modern law is dependent on the remedy sought, in tracing the development of fault liability it is necessary to look in particular at actions for damages. During the nineteenth century, in the vast majority of actions grounded on nuisance, the remedies sought were those intended to effect abatement rather than damages. There are cases in which no damages were sought even though physical harm to property was alleged.[58] No very clear impression of any requirement to prove fault emerges from the relatively few actions for damages raised. In neither *Skene* v. *Maberleys*[59] nor *Hamilton* v. *Charles Tennant & Co*[60] were fault or wrongfulness pled. By contrast, in *Collins* v. *Hamilton*[61] the pursuers undertook, but failed to prove nuisance, loss and fault. In *Cooper & Wood* v. *North British Railway Co*[62] the defenders' argument that 'wrongfully' should be inserted in the issues was repelled. In *Armistead* v. *Bowerman*[63] the pursuer averred that the defender had

[54] *Duke of Buccleuch* v. *Alexander Cowan & Sons* (1866) 4 M 475.

[55] *Logan* v. *Wang (UK) Ltd* 1991 SLT 580.

[56] Whitty, above, n. 11, para. 144. See also E. Reid, 'The Basis of Liability in Nuisance', 1997 JR 162, 165–6.

[57] A. T. Glegg, *The Law of Reparation* (Edinburgh, Green, 1892), pp. 281–2. The term 'negligence' here should be read broadly to mean fault.

[58] E.g. *Willoughby d'Eresby's Trustees* v. *Strathearn Hydropathic Establishment Co* (1873) 1 R 35; *Allison* v. *Campbell & Co* (1890) 6 Sh Ct Rep 80; *Houldsworth* v. *Wishaw Magistrates* (1887) 14 R 920; *Cunningham* v. *Meldrum* (1894) 10 Sh Ct Rep 154; *Ireland* v. *Smith* (1895) 33 SLR 156, 3 SLT 180; *Countess of Seafield* v. *Kemp* (1899) 1 F 402, 6 SLT 10.

[59] (1820) 2 Murr 352. [60] (1839) 1 D 502. [61] (1837) 15 S 895.

[62] (1863) 1 M 299; (1863) 2 M 116. In the context of the case 'wrongfully' meant in excess of the powers in the Railways Clauses Consolidation (Scotland) Act 1845 s. 16.

[63] (1888) 15 R 814. The loss in this case was destruction of fish ova. The defender, whose logging operation upstream had silted the water supply, was held not liable as he had conducted an ordinary operation in an ordinary manner.

conducted his operations in a 'wrongful, reckless and negligent manner'. The Lord Ordinary's finding of negligence was overturned on appeal and the pursuer's case was lost. There appears to have been no concern with fault or wrongfulness in *Blantyre* v. *Clyde Navigation Trustees*.[64] Leaving the case of *Chalmers* v. *Dixon* to be considered in due course, when nineteenth-century actions for damages grounded on nuisance are examined, no consistent approach to pleadings is found, neither is there any clear requirement that fault be proved. Broun, writing in 1891, stated: 'Where the action concludes solely for damages, the pursuer must prove damage.'[65] His authority for this point is *Collins* v. *Hamilton*. Broun added nothing about proving fault.

Actions for damages grounded in nuisance arose in the nineteenth century only where tangible harm was consequent on air or water pollution. This accords with a narrow view of common law nuisance that pertained throughout the nineteenth century in which nuisance consisted of pollution of air, pollution of water, unusual noise, unnatural heat and vibration.[66] In actions that were not grounded on nuisance, where damages were sought in respect of property harm or indeed personal injury resulting from uses or states of property, the general requirement was for proof of loss and fault.[67] It can be seen that property harm arising from nuisance was treated differently from property harm arising in other ways.

Although the requirement for proof of fault was established in the general case[68] at a relatively early stage, there were developments around the middle of the nineteenth century which have been seen by some writers as an attempt to introduce a doctrine of strict liability applicable where property harm was consequent upon a hazardous activity.[69] Two cases in

[64] (1867) 5 M 508; (1871) 9 M (HL) 6. [65] Broun, above, n. 33, p. 89.

[66] See Broun, above, n. 33, p. 8. A further two categories suggested by Broun, dangers and indecency, are problematic. See G. D. L. Cameron, above, n. 28, pp. 245–6.

[67] Property harm arising from uses or states of neighbouring property: *Hay* v. *Littlejohn* (1666) Mor 13974; *Sibbald* v. *Lady Rosyth* (1685) Mor 13976; *Callendar* v. *Eddington* (1826) 4 Murr 108; *Douglas* v. *Monteith* (1826) 4 Murr 130; *Weston* v. *Incorporation of Tailors of Potterrow* (1839) 1 D 218; *Thomson* v. *Gray* (1842) 5 D 377. Personal injury arising from use or state of property: *Gardner* v. *Ferguson* 1795 unreported; *Innes* v. *Edinburgh Magistrates* (1798) Mor 13189, 13967; *Black* v. *Cadell* 9 Feb 1804 FC, Mor 13905, (1812) 5 Pat App 567; *Chapman* v. *Parlane* (1825) 3 S 401.

[68] I.e., where property harm arose through some means other than nuisance.

[69] For the most recent example see R. Zimmermann and P. Simpson, 'Liability among Neighbours' in K. Reid and R. Zimmermann (eds.), *A History of Private Law in Scotland* (Oxford, OUP, 2000) vol. II *Obligations*.

particular, *Cleghorn* v. *Taylor*[70] in 1856 and *Kerr* v. *Earl of Orkney*[71] in the following year, have been taken to suggest that there might be liability in damages irrespective of fault. The emphasis placed upon fault as the essential basis for liability in reparation in two subsequent cases, *Campbell* v. *Kennedy*[72] in 1864 and *Laurent* v. *Lord Advocate*[73] in 1869, is generally regarded as a judicial reaction against these earlier cases.

Scottish judges of the time were apparently divided on this issue.[74] While little immediate further support appears to have been gained for a doctrine of liability irrespective of fault, the notion persisted that fault could in some circumstances be inferred. This uncertainty regarding the need to prove fault arose in the context of property harm resulting from uses of property in general and was not related in particular to nuisance. The case that tied inferred fault to nuisance was *Chalmers* v. *Wm Dixon Ltd*, decided in 1876.[75] Grounding on nuisance, a farmer sued for damages in respect of harm to his crops and the health of his family caused by smoke. *Chalmers* was unlike other nuisance cases of the time because the smoke did not emanate from a deliberately conducted activity, but had arisen by accident. A heap of industrial refuse for which the defenders were responsible had combusted. The defenders focused inquiry on their lack of culpability.

The Court found for the pursuer. The reasoning employed may be summarised as follows. In the context of a dangerous and non-natural use of land, it was possible to distinguish authorities on natural uses of land which required proof of fault for liability. The governing authorities in the context of dangerous *opera manufacta*, *Kerr* v. *Earl of Orkney*, and for non-natural user, *Rylands* v. *Fletcher*,[76] were taken to support the proposition that liability might arise without proof of fault. In the circumstances of the case, the pursuer in *Chalmers* could be relieved of the burden of proving fault, a burden that could not have been discharged without great practical difficulty. Fault on the part of the defenders could be inferred, but fault remained the basis for liability.

Until the House of Lords ruling in *RHM Bakeries (Scotland) Ltd* v *Strathclyde Regional Council* in 1985,[77] it was by no means clear that liability in reparation for nuisance required proof of fault. This rendered

[70] (1856) 18 D 664. [71] (1857) 20 D 298 [72] (1864) 3 M 121. [73] (1869) 7 M 607.

[74] For detailed discussion see Zimmermann and Simpson, above, n. 69.

[75] (1876) 3 R 461. [76] (1868) LR 3 HL 330.

[77] *RHM Bakeries (Scotland) Ltd* v. *Strathclyde Regional Council* 1985 SC (HL) 17, 1985 SLT 214.

nuisance an anomalous ground of action in the law of delict.[78] While the applicability of the ruling in *Duke of Buccleuch* v. *Cowan* is now restricted to actions for remedies other than damages, it was not always seen in this way and so Mitchell, writing in 1930, considered nuisance in terms of illegality, that is wrongful use of property in which the courts were unconcerned with fault, at least not in the form of negligence.[79] Mitchell presented nuisance and non-natural user separately, liability for harm arising from non-natural user being based on inferred negligence on the authority of *Chalmers* v. *Dixon*. After all, *Chalmers* did not truly belong in the wrongful category given the accidental nature of the harm. In Mitchell's analysis, liability for harm arising from natural uses of property that were not per se wrongful[80] depended on proof of negligence. Early to mid-twentieth-century cases involving property harm, for example through flooding or withdrawal of support, generally depended for liability on proof of negligence and were not at the time regarded as involving nuisance.[81]

Perceptions of liability in nuisance in general may have been distorted in favour of liability without fault by a combination of factors. First, there appear to have been no actions for reparation in respect of 'typical'[82] forms of nuisance between 1863[83] and 1954. Thus, for over 90 years,

[78] The other major exception to the normal rule, that liability is based on fault concerned liability for animals which could be strict depending on circumstances. Strict liability for damage done by animals is now on a statutory footing, Animals (Scotland) Act 1987. Liability in defamation rests on malice, but malice is presumed from the defamatory nature of the statement so while liability is in effect strict, by a legal fiction it rests on fault.

[79] W. Mitchell, above, n. 31, vol. x, para. 692.

[80] I.e., gave rise to property harm, but not to nuisance as such.

[81] E.g. *Hill's Trustees* v. *Edinburgh Magistrates* 1912 1 SLT 448; *McCormick* v. *Fife Coal Co Ltd* 1931 SC 9. It has been widely assumed that liability in the flooding case *Caledonian Railway Co* v. *Greenock Corporation* 1917 SC (HL); [1917] AC 556 was found irrespective of fault. This is incorrect. The pursuers sought to prove negligence at first instance and succeeded in so doing. See further E. Reid, 'Liability for Dangerous Activities: A Comparative Analysis' (1999) 48 ICLQ 731, 748 note 102; G. D. L. Cameron, 'Strict Liability and the Rule in *Caledonian Railway Co* v. *Greenock Corporation*' (2000) 5 SLPQ 356.

[82] Meaning broadly, where the use of property was affected by smoke, water pollution, noise, heat or vibration.

[83] *Cooper & Wood* v. *North British Railway Co* (1863) 1 M 499 (see above, note 24). The complaint concerned fumes from foundries which, it was alleged, had 'completely destroyed Baileyfield as a residence'. *Chalmers* v. *Dixon*, as noted above, was not a typical case. Given the circumstances in *Armistead* v. *Bowerman* (1888) 15 R 814 it does not serve well as a typical nuisance case. While it involved water pollution this was a result of stirring up silt rather than a discharge of effluents. *Blantyre* v. *Clyde Navigation Trustees* is also not typical. It concerned silting of the river Clyde by sewage deposits impeding

there was no real opportunity for judicial discussion on whether fault was required for reparation in nuisance in general; *Chalmers* v. *Dixon* only truly supporting a limited proposition that there is no onus on pursuers to prove fault where harm results from dangerous and non-natural use of land. In 1954 in *Watt* v. *Jamieson*, reparation was sought when sulphurous fumes from a water heater caused extensive damage to an upper property. Lord President Cooper seemed to regard nuisance as falling outside the fault doctrine, although he did not discuss the point in any detail.[84] Lord Cooper drew no distinction between claims for damages and other remedies and was criticised subsequently on this basis. Professor Sir T. B. Smith argued that claims for reparation fell within delictual principles and therefore required fault, whereas claims for interdict fell within the law of property and did not require fault.[85]

Second, the actions for damages that did feature in the interim period arose in respect of dangerous nuisances[86] or non-natural user[87] and these were determined without reference to fault. In some cases, claims based on fault were allowed as alternative pleas to nuisance emphasising that liability in nuisance was not seen to depend on fault.[88] In this fashion, the strict liability perception of nuisance gained ground coupled with the association between nuisance and non-natural user.

The developing association between nuisance and non-natural user was ended in *Watt* v. *Jamieson* when the defender's contention, that he could

access. The case turned on interpretation of the Clyde Navigation Acts of 1758, 1840 and 1858. *Fleming* v. *Gemmill* 1908 SC 340 in which the defenders had fouled a stream by using sinks to dispose of foul effluent would represent a typical nuisance case were it not for the awkward fact that the action was neither grounded nor determined in nuisance (see text at n. 49 above).

84 'It appeared to me that the defender's argument…tended to confuse nuisance as a cause of action with culpa and the special aspect of culpa which is generally described as the rule in *Rylands* v. *Fletcher*.' 1954 SC 56, 57.

85 T. B. Smith, *Short Commentary* (Edinburgh, Green, 1962), p.534: 'It is fully in accordance with the Civilian tradition of our law…that interdict should be granted when a man makes unreasonable use of his property. The wrong and the remedy are within the scope of the law of Property. Claims for damages fall, however, within the scope of the law of Delict.' The text is quoted at note 142 below.

86 E.g. *Slater* v. *McLellan* 1924 SC 854.

87 Some non-natural user cases were determined on the basis of *Rylands* v. *Fletcher* rather than nuisance e.g. *Gemmill's Trustees* v. *Alexander Cross & Sons Ltd* (1906) 16 SLT 576; *Western Silver Fox Ranch Ltd* v. *Ross & Cromarty County Council* 1940 SC 601; in other cases non-natural user was clearly associated with nuisance e.g. *Blair* v. *Springfield Stores* (1911) 27 Sh Ct Rep 178.

88 E.g. *Hay* v. *Waldegrave Leslie* (1896) 4 SLT 124; *Giblin* v. *Lanarkshire County Council* 1927 SLT 563. In *Western Silver Fox Ranch* (above, note 87) alternative claims based on *Rylands* v. *Fletcher* and negligence were upheld.

not be liable in nuisance for an ordinary administration of his property, was rejected.[89] The relationship between nuisance and non-natural user may have been vague and problematic, but it served to some extent to keep the scope of nuisance within bounds. With this constraint on nuisance removed, no sufficient criteria remained to distinguish between property harm cases for which proof of negligence was required and those that fell under the doctrine of nuisance.[90]

Actions for damages involving physical harm to heritable property that would earlier have been grounded on negligence came, in the latter half of the twentieth century, to be pursued in nuisance. In effect, nuisance offered a pleading shortcut if fault did not have to be proved. In particular, where property harm took the form of flooding or withdrawal of support, actions now tended to be grounded on nuisance.[91]

Fault was affirmed as the essential basis for liability in reparation in nuisance by the House of Lords in 1985 in a judgment that overturned the unanimous decision of the bench in the Inner House. In *RHM Bakeries (Scotland) Ltd* v. *Strathclyde Regional Council*,[92] the pursuers sought damages in respect of flooding of their property caused by a collapsed sewer, for which the defenders were responsible. Lord Fraser dealt in his speech with the authorities that were said to support liability without fault. *Kerr* v. *Earl of Orkney* and *Chalmers* v. *Dixon* were judicially interpreted in terms of inferred fault. *Rylands* v. *Fletcher* was cast as the villain of the piece and was declared not to be part of Scots law.[93]

Lord Fraser, however, sought to preserve inferred fault in the following dictum:

[89] The defender argued that: 'an action for nuisance will not lie in Scotland where the type of user complained of involves only a normal, natural and familiar use of the property'. This looks like an attempt to revive the Hole v. Barlow doctrine that no action lies for the reasonable exercise of a lawful trade in a lawful place, (1858) 4 CB (NS) 334. This doctrine was rejected in English law in *Bamford* v. *Turnley* (1860) 3 B & S 62, (1862) 3 B & S 66 and in Scots Law in *Inglis* v. *Shotts Iron Co* (1882) R (HL) 79.

[90] The broadening in the scope of nuisance that takes place is attributable to a combination of factors. See further G. D. L. Cameron, above, n. 28.

[91] The first flooding case grounded on nuisance was *Gourock Rope Works* v. *Greenock Corporation* 1966 SLT 125, the first support case was *McNab* v. *McDevitt* 1971 SLT (Notes) 41.

[92] 1985 SC (HL) 17, 1985 SLT 214.

[93] 'The doubt about whether culpa is the essential basis in Scots law for the liability of the proprietor of land to a neighbour arises from the fact that the English decision in *Rylands* v. *Fletcher* has sometimes been referred to as if it were authoritative in Scotland. In my opinion, with all respect to eminent judges who have referred to it in that way, it has no place in Scots law, and the suggestion that it has, is a heresy which ought to be extirpated' (per Lord Fraser, ibid., p. 217).

> The view that I have expressed does not by any means imply that, *in a case such as this*, a pursuer cannot succeed unless he avers the precise nature of the fault committed by the defender which caused the accident. It would be quite unreasonable to place such a burden on the pursuer, who in many cases will have no knowledge, and no means of obtaining knowledge of the defender's fault. As a general rule it would be relevant for a pursuer to make averments to the effect that his property has been damaged by a flood caused by an event on the defender's land, such as the collapse of a sewer which it was the defender's duty to maintain, that properly maintained sewers do not collapse and that the collapse is evidence that the defender has failed in his duty to maintain the sewer. The onus will then be on the defender to explain the event in some way consistent with absence of fault on his part.[94]

Having rejected liability without fault, Lord Fraser appears to have sought to preserve the doctrine of inferred fault from *Chalmers* v. *Dixon*, for the same reason given in that case, that is the need to avoid placing undue burdens of proof on pursuers. However, while in *Chalmers* the decision was reached in the specific context of a dangerous *opus* and non-natural user, in Lord Fraser's dictum the context, 'a case such as this', is, to say the least, vague. It was left unclear in what circumstances a claim should proceed according to the normal requirements for proof of fault and when fault might be inferred. The weakness in this formulation was revealed when it was put to the test in *Argyll and Clyde Health Board* v. *Strathclyde Regional Council*.[95] The pursuers' property was flooded when a water pipe in the control of the defenders burst. The analogy with the circumstances in *RHM Bakeries* was obvious. If there was ever to be 'a case such as this', this was it.

The pursuers' plea, that properly maintained water pipes do not burst, was held irrelevant by Lord McCluskey in the Outer House. The defenders were entitled to specification of the way in which they were at fault. In the absence of averments on what a proper maintenance regime should be, and the way in which the defenders' conduct fell short of this, no sufficient case in fault had been averred. In short, in the absence of averments on the standard of care, the defenders were entitled to be absolved. It was clear that in substance the pursuers' contention was that the defenders had been negligent. The harm was alleged to have arisen from a failure to maintain with the inference that had proper care been taken, then harm would not have arisen.[96]

94 *RHM Bakeries (Scotland) Ltd* v. *Strathclyde Regional Council* 1985 SLT 214, 219. Italics added.

95 1988 SLT 381.

96 In *RHM* Bakeries the nature of fault is slightly different: the defenders did not respond sufficiently quickly to repair a burst sewer. This could be viewed in terms of allowing the

It may be this decision that led the defender in *Kennedy* v. *Glenbelle*[97] to argue that the pursuer could not succeed in an action grounded on nuisance unless he was able to prove negligence on the part of the defender. This provided the Inner House with the opportunity to address issues not covered in *RHM Bakeries*: the nature of fault in nuisance and the respective circumstances in which actions should be resolved according to the doctrine of nuisance and those to which the ordinary rules of negligence apply.

While liability for reparation in nuisance rests on fault, fault is a generic term and not a synonym of negligence. The Inner House adopted a model of fault from Whitty's entry in the *Stair Memorial Encyclopaedia*.[98] Whitty in turn had borrowed this model from the *Second Restatement of the Law of Torts*.[99] In this model, fault takes the form of negligence when conduct creates a risk that harm to the defender will result if insufficient care is taken. Fault takes the form of intention where harm to the defender is the virtually certain consequence of conduct irrespective of care taken. In between intention and negligence lies recklessness, where harm to the defender is less than certain, but substantially likely or, put another way, where the risk of harm is so high that it will most likely materialise irrespective of care taken. Fault, in the Scots view of this model, is seen in terms of a continuum,[100] with the form taken by fault changing from intention to negligence as the likelihood of harm varies from a near certainty to a mere risk and as the harm becomes avoidable with the exercise of sufficient care. Since fault operates on a continuum, there is no clear line of demarcation between intention and negligence: one shades into the other under the veil of recklessness.

In holding that fault in nuisance was relevantly averred in terms of 'a deliberate act done in the knowledge that harm would be the likely result', the Court in *Kennedy* located fault in nuisance in terms of intention or recklessness. While not in ignorance of the potential consequences, the defender had nevertheless instructed the removal of a supporting wall. The resultant settling in the building with damage to upper floors was more or less inevitable regardless of care taken in the operation.

continuation of a state of affairs in the knowledge that it is causing harm amounting to nuisance.

[97] 1996 SC 95, 1996 SCLR 411.

[98] Whitty, 'Nuisance', above, n. 11, (1988) paras. 2087, 2089. Paras. 87, 89 in (2001) Reissue.

[99] American Law Institute 1979.

[100] Whitty, above, n. 11, para. 89.

Lord President Hope set out explicitly to differentiate nuisance from negligence and made it clear that, where fault takes the form of negligence, 'negligence will provide an equivalent remedy'.[101] It can be concluded that, in the context of physical damage to property, the scope of nuisance is not limited by the nature or source of the harm, but by the nature of the fault to which the harm is attributable. Nuisance emerges from *Kennedy* as a delict in which liability is based on intentional fault. Thus, nuisance serves to provide reparation in respect of property harm caused intentionally or recklessly, but not by accident or through the exercise of insufficient care.

Following *Kennedy* and a small number of subsequent cases, it is now possible to provide a coherent summary of fault in nuisance in Scots law. The first point to note is that in any action grounded on nuisance, nuisance must first be established. This is sufficient if the remedy sought is not damages. Where damages are sought, fault must be proved in addition.[102] Liability arises in respect of harmful acts or operations deliberately undertaken. Intention, in this context, means that the act is intentional. It does not mean that harm to the victim is intended. Motive is, in the general case, irrelevant in delict.[103] The conduct must be deliberate and carried out in the knowledge that harm would be the outcome, but knowledge may be established constructively; actual knowledge is not required.[104] Allowing the continuation of an activity or state of affairs, in the knowledge that it is causing harm amounting to nuisance, is, likewise, culpable.[105]

Finally, there is a further form of fault, noted in *Kennedy* as 'conduct causing a special risk of abnormal damage'.[106] Lord Hope considered that this might be a form of recklessness. It may be that this element of fault requires to be more fully worked out. On the basis of present authorities, it may be stated that where hazardous works are instructed and harm results from the operation, the party instructing the works cannot evade liability by pleading that he engaged a competent contractor to carry out the work.[107] It seems that this form of fault is applicable where there is a

[101] 1996 SCLR 411, 416D. [102] Ibid. 414F–G.

[103] It is relevant in use of land *in aemulationem vicini* in which liability is based on malice. It is also relevant in conspiracy.

[104] *Anderson* v. *White* 2000 SLT 37.

[105] See text at note 57 above. This is also the best explanation of fault in *Powrie Castle Properties* v. *Dundee City Council* 2001 SCLR 146.

[106] 416D.

[107] *Noble's Trustees* v. *Economic Forestry (Scotland) Ltd* 1988 SLT 662; *Hamilton & Hamilton* v. *Wahla and Ryeside Construction Ltd*, unreported. Glasgow Sheriff Court 28 April 1999, www.scotcourts.gov.uk A3944/97E.

very high risk of serious harm. This rule does appear to operate on the cusp of strict liability. It is also a variation on the normal rule of vicarious liability, that one is responsible for the delicts of employees, but not independent contractors.

It might appear to the casual observer that liability for reparation in nuisance was strict until 1985. The truth, of course, is considerably more complicated. The general principle governing liability in reparation, laid down by Stair at the end of the seventeenth century and becoming operative in Scotland from the mid-eighteenth century, was Aquilian, *damnum iniuria datum*. Liability in reparation for property harm in the general case was based on proof of loss and fault or wrongfulness before the commencement of the period on which this study concentrates. The basis on wrongfulness of liability for nuisance without further proof of fault satisfied the doctrinal requirement that *damnum* should arise from *iniuria*, but the integrity of this approach depended upon a process by which nuisance was established. That is, while *damnum* indicated *injuria*, in order to do so the *damnum* had to take the particular form of nuisance. When it did, the defender's conduct could be said to be wrongful. This analysis, applied in the context of deliberately conducted activities or states of affairs and consciously allowed to persist in the knowledge of infringement of neighbours' rights, appears doctrinally unobjectionable.

The analysis breaks down, however, if this approach is applied in the context of property harm in general, rather than being restricted to cases where nuisance is established. This indeed is what happened. By the latter half of the twentieth century, sight had been lost of the essential character of nuisance as a state of affairs, rendering the occupation of property uncomfortable or inconvenient, and nuisance had come to embrace within its scope property harm arising from use of property in a much more general sense than it was understood during the nineteenth century. While a state of affairs amounting to nuisance could tenably be seen as wrongful per se, liability for property harm arising from insufficiency of care ought properly to be based on proof of fault. In terms of delictual principle, liability in nuisance became aberrant.

The eventual triumph of fault in nuisance can be seen as driven by a need to rule on a doctrinal anomaly. *RHM Bakeries* resolved a debate in which some writers had argued against fault as the essential basis for liability in the common law of Scotland, citing nuisance and other associated cases, such as *Cleghorn* v. *Taylor*,[108] *Kerr* v. *Earl of Orkney*[109] and *Caledonian Railway Co* v. *Greenock Corporation*,[110] to support an argument that liability could be strict.[111]

It can be seen that Lord Fraser's formulation of inferred fault delivered in *RHM Bakeries* is indistinguishable from the rules of *res ipsa loquitur*.[112] The point demonstrated in *Argyll & Clyde Health Board* was that *res ipsa loquitur* does not apply in particular to nuisance. Once *Kerr* and *Cleghorn* are examined, it may be considered that inferred fault was nothing more nor less than an early attempt to introduce the doctrine of *res ipsa loquitur*.[113]

The first point that must be appreciated about *Kerr* is that the relevant dictum[114] was strictly *obiter*. The circumstances in *Kerr*, the collapse of a dam within four months of completion on which the defender had little or nothing to say regarding care taken in construction, were so eloquent of negligence that it would have been otiose to seek proof of fault and unjust to impose such a burden on the defender.[115] In the event, this was not necessary because the noble defender made good the losses that arose as a direct consequence of the collapse of the dam; he had rebuilt the mill that had been washed away in the flood. The pursuer's remaining claim was for business losses he claimed to have incurred while operating from alternative premises while the new mill was being built. He was unable to prove these losses and lost the action.[116]

[108] (1856) 18 D 664. [109] (1857) 20 D 298.

[110] 1917 SC (HL) 56; [1917] AC 556. See note 81 above.

[111] E.g. W. A. Elliott, 'What is Culpa?' 1954 JR 6; K.W.B. Middleton, 'Liability Without Fault' 1960 JR 72; G. MacCormack, 'Culpa in the Scots Law of Reparation' 1974 JR 13.

[112] See *Ballard* v. *North British Railway Co* 1923 SC (HL) 43.

[113] See E. Reid, 'Liability for Dangerous Activities' (1999) 48 ICLQ 731, 749.

[114] The dictum is found at (1857) 20 D 298, 302. It is summarised in the rubric thus: 'Where a party erects a *novum opus* on a stream for the purposes of collecting the water in a dam, he is bound to erect it as to render all property lower down the stream as secure as it was before, and if the dam should give way and do injury – even though in consequence of an extraordinary fall of rain – he will be held liable in damages, and no proof of care in the construction of the work will relieve him.'

[115] Per Lord Justice-Clerk Hope, ibid., 303: 'I never saw a case of such water-works in which the maker had less to say in order to free himself from liability. But in stating that, I am not prepared to say that any proof of the skill and care with which a new operation was conducted will be relevant when such a dam gives way immediately after its construction. Its entire failure is proof that it was not constructed so as to afford the security against risk, which the maker was bound to provide.'

[116] *Kerr* v. *Earl of Orkney* has long been misrepresented in Scots legal writing. The original source of misunderstanding may be the erroneous treatment of the case in J. Guthrie-

Cleghorn is in some respects similar. A chimney of recent construction collapsed and passed through the building beneath, destroying china in the pursuer's shop. Clearly, somebody was negligent; whether it was correct in principle to hold the owner of the upper property who had instructed the building of the chimney liable for the builder's negligence may be doubtful. The issue of liability of a proprietor without proof of fault was addressed subsequently in *Campbell* v. *Kennedy*,[117] in which the view that liability might arise *ex dominio solo* was rejected.[118] Thus, the potential effect of *Cleghorn* on the law was promptly quashed. *Cleghorn* was rationalised in *Campbell* in terms of an inference of fault.[119] In considering *Kerr*, *Cleghorn* and *Campbell*, the subject of inquiry is liability for property harm in general; analysis has not yet ascended into the specialised territory of nuisance. The presence of the maxim *sic utere tuo ut alienum non laedas* in opinions in both *Cleghorn*[120] and *Campbell*[121] has led some commentators to regard them in terms of nuisance, but the circumstances are quite unlike nuisance cases of the time.

Kerr, unfortunately, was given a significance it never merited by a long-running association with *Rylands* v. *Fletcher* originating in *Chalmers* v. *Dixon*. Bearing in mind that in *Kerr*, nothing was actually determined on the basis of Lord Justice-Clerk Hope's observations, what should have passed as a hypothetical statement presaging the development of the rule *res ipsa loquitur* became instead a doctrine of inferred fault bound up with nuisance. The presence of *Rylands* v. *Fletcher* in the reasoning employed in *Chalmers* created the possibility of strict liability in the sense of liability irrespective of fault. A tendency by Scottish commentators to interpret *Rylands* in terms of inferred fault is evident,[122] but this is an apologist's stance. As became clear in the English case of *Read* v. *Lyons*,[123] *Rylands* revived an old rule that a man acts at his peril. While *Chalmers* may have truly supported only inferred fault, sight of this could be lost and the view of *Rylands* liability, described as liability in nuisance and applied in cases such as *Giblin* v. *Lanarkshire County Council*, was very much liability irrespective of fault. The decline and fall of the rule in *Rylands* v. *Fletcher* in Scots law may be attributable to the revelation of its

Smith, *A Treatise on the Law of Reparation* (1864), 396. Had it heralded a new doctrine of strict liability one might have expected some mention of the case in Shaw's edition of Bell's *Principles* (Edinburgh, Clark, 1899). There is none.

[117] (1864) 3 M 121. [118] See Lord Neaves, ibid., 125.

[119] See Lord Justice-Clerk Inglis, ibid., 126. [120] Per Lord Cowan, (1856) 18 D 664, 698.

[121] Per Lord Justice-Clerk Inglis (1864) 3 M 121, 126.

[122] E.g. Bell, *Principles*, 10th edn (1899) para. 970. [123] [1947] AC 156.

true nature in *Read* v. *Lyons*. Following this case Lord President Cooper urged caution:

> It may be permissible to utter yet another warning against the dangers to our native principles which attend the incautious use of English precedents bearing upon this highly controversial branch of law ... we cannot ignore the wide distinction in principle between the two systems without destroying the very basis of the Scots law of Delict.[124]

One can see the strength of the association between nuisance and inferred fault in Lord Fraser's attempt to preserve this doctrine in *RHM Bakeries*. As demonstrated in *Argyll & Clyde Health Board* the association is, however, misconceived. The operation of *res ipsa loquitur* is restricted to circumstances in which it is appropriate, that is where a cause is undiscoverable.[125] It enjoys no particular association with nuisance, indeed, given the *Kennedy* formulation of fault in nuisance in which liability depends on deliberate acts and knowledge of harmful consequences, it is hard to see any application in nuisance for *res ipsa loquitur*. The element of *Chalmers* that is preserved in *Kennedy* is the peculiar rule on liability for hazardous activities expressed as conduct causing a special risk of abnormal damage. No doubt this element will lead to further discussion in the future.

So far as the requirement of fault for liability in nuisance is concerned, on one view Scots law has taken 132 years to return to the point reached in 1864 in *Duke of Buccleuch* v. *Cowan*. Then, the sole requirement was for the establishment of nuisance. In *Kennedy* the need to establish nuisance is re-emphasised and while there is now a further need to prove fault, when fault can be established in terms of a deliberate act done in the knowledge that harm would follow, it is apparent that liability in nuisance still proceeds according to notions of wrongfulness rather than negligence, even though wrongfulness is described in terms of intention and recklessness. The additional requirement to prove fault is necessitated by changes that have taken place in the scope of nuisance. Since 1950, the majority of reported actions for damages grounded on nuisance have involved flooding or the ingress of water, or withdrawal of support. These are all circumstances that previously would not have been considered as nuisance. In order to prevent nuisance from being used as a pleading shortcut in cases where liability depends properly upon negligence, it has been necessary to require proof of fault in nuisance.

[124] *McLaughlan* v. *Craig* 1948 SLT 483, 490–1.

[125] *McQueen* v. *Glasgow Garden Festival (1988) Ltd* 1995 SLT 211.

Following *Kennedy*, the form taken by fault will determine whether the action should be resolved under the rules of nuisance or according to the ordinary principles of negligence.

6.5 Location of nuisance in the common law

Professor Sir T. B. Smith wrote of nuisance in 1962: '[I]t is thought that there is still a tendency to confuse a remedy for the protection of property with a claim in delict.'[126] The taxonomical uncertainty he identified remains unresolved.[127] In the *Stair Memorial Encyclopaedia of the Laws of Scotland*, nuisance has its own section rather than being included with either obligations or property, for the precise reason that its true location could not satisfactorily be determined.

Nuisance arrived in Scots law too late for consideration by Institutional Writers other than Bell. Bell located nuisance unambiguously within property. 'The land-owner's right to the absolute use of his property is qualified by the law of nuisance.'[128] That nuisance was seen as a restriction on absolute property rights follows from the fact that this was the lacuna in the common law which nuisance was adopted to fill. The need for some restriction on property use along the lines of nuisance was noted in what may be regarded as the earliest writing on the doctrine in Scots law. This was a note appended by Lord Kames to the report of *Kinloch v. Robertson*.[129]

> The connection of close neighbourhood in a burgh introduces new duties among the inhabitants. Neighbours in town must submit to ordinary inconveniences from each other; but they must be protected against extraordinary disturbances, such as may render their property useless to them, or at least uncomfortable. Close neighbourhood introduces this temperament in equity, but not in such a manner as to deprive his neighbour of the use of his property. The only difficulty in matters of this kind is to bring this temperament under a general rule. If this cannot be done, the matter must be left to the discretion of Judges; *for when a man exceeds just bounds in the use of his property, justice demands a remedy.*[130]

[126] *Short Commentary on the Law of Scotland*, p. 531.

[127] D. Visser and N. Whitty, 'The Structure of the Law of Delict' in K. Reid and R. Zimmermann, *History of Private Law in Scotland* (Oxford, OUP, 2000) vol. II, 422, 426: 'The place of nuisance … remains uncertain'.

[128] Bell, *Principles* (Edinburgh, Clark, 1899) para. 241.

[129] (1756) Mor 13164.

[130] Italics added.

The idea of nuisance as a restriction on absolute rights of land use persisted throughout the nineteenth century. 'There is no doubt that a man can use his property in the way that he thinks best; but it is equally true that he is not entitled to put a nuisance on it.'[131] An Act of 1838 referred to 'questions of nuisance or damages arising from the alleged undue exercise of the right of property'.[132] Some fifty years later, Guthrie-Smith wrote in the following terms: '[W]hen a man exposes his neighbours to noise, smoke, unwholesome smells, or offensive vapours, or discovering a valuable seam of clay in his property starts a brickwork, he exceeds the liberty which the law gives him in the enjoyment of his property.'[133] Bell's view of nuisance as quoted above was repeated in subsequent editions.[134] It may be noted, however, that no doctrine of abuse of rights of general application was ever developed in Scots law.[135]

The tendency to write of nuisance in terms of abuse of rights did not survive into the twentieth century when it became more usual to describe nuisance in terms of an interference with rights incidental to land ownership.[136] This may indicate a shift in view among writers, but it was of course always possible to describe nuisance as an invasion of rights. This is most clear in cases involving water pollution in which the pursuer's natural right to water fit for primary purposes could be vindicated by an interdict preventing further pollution:

> The erection of a mining village may be a fitting and proper use by the respondents of their own property, but in that use they are not entitled to invade the rights of their neighbours by destroying the flow of pure water which has hitherto been enjoyed. They must make their arrangements for disposing of the sewage without invading the rights of the lower heritors, or otherwise discontinue a use of the subjects which involves an invasion of those rights, and which on that account is not a proper or lawful use of their property.[137]

131 *Arrott* v. *Whyte* (1826) 4 Murr 149 per Lord Gillies at 158.

132 Sheriff Courts (Scotland) Act (1838) 1 & 2 Vict. c. 119 s. 15.

133 J. Guthrie-Smith, *The Law of Damages*, 2nd edn (Edinburgh, Clark, 1889) p. 216.

134 E.g. para 973 in 5th edn (1860) and 10th edn (1899).

135 See E. Reid, 'Abuse of Rights in Scots Law', (1998) 2 *Edin LR* 129; E. Reid, 'Strange Gods in the Twenty-First Century: the Doctrine of Aemulatio Vicini' in E. Reid and D. Carey-Miller (eds.), *A Mixed Legal System in Transition* (Edinburgh, EUP, 2005).

136 See W. Mitchell, above, n. 31. vol. x, para. 687; D. M. Walker, *Delict*, 2nd edn (Edinburgh, Green, 1981) p. 956; Whitty, above, n. 11, para. 5: 'The modern approach in Scots law is that nuisance has reference to the invasion of an interest rather than to the thing, condition or activity causing the invasion.'

137 Per Lord Shand, *Caledonian Railway Co* v. *Baird & Co* (1876) 3 R 842.

Actions arising from water pollution were grounded in nuisance from 1791,[138] although it may be noted that some actions to vindicate this right were brought without any reference to nuisance right up into the twentieth century.[139] Although a right, expressed in general terms, to comfortable enjoyment of property is surely implied in the early authorities,[140] it proves difficult to trace early instances in which this is made express. Broun approached the issue in terms of infringements of specific rights by divining, for example, a right to clean air by analogy with the right to clean water.[141]

Nuisance was a doctrine selectively borrowed from the English law of torts to make up for a deficit in the Scots law of property. As noted, the remedies sought were those intended to effect abatement. From the point at which damages came to be sought, it was inevitable that the law of delict would come into play. Whitty provides a rationalisation of the location of nuisance in Scots law which is contingent upon the remedy sought:

> *Primo*, the main role is as a doctrine of property law or neighbourhood protecting interests in the use or enjoyment of land or public places from present or future interference, the main remedies being interdict, declarator and decree *ad factum praestandum* for abatement. *Secundo*, nuisance has also a role as a doctrine in the law of delict or reparation, applicable to situations where (as in the case of interdict) the defender's conduct is intentional in the sense that he knows that the harm is certain, or virtually certain, to result from his conduct.[142]

This may serve as a rationalisation, but nuisance in property and nuisance in delict are not truly separate. Since nuisance is a wrong, it may aptly be located in delict irrespective of the remedy sought. The commission of a wrong in the form of nuisance gives rise to an obligation on the defender's part to repair the wrong, by abating the nuisance or by making reparation.[143] Thus, although early writing located nuisance in property law,

[138] *Miller* v. *Stein* (1791) Mor 12823, *Russell* v. *Haig* (1791) Bell Oct Cas 338.

[139] E.g. *Barrie* v. *Pollock* (1891) 7 Sh Ct Rep 273; *Fleming* v. *Gemmill* 1908 SC 340.

[140] See early definitive statements on nuisance at note 30 above.

[141] Broun, above, n. 33, p. 28.

[142] N. Whitty, 'Nuisance', above, n. 11, para. 17. Cf T. B. Smith, note 39 above. Whitty gives a third, possible, but doctrinally inconsistent role for nuisance in the context of harm unintentionally caused (*Short Commentary* (1962) 534): 'It is given fully in accordance with the Civilian tradition of our law … that interdict should be granted when a man makes unreasonable use of his property. The wrong and the remedy are within the scope of the law of Property. Claims for damages fall, however, within the scope of the law of Delict.'

[143] Per Lord President Inglis, *Stevenson* v. *Pontifex & Wood* (1897) 15 R 125, 129: '[H]e who commits the nuisance is under a constant legal obligation to abate it.'

nuisance, even in its earliest phase, can be described in terms of the law of obligations and since the obligation arises from a wrong it is a delictual obligation.[144] The right to comfortable enjoyment of property has a dual existence as both a right of property and a reparable interest. Indeed, the proper location of reparable wrongs against property in general is inherently ambivalent.

The right to reparation depends upon a wrongful or culpable invasion of a reparable interest. Conversely, the duty to make reparation arises out of wrongdoing.[145] Reparable interests in Scots law include the right to goods and possessions.[146] Thus, so long as *damnum* can be shown, a wrongful invasion of a right in property, for example by culpable destruction of that property, gives rise to a delictual action for reparation. In addition to the general action for damage and interest, Stair listed nominate delicts operative at his time.[147] These may be seen as the working out of the general principle of delictual liability in specific contexts.[148] Of the twelve delicts listed, four (spuilzie; intrusion; ejection; and molestation)[149] were constituted by wrongful invasions of property rights.

Elements of ambivalence similar to those in nuisance are found in other wrongs against property. The close relation of property law and delict can be illustrated by considering property harm caused by water. Flooding of neighbouring property caused by some operation or *opus manufactum* did not, in Scotland, fall to be considered in terms of nuisance before 1966.[150] Prior to this, such cases might be dealt with under property law doctrines such as encroachment or the natural servitude on lower property to receive water flowing from higher ground; or in delictual terms with liability arising from fault.[151]

Two cases of the mid-nineteenth century may be contrasted. In both, property harm to opposite heritors was alleged to follow from operations to protect river banks. In *Lindsay* v. *Thomson*,[152] the Court refused to

[144] Though note that nuisance may arise in breach of the terms of a feu charter or lease in which case the obligation is contractual rather than delictual in character.

[145] Stair, *Institutions*, I, 9, 2 and 5; cf. *Justinian*, Institutes, 3, 13.

[146] Stair, *Institutions* I, 9, 4. [147] Stair, *Institutions*, 1, 9,5.

[148] See Visser and Whitty, 'The Structure of the Law of Delict' in K. Reid and R. Zimmermann (eds.), above, n. 69, vol. 2, ch. 15, 437; M. Hogg, *Obligations*, 2nd edn (Edinburgh, Avizandum, 2006), para. 3.14.

[149] Encroachment.

[150] *Gourock Rope Works* v. *Greenock Corporation*. See text at n. 91.

[151] Henderson, Kerr, Samuel, Weston, Campbell, Moffat etc: see Cameron, 'Scots and English Nuisance', above, n. 28 at p. 107.

[152] (1866) 5 M 29.

order the removal of an embankment built beneath the high water mark for spring tides of a non-navigable estuary without proof of damage to the pursuer and proof that the damage was wrongfully caused. By contrast, in *Morris* v. *Bickett*,[153] the pursuer was entitled to interdict the construction of protective works on the *alveus* of a stream with no requirement to show damage or wrongfulness. While a distinction may be drawn between building on the *alveus* and building on the shore, it is clear that *Morris* was regarded in terms of encroachment and resolved according to property rights, whereas in *Lindsay*, with the requirement to show both loss and fault, the approach taken is clearly delictual even though the remedy sought was not reparation, but removal.

The ambivalence that is found generally in property-related delicts is, perhaps, more acute in nuisance than in, say, encroachment or trespass. The reason may be that the remedy sought is seldom damages except in nuisance. While claims for damages relative to actions for interdict or other remedies were rare throughout the nineteenth century, in the latter half of the twentieth actions for damages came to outnumber those for other remedies. In trespass, by contrast, there have been relatively few actions for damages since a bare trespass does not give rise to such an action. Damages for trespass tend to have been claimed where the agent of harm has been straying animals[154] and liability determined according to common law rules peculiar to animals.[155] In encroachment the remedy sought is more likely to be for removal of walls or for boundaries to be otherwise restored.

The ambivalent location of nuisance has a practical consequence in the context of prescription. The law is statutory.[156] There is uncertainty regarding which provisions are applicable as regards both prescription of the right to object to nuisance and prescription of the obligation to make reparation. If the obligation to make reparation arises from land then the prescriptive period should be twenty years under s. 7. It has been argued strongly, however, that this obligation does not arise from land, but from fault[157] and so it should prescribe after five years under s. 6. Equally, it is not clear whether s. 7 which applies to obligations, or s. 8 which applies to other rights relating to property, is applicable to prescription of the right to object to nuisance.[158]

153 (1864) 2 M 1082, (1866) 4 M (HL) 44.

154 Or where there has been assault.

155 Liability for damage done by animals is now regulated by the Animals (Scotland) Act 1987 and provided the statutory rules apply to the circumstances liability is strict. The common law is not disabled by the Act.

156 Prescription and Limitation (Scotland) Act 1973.

157 D. Johnston, *Prescription and Limitation* (Edinburgh, Green, 1999), 6.62–6.63.

158 See ibid., 7.14; N. Whitty, above, n. 11, paras. 123–6.

This uncertainty derives from the fact that nuisance was originally conceptualised in terms of property rights rather than obligations.

6.6 Administrative regulation

While the majority of this chapter has been given over to considering the development of Scots nuisance in the common law, the treatment of the subject is incomplete without some consideration of the development of nuisance in statutory regulation of towns, particularly during the course of the nineteenth century. As noted earlier, nuisance made its way into the common law by the process that saw sheriffs and justices of the peace assume jurisdiction and nuisance designated for trial by jury, but its origins lay in municipal regulation.

Nuisance continued to feature as an aspect of municipal regulation and, although the office and common law powers of Deans of Guild were circumscribed, the regulation of nuisances was placed on a statutory footing with powers of enforcement being given in towns to Commissioners of Police whose responsibilities operated in parallel with those of councils. Whereas the concern of the common law was with rights and wrongs, statutory nuisance operated in the broader context of ordering an urban environment that was experiencing a continued rapid rise in population with consequent problems of overcrowding, sanitation and public order. The growth of towns during the nineteenth century gave rise to a need for regulation on a wide variety of points, from mundane matters such as naming streets and numbering houses to vital issues such as the provision of water and drainage. Thus, provisions on dunghills and nuisances generally may be found in the Burgh Police legislation of the nineteenth century alongside ones on street lighting, regulation of building, fair trading and offences such as prostitution or urinating in the street.

Aside from general concerns to order the urban environment, the most significant driving factor behind legislation was public health. This concern was prompted especially by the cholera epidemics that took place from 1831 to 1832, 1848 to 1849 and 1853 to 1854. Although the miasmic theory of contagion prevailed at the time, this view was subject to attack[159] and advances in epidemiology indicated the role played by contamination of food and water in spreading the disease.[160] While cholera was the

[159] Notably by Louis Pasteur.

[160] J. Snow, *On the Mode of Communication of Cholera* (London, John Churchill, 1849 and 1855).

most dramatic and immediate problem of the time, there were epidemics of other diseases (influenza in 1837, typhus in 1847) and generally poor health. Infant mortality in towns was high due to outbreaks of diarrhoea, measles and scarlet fever. Clearly, steps required to be taken so that towns were provided with clean water and sewerage and sanitation in general had to be improved. Effective mechanisms for implementing, enforcing and paying for such measures had to be established, but this took time. For the majority of Scotland's urban population in the biggest cities, severe overcrowding and poor sanitary conditions remained the norm until into the twentieth century, but significant advances were made during the nineteenth. While in the 1860s the death rate for Scotland's four largest cities, Glasgow, Edinburgh, Aberdeen and Dundee, had been fifty-seven per cent higher than for rural areas, the rate began to fall from the mid 1870s and by 1911 the gap between urban and rural death rates was down to seventeen per cent.[161]

Municipal regulation of the largest cities was based on local Acts of Parliament[162] and this situation prevailed throughout the nineteenth century, although they were subject also to Acts of general application such as the Public Health (Scotland) Acts of 1867 and 1897. The first public and general Burgh Police Act was passed in 1833. This Act empowered burghs to establish Commissioners of Police and to raise money to operate the regulatory regime provided for by the Act. There was no obligation on any burgh to adopt the provisions of the Act and it applied only to Royal Burghs and Burghs of Barony and Regality. There were, however, many sizeable towns that had emerged in the period since 1750 that did not have this status. Since 1832 there had been a new class, the Parliamentary Burgh, that had been established in the course of revising the franchise.[163] The Burgh Police (Scotland) Act of 1847 empowered the thirteen Parliamentary Burghs, towns such as Paisley, Greenock, Leith and Kilmarnock, to adopt the provisions of the 1833 Act. The empowerment to

161 G. Morton and R. J. Morris, 'Civil Society, Governance and Nation, 1832–1914' in R. A. Houston and W. J. Knox (eds.), *The History of Scotland*, vol. 2 (London, Allen Lane, 2006) p. 512. On sanitary conditions and overcrowding see also I. G. C. Hutchison, 'Workshop of Empire' in J. Wormald (ed.), *Scotland: A History* (Oxford, OUP, 2005), pp. 225 ff.

162 The use of Local Acts was not restricted to the bigger cities. They were used widely for general purposes of improvement. Schedule III of the Burgh Police (Scotland) Act 1892 lists Local Acts of Parliament in force at the time in twenty-three burghs ranging in size from the relatively large, such as Ayr and Paisley, to the small, such as Broughty Ferry and Rothesay.

163 Representation of the People (Scotland) Act (1832) 2 & 3 Wm IV c. 65.

adopt Burgh Police legislation was extended to all places with a population of 1,200 or greater by the Burgh Police (Scotland) Act 1850 and from this point the term 'burgh' appears to have lost any special significance and is used to refer generally to populous places. The empowerment was further extended to all places with a population of 700 or greater by the Police and Improvement Act of 1862.

These were empowering statutes only. It was not until the consolidating Burgh Police (Scotland) Act of 1892, which repealed the Acts of 1833, 1847, 1850 and 1862, that the statutory regime became mandatory. Even at this stage, the Act was not obligatory on Edinburgh, Glasgow, Aberdeen, Dundee and Greenock which were empowered to adopt the Act in whole or in part. The 1892 Act authorised the establishment of Dean of Guild courts in all burghs with a jurisdiction that was primarily concerned with examining and authorising plans for new buildings, alterations to existing buildings and the repair, demolition or sale of ruinous buildings, but extended generally to protecting the interest of the public.[164]

The relation between the law on 'the abatement of nuisances' and public health had been considered in a report in 1840.[165] Broadly, it was concluded that neither the common law nor the statutory regimes extant at the time were adequate vehicles for the promotion of public health. With no law of public nuisance, common law actions depended upon mobilisation of the law by individuals. Actions in the Jury Court were expensive and subject to delay. Where the source of nuisance was long standing, actions could be defended relatively easily on grounds of prescription or acquiescence and, at the time, the argument that the complainer had come to the nuisance was regarded as a valid defence.[166] Where they were in operation, powers under the burgh police regimes of the time were limited and enforcement posed serious difficulties.

Subsequent to this report, the geographical coverage of burgh police regimes was extended, as noted above, and the successive statutes indicate progressively more comprehensive and detailed public health regimes. While it had not been incumbent on any burgh to adopt the provisions of the 1833 Act, the provisions themselves were empowering rather than mandatory. Under the Act it was lawful, for example, for proprietors, at their own

[164] See J. Campbell-Irons, *The Law and Practice of the Dean of Guild Court* (Edinburgh, Green, 1895), p. 60.

[165] J. Hill-Burton, *On the State of the Law as Regards the Abatement of Nuisances and the Protection of the Public Health in Scotland with Suggestions for Amendment* (1840).

[166] *Duncan* v. *Earl of Moray* 9 June 1809 FC. This rule changed: see *McCallum* v. *Forth Iron Co* (1861) 23 D 729; *Fleming* v. *Hislop* (1886) 13 R (HL) 43.

expense, to install foul water pipes leading from their houses into a common sewer and authority was granted to make a drain where none existed, but there was no requirement to do so.[167] Similarly, Commissioners of Police were granted the authority, but were not required to construct main drains or common sewers;[168] to employ 'scavengers' to clean the streets and remove ordure;[169] and to make provision for the supply of clean water.[170]

By contrast, a more extensive regime was provided for in the Act of 1850. Whereas the 1833 Act had empowered Commissioners to appoint watchmen and police constables,[171] under the later Act the appointment of a Superintendent of Police and constables was mandatory.[172] Burghs which adopted the Act were also empowered to appoint Inspectors of Nuisances and Officers of Health.[173] The provision of sewers and drains by the Commissioners became mandatory.[174] Whereas the 1833 Act contained a very generally expressed right to levy sums for the purposes of the Act,[175] detailed powers to levy rates for specific purposes were provided in 1850.[176] In general, the later Act made provision for a more thorough regime on street cleansing and the removal of rubbish and ordure; the provision and emptying of privies and cesspits; the disposal of corpses; slaughtering of animals; and for the identification and removal of nuisances that endangered health. No new noxious or offensive trades[177] were to be established without the consent of the Commissioners who were required to pass by-laws to prevent or diminish the 'noxious or injurious' effects of such activities. Inspectors of Nuisances and Officers of Health were given powers to inspect premises in which food was sold, with penalties imposed for keeping food unfit for human consumption.[178]

In addition to the Burgh Police Acts, specific legislation of general application was enacted to address the issue of public health. The Nuisances Removal (Scotland) Act was passed in 1856 in order to make

[167] S. 95. [168] S. 96. [169] S. 111. [170] S. 115. [171] S. 74.

[172] S. 85. The duties of the Superintendent of Police included the 'suppression of nuisances': s. 86.

[173] Ss. 218 and 221, respectively. [174] Subject to impossibility: see s. 244.

[175] S. 44. There was also reluctance on the part of Police Commissioners in some places to levy rates on property owners in general to alleviate the problems of the slums. See T. M. Devine, *The Scottish Nation 1700–2000* (London, Allen Lane, 1999), p. 336.

[176] Ss. 63–84.

[177] Namely: blood boiler, bone boiler, tanner, slaughterer of cattle, horses or other animals, soap boiler, tallow melter, tripe boiler or other noxious or offensive business, trade or manufacture (s. 180).

[178] Ss. 81, 82.

more effective provision for enforcement than had been achieved by the Nuisances Removal and Diseases Prevention Acts of 1848 and 1849. The Public Health (Scotland) Act followed in 1867.[179] Until the passage of this Act, very little provision had been made for public health outside towns. Now Parochial Boards were given powers for the removal of nuisances, the prevention of diseases and the provision of sewerage and water supplies. The 1867 Act was repealed by the Public Health (Scotland) Act of 1897 which nevertheless re-enacted many of the provisions of the earlier Act. The 1897 Act established a supervisory body, the Local Government Board for Scotland, with powers of compulsion and incentive. This body was replaced in 1919 by the Scottish Board of Health[180] whose powers and duties were in turn transferred to the Department of Health for Scotland under the Reorganisation of Offices (Scotland) Act of 1928.[181] Although subject to many subsequent refinements, the 1897 Act provided a basic structure for public health that remained in place until towards the end of the twentieth century.

It can be seen that the developing public health regime was tied in with the development of local government more generally. By the end of the nineteenth century, municipal regulation had made substantial advances: 'the quality and efficiency of burghal administration had improved immensely during the nineteenth century, and was by 1900 the recognisable precursor of the modern system of local government'.[182] The powers previously exercised by Commissioners of Police had been vested in Town Councils under the Burgh Police (Scotland) Act of 1892 and Town Council (Scotland) Act of 1900, thus ending the system of parallel responsibility that had operated under earlier burgh police regimes. The development of administration in rural areas had lagged behind the towns, but was reformed by the Local Government (Scotland) Act of 1889 which established County Councils. Further fundamental revisions of local

[179] An earlier Public Health (Scotland) Bill of 1849 had been defeated. Opposition to the Bill was motivated by the view that poor health was attributable, not to sanitation, but to poverty. See G. Morton and R. J. Morris, above, n. 161, 542–3. Another perspective held that the 'urban crisis' was a moral problem: '[I]t was believed that the horror of the slums came about because of the irreligion of the masses and the destructive effect that this had on the character of the poor who were regarded as the victims of their own failings.' Per T. M. Devine, *The Scottish Nation 1700–2000* (London, Allen Lane, 1999), p. 335. See further ibid., p. 344.

[180] Scottish Board of Health Act 1919.

[181] This later became part of the Scottish Home and Health Department under the Reorganisation of Offices (Scotland) Act 1939.

[182] J. McFadden, 'Local Government' in *Stair Memorial Encyclopaedia of the Laws of Scotland* (Edinburgh, Butterworth, 1999) Reissue, para. 29.

government took place during the twentieth century under the Local Government (Scotland) Acts of 1929, 1973 and 1994.

In the latter half of the nineteenth century, a number of statutes were passed to regulate specific activities or operations likely to give rise to pollution. Examples include the Smoke Nuisance (Scotland) Act of 1857; the Alkali Act of 1863; the Locomotives Act of 1861; and the Rivers Pollution Act of 1876. Such legislation meant that taking action to abate pollution was no longer dependent upon mobilisation of the common law by individual citizens. Regulatory regimes varied; in some instances penalties could be imposed for infringement. The nineteenth-century legislation was subject to much subsequent amendment and its effectiveness must be highly doubtful. Smoke pollution in particular was problematic in British cities until the Clean Air Acts of 1956 and 1968 which had been prompted by an especially bad smog in London in December 1952.[183] These Acts, along with the Control of Pollution Act of 1974 and a mass of delegated legislation, established a regulatory framework for a broad range of environmental controls.[184]

Until the final decade of the twentieth century, the approach to environmental regulation was piecemeal inasmuch as separate regimes applied to pollution of water, pollution of the air and waste disposal. Regulatory responsibilities were widely distributed. The Environmental Protection Act of 1990 and the Environment Act of 1995 brought in a new era of integrated pollution control to ensure, as one commentator has put it: 'that pollution is not merely transferred from one medium to another and that the best environmental option can be chosen'.[185] The 1995 Act, moreover, created a single body, the Scottish Environmental Protection Agency,[186] which has taken over many regulatory functions previously exercised by Local Authorities, River Purification Boards and Her Majesty's Industrial Pollution Inspectorate.

The removal of nuisances, or things that might give rise to complaints of nuisance, was a natural subject for legislation that promoted the good ordering of neighbourhood generally and became of increasing significance when the focus of concern shifted to public health. The later Burgh Police Acts and Public Health Acts alike contain many provisions relating to nuisances. It may be observed that a broader concept of nuisance

183 These Acts implemented the recommendations of the Beaver Committee which examined the causes and effects of air pollution, Cmd 9011 (1953) and Cmd 9322 (1954).

184 See further C. T. Reid, *Environmental Law in Scotland* (Edinburgh, Green, 1997), pp. 1 ff.

185 Ibid., p. 4.

186 Ss. 20 ff.

was employed in this context than the common law would appear to support and there are references in the legislation to English forms of nuisance that were not found in Scots law.[187] The term nuisance was not used with reference to an invasion of anybody's rights, but refers to the object of complaint. Thus, nuisances are defined in the Nuisances Removal (Scotland) Act of 1856 to include:

> Any insufficiency of size, defect of structure, want of repairs, or other matter or circumstance rendering any building or part thereof unwholesome or unfit for human habitation; any pool, watercourse, ditch, privy, urinal, cesspool or ashpit so foul as to be injurious to health; any animal so kept as to be injurious to health; any accumulation or deposit within fifty yards of any dwelling house within the limits of any burgh offensive or injurious to health; any work, manufactory, trade or business offensive or injurious to the health of the neighbourhood. [188]

Statutory nuisances continue to be understood in this fashion. Statutory regulation of nuisance is now found in the Environmental Protection Act of 1990.[189] Statutory nuisances are listed as follows:

(a) any premises in such a state as to be prejudicial to health or a nuisance;
(b) smoke emitted from premises so as to be prejudicial to health or a nuisance;
(c) fumes or gases emitted from premises so as to be prejudicial to health etc;
(d) any dust, steam, smell or other effluvia arising on industrial trade or business premises so as to be prejudicial etc;
(e) any accumulation or deposit which is prejudicial etc;
(f) any animal kept in such a place or such a manner as to be prejudicial etc;
(g) noise emitted from premises so as to be prejudicial etc;
(ga) noise that is prejudicial to health or a nuisance and is emitted from or caused by a vehicle, machinery or equipment in a street or in Scotland, road;
(h) any other matter declared by any enactment to be a statutory nuisance.

[187] E.g. Burgh Police (Scotland) Act 1850 s. 96 refers to a pigsty placed so as to be a 'common nuisance' and s. 141 empowers Commissioners to direct any prosecution for 'public nuisance'.

[188] S. 8. [189] As amended by the Environment Act 1995 schedule 17.

Identification and enforcement of statutory nuisance falls to local authorities, who have powers to investigate complaints and issue abatement orders requiring remedial measures to be taken.[190] Breach of an abatement order is a criminal offence.[191] The Environment Act is the successor to earlier Public Health legislation and while some provisions remain more or less identical to those found in the Act of 1867,[192] others reflect the circumstances of the time so the 1990 Act contains no reference to dung heaps. There are, in addition, provisions in the Civic Government (Scotland) Act 1982 that apply where annoyance is caused to others by animals or by playing loud music.[193]

While building in burghs had long been subject to regulation, this did not extend to the planned designation of land for particular purposes or to development control. Planning in the modern sense originated in 1909 with the Housing and Town Planning Act of that year. This and subsequent Acts[194] empowered local authorities to draw up plans for land that was likely to be developed. Many did not and since the regime applied only to land designated by local authorities it did not apply right across Scotland. In terms of planning, this legislation was largely ineffective. The 1919 Act was, however, significant in prompting the provision of municipal housing which proved to be the only truly effective measure in combating the severe overcrowding that had prevailed in the previous century.[195]

Although subject to much statutory amendment, the modern planning regime originates with the Town and Country Planning (Scotland) Act 1947 which repealed much of the prior legislation. This Act implemented a further and significant restriction on absolute rights of land use by effectively appropriating to the state the right to develop land. The production of plans by local authorities was made obligatory. Since 1947 applications for development or change of use have been processed with regard

[190] Local authorities are under a duty to investigate complaints and to issue abatement notices where nuisance is found: s. 80. section 82 enables individuals to make direct applications to the sheriff court.

[191] S. 80(4).

[192] The definition of statutory nuisances under the Act is found in s. 16.

[193] Where animals cause annoyance, for example where a dog barks persistently, this is an offence under s. 49(1). An order may be sought from the District Court requiring abatement under s. 49(2). Where a person causes annoyance by playing a musical instrument or singing or performing or playing a radio or hifi and refuses to desist having been required to do so by a constable in uniform this is an offence under s. 54(1).

[194] Housing and Town Planning (Scotland) 1919; Town Planning (Scotland) Act 1925; Town and Country Planning (Scotland) Act 1932.

[195] 'No single piece of legislation has contributed so much to the shape and development of urban Scotland in the twentieth century.' Per T. M. Devine, *The Scottish Nation 1700–2000* (London, Allen Lane, 1999), p. 347.

to the development plan and any other material considerations. The Act imposed a presumption in favour of development, placing the burden on local authorities to find grounds for objection.

Planning law is a mass of regulation and amendment well beyond the scope of the brief resume space allows here. Significant points in the development of planning subsequent to the 1947 Act are noted briefly. Given the hideous quality of many of the buildings constructed in the 1960s, public concern prompted consolidating and reforming legislation during the 1970s.[196] One result was an increase in the requirements to advertise proposed developments and an augmentation and widening of the consultation process. In the market-led economy of the 1980s, the planning process became slanted in favour of developers, as many orders were passed cutting red tape and facilitating the circumvention of development plans, and enforcement became a weak link in the system.[197] This changed during the 1990s. In 1994 the enforcement powers of local authorities were enhanced and the civil powers of authorities to interdict development were clarified. The Town and Country Planning (Scotland) Act of 1997 strengthened the position of development plans with the presumption that development must accord with the plan unless material considerations indicate otherwise.[198] Environmental Assessment, whereby planning authorities must consider the environmental impact of proposed developments such as oil refineries, chemical works, power stations and waste disposal facilities, was introduced in 1988.[199]

Although Scotland has separate planning legislation from England, the provisions are essentially parallel and the regimes effectively similar. There are a large number of minor deviations, mostly consequential on jurisdictional differences, for example in aspects of procedure. The regimes are the same in nature and fundamentally different from other planning regimes that operate in North America and in continental

[196] E.g. the Town and Country Planning (Scotland) Act 1972; Local Government (Scotland) Act 1973; Town and Country Amenities Act 1974; Town and Country Planning (Scotland) Act 1977.

[197] Planning legislation during the 1980s included the Local Government, Planning and Land Act 1980; Local Government (Miscellaneous Provisions) (Scotland) Act 1981; Town and Country Planning (Minerals) Act 1981; Local Government and Planning (Scotland) Act 1982; Town and Country Planning (Compensation) Act 1985; Town and Country Planning (Amendment) Act 1985; Housing and Planning Act 1986.

[198] S. 25.

[199] Environmental Assessment (Scotland) Regulations 1988 (SI 1988 No. 1221) implementing EC Directive 85/337 later amended by SI 1994 No. 2012. Extension to the scheme was required by EC Directive 97/11.

Europe. One characteristic feature is that land in the United Kingdom is not zoned in the way found in other jurisdictions. Development plans delineate and designate one area for industrial or commercial purposes and another for residential. Such designations are, however, given the status of material considerations in the planning process and developers may rely on other material considerations to argue that permission should be granted for a development or change of use that does not accord with the area's designation in the plan. Because planning is an administrative process, rules of natural justice have been introduced through litigation for judicial review, This means, inter alia, that every case must be determined on its merits.[200]

Planning is an aspect of neighbourhood regulation that has emerged relatively recently. Broadly, it enables local authorities to designate land for particular uses and to deny applications for changes of use that are deemed unsuitable for the particular locality. As a significant means for preventing uses of land that might cause disturbance to neighbours, planning is essentially proactive.

6.7 Conclusions

In the new thinking of the Enlightenment, changing circumstances required a pragmatic development of the law. The mid-eighteenth century saw an increase in urban population[201] coupled with a desire for general social improvement. Greater numbers of people living in close proximity gave rise to a need to regulate their activities to preserve good neighbourhood. The initial response came from within the Royal Burghs in the exercise of pre-existing powers of municipal regulation. A need within the common law was identified for a restriction on absolute powers of land use in circumstances in which there were no inhibitions in the form of servitudes and over and above that already provided by the doctrine of *aemulationem vicini*. Recourse was made to English law to furnish a doctrine that would serve although there was no wholesale translocation of the English tort of nuisance.

[200] The author is grateful to Andrea Ross, senior lecturer at the University of Dundee, for providing a helpful overview of planning legislation. Errors are the sole responsibility of the author.

[201] '[L]ate eighteenth century Scotland appears to have been urbanizing at a faster rate than almost any place in Europe.' R. B. Sher, *Scotland Transformed*, note 5 above, p. 195. The trend continued: 'By the early twentieth century Scotland, after England, had become the most urbanized country in the world.' T. M. Devine, *The Scottish Nation 1700–2000* (London, Allen Lane, 1999), p. 328.

While nuisance was initially conceived in terms that may fairly be described as abuse of rights, the corollary of this was that the commission of nuisance was a wrong against the property rights of the victim. The commission of nuisance gave rise to an obligation to abate the nuisance or to make reparation although this rationalisation of nuisance in terms of obligations does not appear in the earlier analyses of the doctrine. Like other wrongs against property rights, nuisance has a dual existence in the laws of property and delict.

The eventual ruling that liability in damages for nuisance was based on fault appears attributable to a need to resolve a doctrinal anomaly rather than to any other cause. Perhaps the issue would have been resolved earlier had there been a greater volume of litigation, but the primary aim of litigants in Scotland has always been to effect abatement or removal, for which proof of fault has never been required. It is only since nuisance has been viewed as sufficiently broad to found claims arising in respect of property harm more generally that actions for damages have come to form a significant proportion of the whole. Once this happened, it was perceived that nuisance could be used to circumvent the normal rules of fault liability, hence the need to resolve the issue.

While common law nuisance has been invoked by proprietors to provide a solution to unwanted invasions of their right to the comfortable enjoyment of property, its wider significance and utility must be doubtful. Clearly, it was an ineffective device to meet the needs of the nineteenth-century urban environment. The development of municipal regimes and public health legislation effectively placed within the hands of the regulatory bodies the responsibility for the control of matters that might otherwise have given rise to common law actions. In any case, those inhabitants with sufficient income to contemplate civil litigation moved out of the most crowded and industrialised areas with the coming of the trams and railways. The right to comfortable enjoyment of property was effectively useless to the majority of the population with the greatest need for it, the urban poor. The sanitary conditions of those without the wherewithal to move to residential areas were alleviated in time, not so much by either the common or statutory law of nuisance, but by the big municipal projects, the piping into cities of fresh water[202] and the provision of municipal housing.

[202] E.g the water supply to Glasgow from Loch Katrine was opened by Queen Victoria in 1859. Waterworks were instituted in Aberdeen in 1866 and in Dundee in 1869.

It is difficult to escape the view that common law nuisance might have been made more or less redundant by its statutory counterpart.[203] Indeed, in nuisance, the common law may fairly be regarded as a residuary mechanism to be mobilised when statutory authorities do not or will not act to effect abatement. Oddly enough, and by a curious route, common law nuisance has found a new niche. Attributable largely to doctrinal research on the subject by Whitty and to the creativity of Lord President Hope, nuisance now has a specialised position in the law of reparation whereby it can be invoked to provide compensation for property harm arising through forms of fault other than negligence.

[203] Different perspectives on the nature of the legislative reforms of the nineteenth century have been offered. E.g.: 'Intrusion into Scots law was more subtle, but also more substantial. A wave of legislation opened up new areas – in public health, working conditions in factories, the protection of investors – which had not previously been covered, by Scots law or any other. The inexorable process was not so much Anglicisation as an assault by the collective British state, which has continued into the twentieth century.' M. Lynch, *Scotland – A New History* (London, Century, 1999), p. 357.

7

Relations between neighbours in Spanish law 1850–2000

ANICETO MASFERRER*

Aristotle's expression *zoon politikon* neatly captures the essentially social nature of mankind. Ever since the first nomadic camps, which later became the Greek *polis* and the Roman *civitas*, man has lived and developed in the cradle of society,[1] coexisting with each other in close proximity as equals.

If the primary purpose of private law is to provide a principled framework which offers solutions to the conflicts arising out of individuals' relationships, then relationships between neighbours is likely to be one of the most paradigmatic areas of private law. It would certainly be difficult to think of a more human and everyday sphere than that of those who share a neighbourhood, a building or a communal wall.

It comes as no surprise then that neighbourhood relationships have resisted assault over the ages, relying on a long-standing culture which is evident from Roman times until the present day.[2]

This chapter will not try to investigate relationships between neighbours in general, nor to adopt with an extensive chronological point of view in mind, but rather it will aim towards a thematic overview of one

* I am indebted to Salvador San Onofre, a Spanish student who helped me with Spanish materials while I was working at the University of Cambridge (as Herbert Smith Visiting Professor, February–July 2005); a thousand thanks also to Matthew Dyson, PhD Law student at the University of Cambridge, because without his contribution it would have been impossible for me alone to achieve an English version that a reader could not only bear but even enjoy; and I also thank Professor Raquel Evangelio Llorca for her clear and helpful comments on an earlier draft of this article (finished at Harvard Law School, USA, 2 October 2006).

[1] Martin Garrido Melero, 'Reflexiones sobre las relaciones de vecindad en Cataluña', (1992) 611 *Revista Crítica de Derecho Inmobiliario* 1553.

[2] L. Díez-Picazo and Ponce de León, *Fundamentos de Derecho Civil Patrimonial* (Madrid, Civitas, 1983), vol. II, p. 114; according to these authors, relationships between neighbours, 'translated into legal terminology, are always relationships between bad neighbours'.

particular area: nuisance.[3] Without doubt, this area constitutes a very important part of the wider picture of relationships between neighbours. It was central to its development, from the time of Codification (1850) to the present day, although there will also be passing references to its historic development from the period of Roman law to 1850.

Despite the extremely frequent nature of the disputes arising from relationships between neighbours, Spanish legal scholars took a long time to bring significant attention to bear on the matter. It was not until the 1990s that detailed monographs of a reliable standard became available, the reading, digestion and citation of which became a necessity for those wishing to penetrate this field.[4]

Since the Middle Ages, the status of neighbour relations can be said to have developed in three distinct socio-economic phases: (1) *feudal society*, with its rural character driving the law of property; (2) *industrial society*, which gave rise to a working-class zone of new forms of construction of 'honeycomb' houses as well as those which might be called a type of farm, organised by ownership in the form of condominium; and (3) *modern society*, that in which we now live and whose potential to cause harm we do not yet fully understand.

As a result, it is obvious that these types of localities (rural, industrial and modern) have nuisances or emissions that are specific to each context. Indeed, in the twenty-first century rural conflicts between farms have given way to others of greater importance, and the first set, which still occur with some frequency today, have passed into oblivion. Now neighbours often exist in a commonhold relationship, living close

[3] Although the expression 'emission' (in Spanish, *inmisión*), rather than 'nuisance', is more common in Spanish private law, I will use the latter because it is the most common word used in the Anglo-American law tradition. In this regard, 'nuisance' comes from Latin *nocere* and means to hurt or harm, from which also come the nouns annoyance and noise and the adjectives noisome and noxious (J. H. Baker, *An Introduction to English Legal History*, 4th edn (London, Butterworths, 2002), p. 422).

[4] Prior to the 1990s, see, among others, the extensive works of Mariano Alonso Pérez; in the 1990s themselves, it is worth highlighting the detailed treatment of this area by E. Algarra Prats, *La defensa juridico-civil frente a humos olores, ruidos y otras agresiones a la propiedad y a la persona* (Madrid, McGraw-Hill, 1995); see also that of F. J. Díaz Brito, *El limite de tolerancia en las inmisiones y relaciones de vecinda* (Navarra, Cuadernos de Aranzadi Civil, 1999); on the *actio negatoria*, J. E. Fernández, *Acción negatoria, inmisiones y defensa de la propiedad* (Madrid, Marcial Pons, 1994); R. E. Llorca, *La acción negatoria de inmisiones en el ámbito de las relaciones de vecindad* (Granada, Ed. Comares, 2000); and, more recently, see María del Rosario Díaz Romero, *La protección jurídico-civil de la propiedad frente a las inmisiones. Especial referencia a la acción negatoria* (Madrid, Civitas, 2003); A. M. Castillo, *El daño causado por el ruido y otras inmisiones* (Madrid, La Ley-actualidad, 2004).

together in buildings, with gases, noise, fumes and irksome smells from large industrial areas and the like causing discomfort and annoyance.

In a largely rural society with a dispersed population, the level of interference in the legal sphere of a neighbour need only be minimal: it is enough to mark out the physical limits in which each individual can act and prohibit certain other conduct which causes harm to neighbours. In the present day, this situation has changed. Industrialisation, the technological era and new forms of urban geography have changed the paradigm from nuisance being an isolated problem to its being one of the main inconveniences of community living.[5]

A study which, like this one, seeks to draw together a short overview of the evolution of nuisance in the Spanish legal tradition must place this in context. Thus, it must pay attention to the impact of socio-economic transformations and the legal regime of nuisance, thereby throwing light on the crucial moments of change and reform in the history of peninsular law and also enabling a comparison between the Spanish experience and that of other states in Europe. However, one should not forget the pan-national scope of the three phases described above (rural, industrial and modern), since later in this chapter certain parallels in the evolution of nuisance in the different legal traditions of Europe will be explored.

For example, one should not be surprised that the normative and doctrinal sources on which the idea and system of nuisance liability are founded remained the same from the first centuries AD until Codification. Furthermore, with the exception of the Anglo-Saxon world, all the relevant legal traditions on the continent have revolved around the *ius commune*, and the legal science of Europe has developed from the same texts: the *Corpus Iuris Civilis* and the *Corpus Iuris Canonici*.

Nevertheless, the focus of this chapter will be the evolution of nuisance from the age of Codification, i.e. from 1850. The techniques common to all the relevant continental legal systems will be looked at (France, Germany, Italy, Spain, etc.), since they each contribute only a few genuine and individual elements which are comparable with those in other European states. These surprising parallel developments in the evolution and theory of the legal regime governing nuisance in the different legal regimes in Europe since Codification can be explained, in my opinion, by three factors. First, there is the common legal tradition (*ius commune*). Second, one can see the powerful influence of the French Civil Code in other states, in particular, of course, in Spain. Third, and final, there is the

[5] Díaz Brito, above, n. 4, p. 15.

supranational effect of the changes in socio-economic structure which gave rise to a series of generally applicable consequences in relation to the law governing neighbours. Indeed, the methodologies used in this context were, if not identical, then strikingly similar and comparable.

The present study, taking a historical perspective, and indeed charting the evolution of a legal institution, can be divided into three parts. The first collates the broad outline of the principal normative and doctrinal threads which give a picture of the evolution of the regime governing nuisance on the peninsula, from Roman control through to Codification. In the second, the paper follows the evolution of the legal institution. The aim of this part is to reconstruct the legal order from the time of Codification to the present. Finally, in the third, there is a series of considerations which aim not only to summarise the most relevant aspects of the regime as it is in force now, but also to suggest some questions (or at least considerations) which might guide the future development of this area of law.

7.1 The principal theoretical trends in the law of nuisance prior to codification

A look at doctrinal history clearly shows that the term 'nuisance' derives from Roman law.[6] In general, from at least the last days of the Republic,[7] Roman jurists were beginning to articulate specific solutions to neighbourly conflicts. These approaches were then brought together by Justinian, and can be found, in particular, in the Digest.[8]

Spanish legal science, based on these Roman law sources, has given thought to this matter on various occasions, although rarely using the

[6] For a wider view on the Roman regulation of nuisance, please see M. Alonso Pérez, 'La protección jurídica frente a inmisiones molestas y nocivas' (1994) *Actualidad Civil* 392; Díaz Romero, above, n. 4, p. 19, note 2; and for a more exhaustive analysis of Roman influences, see Algarra Prats, above, n. 4, pp. 194–208.

[7] 'For the first time in the closing stages of the Roman Republic, the jurist Alfeno Varo formulated the rule which served as the seed for the modern doctrine of nuisance. He did this simply by passing judgment on a dispute between neighbours: *in suo enim alii hactenus facere licet, quatenus nihil in alienum immitat*' (D. 8, 5, 8, 5: Ulp. XVII ad Edictum). In a more modern version, it might read thus: 'Everyone is allowed to act as he wishes in his own legal sphere, so long as he does not unacceptably infringe on the sphere of another' (Mariano Alonso Pérez, 'La tutela del derecho civil frente a las inmisiones molestas y nocivas', *Estudios jurídicos en homenaje al profesor Aurelio Menéndez*, vol. IV (Madrid, Civitas, 1996), p. 4783, footnote 1.

[8] See, *inter alios*, D. 8, 2, 13; D. 8, 2, 19; D. 8, 5, 8.5; D. 8, 5, 17; D. 39, 3, 1, 3 and 8; D. 39, 3, 3 pr.; D. 43, 8, 2, 6; D. 43, 8, 2, 29.

term 'nuisance',[9] and the main legal sources on the peninsula for the last several hundred years reflect this attention.

Thus, one finds express references to the matter of nuisance in both the *Partidas* of Alfonso X ('Alfonso the Wise') (P. V, 32, 19 and III, 32, 7) as well as in the *Fuero Real* (FR 4, 4, 19). However, it was the *Novísima Recopilación* (1805) which drew together references on this matter and is considered to contain 'properly, the direct and clearest antecedents of Art. 590 of the *Código civil*',[10] to the extent that the earlier sources will not be looked at further.

In particular, the *Novísima Recopilación* contained rules about the construction of buildings and of works which might result in harm. Thus, it was forbidden to build pollutant workshops and craft industries within the conurbation of Madrid and its surrounding populations (NoR 7, 40, 5.3).

In like manner, labourers in such industries had to relocate to the outskirts, taking with them all the trappings of their trade (NoR 3, 19, 8).

Furthermore, no trade or craft operating within the *Corte* (king's residence or royal household) could build a blast furnace, except on the outskirts. This was to reduce the risk of fires, and was enforced by the imposition of a fine (NoR 3, 19, 8). This is one example of the *Novísima Recopilación*'s preventative norms: regulations governing the exercise of certain activities to prevent fires and explosions (e.g. NoR 3, 19, 11) and others foreseeing the movement of specific industries located in Madrid (NoR, 3, 19, 1) .

As we enter the period of Codification, we will briefly look at the evolutionary process and the sources of the two unique provisions of the current Civil Code.

Article 590, which enshrined a rule regulating the placing of structures and their protection, was retained substantially unaltered in the *Anteproyecto* of 1882–9, and indeed remains in today's Code. Article 525 of the 1851 Project was accepted by the drafters of the *Anteproyecto* of 1882–9 and made into Art. 592 with only minor changes to its content.

What differences were there then between Art. 592 of the *Anteproyecto* and the final Art. 590 of the Civil Code? There are two main differences: first, that Art. 590 CC does not refer to 'factories which will, by their activities, be dangerous or noxious' but rather to 'factories which, of themselves or by their outputs, might be dangerous or noxious', thus broadening the

[9] The term 'nuisance' was practically unknown in Spanish legislation (except for the reference in the *Liber iudiciorum* VIII, 2, 1–2), apparently appearing for the first time in Spanish case law in a judgment of 12 December 1980. Nevertheless, in academic writing the term has been used more frequently (Algarra Prats, above n. 4, p. 154, note 11).

[10] Evangelio Llorca, above, n. 4, p. 159.

scope of this reference. Second, the rules and guidelines of the current Code refer to a location, while those of 1882–9 refer to the country as a whole.

According to Algarra Prats,[11] Art. 590 flows from the Digest,[12] as well as the *Partidas*,[13] the Fuero Real[14] and the *Novísima Recopilación*.[15]

In the case of Art. 1908, research has not uncovered any Spanish legal precedent, and instead it appears to be derived from the Digest in some way.[16] As a result, this Article does not tally with any norm of the 1851 Project. Its precedent might be located in part in Art. 18 of the *Anteproyecto* of 1882–9, together with Art. 1903 of the 1851 Project. Article 18 has been divided, over time, into Arts. 1907, 1908 and 1909 of the present Civil Code.[17]

7.2 The legal regime governing nuisance

In contrast to other European states, such as Germany and Italy, in Spain nuisance is not regulated in an autonomous and systematic way.[18] This scarcity of legislation has largely been made up for by doctrinal work by commentators and case law. These have elaborated on and developed a legal order dealing with nuisance, working in diverse theories and schools of thought both from the Spanish legal tradition and from other European states.

The Civil Code governing nuisance could be placed between the French model, whose Code lacks provisions in this area, and the German and the Italian models, whose codes expressly regulate this area. This is because the Spanish Code has only one direct reference to the matter of emissions in Art. 1908 (2) and (4), concerning gases and emanations, respectively. This control operates within the context of extra-contractual, or tort, liability (Arts. 1902 and following of the Civil Code):

> ... Equally, occupiers of property are liable for harm caused:
> 2. By excessive *smoke* which is harmful to people or property...
> 4. By emanations from sewers and contact with infectious material which had been dealt with without adequate precautions for the location
>
> (Art. 1908 CC).[19]

11 Algarra Prats, above, n. 4, pp. 157–9.
12 D. 8, 2, 13; D. 8, 2, 19; D. 8, 5, 17.2; D. 9, 2, 27.10; D. 39, 2, 24.12. 13 P. III, 32, 18–19.
14 FR 4, 4, 19. 15 NoR 3, 19, 9–11; NoR 7, 40, 5. 16 D. 8, 5, 8.5–7.
17 Algarra Prats, above, n. 4, pp. 156–7. 18 See footnotes 75 ff.
19 The term 'smoke' (Spanish *humo*) covers, by analogy with Art. 4.1 CC, other forms of emissions such as smells, noise, vibrations, toxic gases and others (Alonso Pérez, above, n. 6, p. 4786).

The second most important Article concerning nuisance is Art. 590:

> No one may build sewers, aqueducts, ovens, forges, chimneys, stables, stores for corrosive materials, steam-powered machinery or installations which, of themselves or by their outputs, are dangerous or noxious, near to a communal well or a neighbour's well without following the distances prescribed by regulations and local custom and without taking any protective measures necessary for the work, as also laid down by regulations. Where there is no regulation, the builder shall take all precautions which are deemed necessary, according to the established opinion of experts, to avoid harm to descendants or neighbouring buildings.[20]

Article 1908, combined with the effect of Art. 590, can be seen to be clearly distinct owing to its finality and location within the Code's framework. However, building on the earlier draft, it draws together ideas with a purely preventative aim in regard to the production of certain nuisances. Nevertheless, where harm results, it is Art. 1908 which must be applied to compensate for the harm, in spite of the fact that measures were taken in order to avoid the harm.

Even if the legislator had not intended to regulate emissions directly by Art. 1908 CC, it is certain that this is the result, comparable with and complementary to Art. 590 CC, that if the defendant (D) were to fail to fulfil the conditions for building, the necessary consequence will be a finding of liability to indemnify for harms and losses under the Aquilian liability of Art. 1902 CC.

In this regard, the STS 12 December 1980 is particularly important, where it is held that:

> Even if the Civil Code does not contain a general norm prohibiting all harmful or noxious emissions, the findings of this Chamber and legal logic are able to supply an interpretation of tort liability based on Art. 1902 CC and the requirements of acceptable neighbourly living and good behaviour according to Arts 590 and 1908 CC, because the main rule is that 'the property cannot reach further than the respect for your neighbour rights' (STS 17 February 1968) (...) In the light of these specific norms, it is fundamental that the practice of an industry, despite its interest for the

[20] This provision should be compared with Art. 305 of the Ley del Suelo (RD-L.1/1992, 26 June) (in this respect, see María Ángeles Parra Lucán, 'La defensa civil frente a las inmisiones: la acción negatoria de los artículos 590 Cc y 305 LS' (1993) I *Aranzadi Civil* 1963 ff.); for a wider view on this Article, see Juan Roca Juan, 'Comentario al artículo 590 del CC', *Comentarios al Código civil y Compilaciones forales*, ed. M Albaladejo García (Madrid, Edersa, 1978), book VII, vol. 2, p. 209; Miguel Coca Payeras, *Comentario del Código Civil* (Madrid, Secretaria General Técnica, Centro de Publicaciones Ministerio de Justicia, 1993), pp. 1496 ff.

> national economy, has to develop its function while taking due account of someone else's property. Even when, following an authorised opinion, the legal order does permit a specific form of economic activity, for the advancement of a particular social interest or to gain a valuable regime, nevertheless it is not authorised to abolish or damage the rights of individuals, without a sufficiently justified counter-value. On the contrary, the public interest does not deny the obligation to prosecute all specific establishments in order to avoid nuisance (or emissions) and to make use of the means by which technology can eliminate them.

By way of introduction, it is worth pointing out that the Spanish system of regulating nuisance is both incomplete and out of date, relying on principle, definition and support from doctrinal as much as from case law sources. Indeed, it was born incomplete, as the above two Articles in the Civil Code demonstrate. It is out of date because it expresses some precepts which correspond more to a rural society (more accurately, that of the 1500s to 1800s) than to an industrial one (that which developed in Spain from the second half of the nineteenth century and into the twentieth). It was the influence of the Code Napoléon, itself modelled on principles of the nineteenth century, which explains this preoccupation with agrarian life. At the time of the drafting of the Civil Code, Spanish industry had scarcely begun to develop, and as a result the regulations on this matter already needed to be phased out almost as soon as they were enacted and came into force in 1889.

In spite of this and other criticisms one might make against the insufficiencies and anachronisms in the Civil Code provisions regulating nuisance, it is undeniable that academic comment has also highlighted certain aspects which are clearly positive.

One of these is the flexible nature of Art. 590. It has allowed situations which were not expressly contemplated in advance to fit within the legal regime.[21] Such Articles allow one to tease out several of the most fundamental aspects of the legal regime governing nuisance in Spanish law. According to the view of Algarra Prats, such rules

> give sufficient foundation for the enunciation of a test to determine which nuisances are, and which are not, tolerable: in particular on the basis of the excessiveness of gases. Finally, they suggest mechanisms to protect against and prevent nuisance in Art. 590 CC as well as to provide the means to indemnify and compensate, by means of tort liability in Art. 1908. This is in the general setting of Art. 1902 CC, which Spanish case law links equally to the means of preventing ultimately harmful situations.[22]

[21] Algarra Prats, above, n. 4, pp. 161–2. [22] Ibid., p. 161.

Another positive aspect, closely related to the one just described, is the benefit of dedicated work by commentators and case law trying to fill in certain gaps which are certainly not unimportant, such as: (1) the nature of a nuisance, or a list of criteria which could be used to formulate one; and (2) criteria and principles which guide the decision as to whether a given nuisance should have to be tolerated or not. One incontrovertible result has been that commentators as well as cases have been rectifying the legislative insufficiencies, in no small part by resorting to the solutions of foreign legal systems, especially the German, Italian, French and English ones.

While these very necessary contributions from academics and cases in order to flesh out a full and effective legal regime to govern nuisance certainly existed, it is also clear that until the 1990s

> in Spain there were very few pieces of work done in this area, but luckily the quality of those that were done is indisputable, as is their contribution to clearing up certain aspects of the matter. Nor, it might be added, is Spanish case law particularly extensive. One swiftly notices the difference in quantity when one compares it with foreign doctrinal and judicial work, especially in Germany and Italy.[23]

There are, for instance, hardly any decisions or principles enunciated by the Supreme Court in the nineteenth century, as we will see. Why should there be this lack of case law, when it is so plentiful in other jurisdictions like those in France and Italy? Contrary to what one might think, this does not reflect the absence of tensions and conflicts between neighbours, but rather that Spanish courts were paying attention to other manifestations of these conflicts.[24]

7.2.1 Location within the legal taxonomy: proprietary and obligations elements

From the point of view of classification, the location of Arts. 590 and 1908 within the Civil Code is not entirely appropriate. The Spanish Civil Code, then following the French model (a model from which the BGB later departed), chose a clear definition for the law of property (Art. 348) and approached its scope from a vertical perspective (Art. 350) rather than defining its contents (a horizontal approach). It then allocated this issue to the class of legal servitudes. This class contained all the delimitations of the law of property, such as servitudes in the public interest, and

[23] Ibid., p. 54, footnote 146. [24] Ibid., p. 7, footnote 19.

those in the interests of individuals (Arts. 552–93). As a consequence, the boundaries of the law of property relating to neighbours are thought of, inaccurately, as legal servitudes, and the rules on nuisance derived from Art. 590 are located amongst those dedicated to servitudes.

Nevertheless, there is clearly a close connection between the laws of real property, neighbours and nuisance, evident because if one seeks to describe a specific aspect of the law as between neighbours,[25] one's efforts will in turn define the content and exercise of an area of the law of property.

Without question, man does not live, indeed could not live, in isolation: such wildness would result in being unwilling to tolerate any nuisance, and certainly not being able to bear 'excessive' or 'intolerable' nuisance. These terms are precisely the means which are used in the attempt to govern the law on emissions (nuisance). Hence the distinction drawn by certain authors between bother (tolerable nuisance) and nuisance (intolerable), or between a mere nuisance (as equivalent to bother) and harmful nuisance (that is, a nuisance which causes loss to a victim for which he can then bring an action in law to gain reparation or compensation,[26] as we shall see later).

On the one hand, the law of nuisance, as one element of the law between neighbours, has followed in the footsteps of the law of real property, whose theory and content has changed over time. However, it is well known that the law between neighbours, with nuisance as an example, does not only concern those who can show title to the property as owner, but also anyone who can show a right to possess the property.

On the other hand, it should not be forgotten that the Spanish law of nuisance also has one foot in the law of tort, and in this sense follows the trends and threads which have arisen in this area since the promulgation of the Code until today.

As a result, nuisance, as an element of relationships between neighbours, can be placed in the framework of the exercise of rights relating to property and of other more limited rights relating to property (Art. 590). At the same time, it seems to end up expanding at its edges into the area of tort law (owing to Art. 1908 CC). In this way, there is a need to focus on two broad strands: the real (law of property) and obligations (tort law).

[25] That nuisance is a specific aspect of relationships between neighbours has been declared expressly for the case law: STS 12 December 1980 (JC, 1980, no. 390, pp. 560 ff.); in this respect, see also Algarra Prats, above, n. 4, pp. 54 ff.

[26] Macías Castillo, *El daño causado por el ruido y otras inmisiones*, pp. 243 ff.

Nonetheless, in practice, it is the obligations thread which developed first and exercised a strong *vis attractiva* on the law of nuisance.[27]

7.2.2 The idea of nuisance: harmful and non-harmful nuisance. The criteria for establishing liability. From fault liability to strict liability

Nuisance amounts to a particular aspect of relationships between neighbours: if we leave behind its definition and evolution (which is roughly parallel to those of the law of property), we can quickly see the key aspects of the notion of a nuisance as set out in doctrinal works, based on legislation, jurisprudence and comparative sources.

The relevant legislative rules currently in force contain no definition of the term 'nuisance'. Equally, nor do the nineteenth-century rules of the Civil Code nor Catalan law from the end of the previous century. In part, this difficulty goes hand in hand with defining a situation such as nuisance that is so subject to change and evolution, and where specific examples vary with time and location.[28] It will not be surprising to learn then that the same situation exists in other European states.

Thus, it is doctrinal works which have tried to offer a definition and whose exploration of the area has been fuelled by casuistic legal reasoning. As a rough and ready definition, a nuisance may be defined as *any interference with the legal sphere of another which causes harm, resulting from the exercise of a proprietary right which was carried out on the owner's land, but which affected the other, or as a spreading of noxious substances which endanger health.* What form do such interferences usually take? Examples from litigation have concerned gases, smells and noxious substances derived from industrial activities, the making of highly irritating noise, moisture in communal walls, edifices which block the light or air from neighbours, emanations, vibrations and the like.

In spite of all this, the largest difficulty in this area is not the lack of a definition, but a means to determine which nuisances are unacceptable and which innocuous. There can only be an action against the nuisance that had caused damage or harm, because the law is not interested in those actions which allege harmless actions (there would not be any legal interest to proceed). As the STS 26 March 1987 pointed out: 'harmless uses of

[27] Algarra Prats, above, n. 4, p. 162; Evangelio Llorca, above, n. 4, pp. 4–5; Macías Castillo, above, n. 26, pp. 235 ff.

[28] Diaz Brito, above, n. 4, p. 21; Evangelio Llorca, above, n. 4, pp. 2 ff.

land between neighbours, advantageous for one and not disadvantageous for the other, are permissible by law'.

This difficulty has, for the most part, been the principal battleground of scholars in Spain and in Europe.[29] This battle has been fought at a supranational level, though indeed the main offerings and contributions have ended up enjoying a prestige far from the Spanish legal system. It is precisely the European scope of these theories that draws us to them. We now turn to examine which of them has become dominant in Spanish law.

Throughout the history of nuisance, there have been various theories which have tried to establish criteria for setting the line that divides tolerable, and therefore legal, nuisances from intolerable and illegal ones. One might put this a different way and seek to establish which situations allow the aggrieved party to bring an action for compensation. The following is a list of these theories.

7.2.2.1 Acts of *aemulatio*

Based on Roman provisions, and leaving to one side the Roman theory of the *inmissio in alienum*, medieval legal thought espoused the theory of *aemulatio*, whose antecedents can be attributed to Cino dei Sinibuldi and was then later adopted by the great glossators, Bartolus and Baldus. This theory describes as an unlawful nuisance, and therefore one which triggers compensation to the victim, all those activities which do not yield some benefit or advantage to the doer, and so which are carried out with the sole intention of causing harm to a neighbour.

Over time, the need for *animus aemulandi* gave way to 'an extraordinary use' requirement, where such an act was considered unacceptable if it caused harm to a third party but reaped no benefit for the doer. The largest problem with this theory was the need to prove the subjective element of the intention to harm (*animus nocendi/aemulandi*), a handicap which was borne by the person who had suffered the loss. In the modern period, this element was amended and a reverse burden of proof brought in: the occupier who causes loss to a neighbour must show that by doing so he benefited in some way; should he be unable to do so, the intention to cause harm will be presumed.[30]

[29] For Spain, see Evangelio Llorca, 'El límite entre las inmisiones permitidas y las prohibidas: Criterios históricos de fijación', pp. 855–921; more recently, see also Macías Castillo, above, n. 26, pp. 78–92.

[30] Díaz Romero, above, n. 4, p. 21; Macías Castillo, above, n. 26, pp. 71–2.

It cannot be doubted that this approach has had influence on the Spanish legal tradition,[31] much as it has in other European jurisdictions.[32] It is a different matter to be able to say that it still has that influence today.

Although the Spanish legal order does not have any discrete provision which explicitly penalises acts of *aemulatio*,[33] the majority of commentators maintain that they are unlawful.[34] In so doing, they invoke case law whose flavour is 'more anecdotal than reliable, and almost always in the form of legal grandiloquence'.[35]

7.2.2.2 Abuse of rights

As the theory described above was in disarray, French jurisprudence in the middle of the nineteenth century came up with a new approach. This theory held that harm of sufficient severity would only be compensated if they exceeded the limits of nuisances which are normal in that locality. This method approached a state of complete irrelevance of the culpability of the wrongdoer, and instead moved towards a quasi-objective liability.[36]

Given the legislative silence in relation to abuse of rights, it was down to doctrinal works and case law[37] to develop this theory, a theory whose influence quickly spread to territories outside France.[38]

In Spain, just as in France, it was left to case law to introduce the notion of abuse of rights into the realm of neighbour relations and nuisance, this time through a later interpretation of doctrine by Calvo Sotelo.[39] Based on this interpretation, the STS 14 February 1944 established abuse of rights in the Spanish legal order:

> Subjective rights beyond their legal limits, frequently defectively limited, have other defects in the moral, teleological and social orders. And the individual who acts under an external legal order and under the appearance of acting as a consequence of his own right, exceeds the limits

[31] At least see P. II, 32, 13 and P. III, 32, 19. [32] § 226 BGB; Art. 833 CC Italy.

[33] Art. 3.1 Catalan Act 13/1990, 9 July 1990, on *actio negatoria*, nuisance, servitudes, and neighbourhood relations.

[34] Evangelio Llorca, above, n. 29, p. 868, footnote 38, where we find many authors who take the same view.

[35] Macías Castillo, above, n. 26, p. 73.

[36] Alonso Pérez, Mariano: 'Las relaciones de vecindad', *Anuario de Derecho Civil*, Tomo XXXVI, Fascículo I, 1983, pp. 56 ff.; Evangelio Llorca, above, n. 29, pp. 870 ff.; Macías Castillo, above, n. 26, pp. 78 ff.; in this regard, the French judgment of the Colmar Court 2 May 1855 became extremely relevant.

[37] Judgment of the Colmar Court 2 May 1855 and others.

[38] §§ 226 and 228 of the BGB; Art. 2 Swiss CC (1907).

[39] J. Calvo Sotelo, *La doctrina del abuso del derecho* (Madrid, Librería General de Victoriano Suárez, 1917).

> imposed by justice, and *bona fide* falls into liability with the subsequent damage to others and to society.[40]

On the basis of precedents, until then only in doctrine and case law, the *Título Preliminar* was amended with a new Art. 7.2 by means of the Decree of 31 May 1974:

> The law does not protect the abuse of rights or the antisocial use of them. All action or omission that, by the intention of its author, by its object or by the circumstances in which it is done, would exceed the normal limits of a right, with nuisance to another individual, will give rise to compensation or to the necessary administrative or judicial measures to prevent the abuse from continuing.

Without wishing to go into great detail, it is worth noting that Spanish commentators are not unanimous about the applicability of this doctrine to the law of nuisance. One school believes that, in default of a specific provision governing nuisance in the Spanish regime, the doctrine of abuse of rights should be applied as a regulatory principle in lieu. Others, on the other hand, understand that it is, like the theory of *aemulatio*, an incomplete answer to all the problems that nuisance throws up. For example, there might arise the situation where one causes harm without the intention of doing so and with some benefit in mind (thus satisfying the subjective criteria), and equally one might produce what should be an actionably noxious nuisance in the exercise of rights which conform to the key criteria here (the objective criteria).[41]

7.2.2.3 'Ordinary obligations' or 'extreme inconvenience'

According to this theory, which also grew out of mid-nineteenth-century French thinking,[42] an occupier cannot be made liable for any inconveniences he causes to his neighbour, since the production of certain irritations is an inevitable part of communal life. Liability can only be imposed for those nuisances which exceed the *mesure des obligations ordinaires du voisinage*.[43]

40 Thanks to this decision, the reinvigorated concept of abuse of rights began to play an important role as an efficient limitation against harmful emissions; see in this respect, for example, STS 24 February 1959 and STS 22 September 1959.

41 Evangelio Llorca, above, n. 29, pp. 886–7.

42 It appeared for the first time in the report of the French Court of Appeal 27 November 1844.

43 Evangelio Llorca, above, n. 29, pp. 888 ff.; J. B. Blaise, 'Responsabilité et obligations coutumières dans les rapports de voisinage', *Revue Trimestrielle de Droit Civil*, 1965, pp. 261 ff.

7.2.2.4 'Normal use': *inmissio* and *Eingriff*

Moved by the insufficient theories of *aemulatio* and abuse of rights, German pandectists came up with a new doctrine for guidance of *inmittere in alienum*, derived from the formula of *Eingriff*, and especially for use in industrial contexts. This approach, supported by Ihering, not only prohibited direct interference, but also any other which, flowing from the actions of the occupier of property carrying out the interference affecting the neighbour, is also a result of excessive use and abnormal activity. This approach necessarily requires that one tolerate inconveniences which flow from normal use and indeed one might have to put up with extraordinary uses, such as those produced by industrial activity.[44]

Two variants of this doctrine have developed, both seeking to differentiate between permissible irritations and prohibited ones according to whether they are of a normal character or not.

7.2.2.4.1 *Inmissio* approach This doctrine, suggested by Spangenberg,[45] holds that the occupier of property may use it as he sees fit so long as he does not cause any harm or nuisance to a neighbour. However, the definition of harm within this approach, or rather the definition of the term used, which was *inmissio*, is limited to tangible substances and materials. Therefore, this doctrine places emphasis on the damage: that it was generated while the occupier was engaged in an extraordinary use of the premises, and of a form which must be borne, i.e. as part of the ordinary and usual use of the property.[46]

7.2.2.4.2 *Eingriff* approach (Ihering) Ihering substituted the idea of *inmissio* for one which covered other kinds of irritations: *Eingriff* (or *influjo*, influx).

Following the classic distinction between direct and indirect nuisances, Ihering wished to prohibit all direct interventions, that is, all those inconveniences which were initiated in the neighbouring property. As to indirect nuisances (those which began in the neighbouring property and then spread to others nearby), a distinction should be drawn between harm to objects (nuisances which damage goods), which should come under the general test of standard and regular use, and harm to subjects

[44] Alonso Pérez, above, n. 4, p. 63; Evangelio Llorca, above, n. 29, pp. 903 ff.

[45] E. Spangenberg, 'Einige Bemerkungen über das Nachbarrecht', *Archiv für die Civilistische Praxis* (1826) 9.

[46] Evangelio Llorca, above, n. 29, pp. 904–5; Macías Castillo, above, n. 26, pp. 82–3.

(nuisances which are harmful to persons), which should conform to the rules applicable to the sensitivity of persons in general.

As a consequence, one must only prohibit indirect encroachments 'when, coming from abnormal use of the property, they are harmful towards property or injurious or noxious to health in a way beyond that which is ordinarily to be tolerated'.[47]

The influence of Ihering's approach was not slow to be recognised, first in his native Germany,[48] and a little later in Italy.[49] In Spain, Ihering's thesis was put into effect in the Catalan Act of 13/1990, Art. 3 of which draws up the criteria for actionable losses and the normal use of property as well as local customs.[50]

7.2.2.4.3 Social necessity (Bonfante) Bonfante developed a theory whereby indirect nuisances, as well as direct ones, should be prohibited where they arise out of an extraordinary use of the land which also exceeded that necessary for the normal enjoyment of life.[51]

This theory holds that 'every interference in the legal sphere of another, by means of or as a consequence of acts in one man's property but which spread to that of another, gives rise to a right to bring an *actio negatoria* to stop the disturbance. It is worth adding here that there would be no need to prove fault in an action brought to gain compensation for the harm caused.'[52]

Bonfante was building up a theory on the basis of the general good of the community as the limiting factor in the law; it is a social factor and a means to balance the presence of nuisances which affect others.

7.2.2.4.4 Judicial discretion According to the work of some French and Italian authors (Gabba and Brugi, amongst others), the best solution would be to leave each occurrence of a dispute concerning nuisance to the discretion of the judge.

While this theory has been criticised,[53] it does produce positive results in the context of a legal system with uncharacteristically little legislative

47 Evangelio Llorca, 'El límite entre las inmisiones ...', p. 905; see also Macías Castillo, above, n. 26, pp. 82–91.

48 § 906 German BGB.

49 Art. 844 CC Italy (1942).

50 Díaz Romero, *La protección jurídico-civil de la propiedad frente a las inmisiones*, p. 28.

51 González-Alegre Bernado, 'La teoría del abuso del derecho como principio informador en las relaciones de vecindad', p. 50.

52 P. Bonfante, *Las relaciones de vecindad* (trans. A. García Valdecasas) (Madrid, Reus, 1932), p. 53.

53 This thesis has been criticised by some authors who, like Bonfante, thought that this violated the classic diversification of the three powers because judges cannot legislate

guidance in this area. It gives judges the task of setting out the limits of legal spheres in each individual case, and in so doing some guidance will be accumulated, for example concerning the time and place of the nuisance.

Part of Spanish legal scholarship holds that the difficulty of this matter is not to determine a fair solution for each moment, but to find a general formula valid for all cases. If there is truly a lack of a universal rule to determine the limit acceptable for every case of emission, it is logical that the work of judges will have a special relevance. In any given case, they are the ones who, by interpreting the law, following the different theories and doctrines which have emerged over the years and using earlier jurisprudence,[54] have to determine if a given emission is *plus quam tolerabile*.[55]

As a conclusion, it should be noted that the Spanish courts have been using almost all these different criteria from 1850 until the present day, as is demonstrated by case law. Furthermore, even the Spanish Supreme Court recognises the diversity of criteria used by courts, as well as the importance of the comparative law in this matter. In this regard, the STS 12 December 1980 is particularly important, where it is held that:

> The problem of the emissions of smoke, gas or toxic exhalation, and the indemnity for the caused damages by the '*inmissio in alienum*', a concrete aspect of relationships between neighbours, derives from comparative law (Art. 844 Italian CC 1942 and Art. 1346 Portuguese CC 1966, for example), making use of the principles of customary law in the use and the tolerance of the troubles, paying attention to the conditions of the place and the nature of the property, standards which also respond to the Law 367.1, *Compilation of the Private Law of Navarre*.

Another question connected to liability is how to ascertain who is liable. Theoretically, strict liability is the principle in property law (Art. 590 CC), while fault liability is the principle in tort law (Art. 1902 ff. CC). Then, taking into account that in Spain cases have to exemplify the protection against nuisance as revolving around tort liability, one could conclude that fault liability played the main role as a juridical principle to be applied. Certainly, it is not necessary to go into great detail to show fault

(González-Alegre Bernado, 'La teoría del abuso del derecho como principio informador en las relaciones de vecindad', p. 54).

[54] Ibid., p. 45.

[55] On the concept and source of the test of reasonable tolerability, see N. R. Whitty, 'Nuisance', *The Laws of Scotland: Stair Memorial Encyclopaedia*. Reissue (Edinburgh, Butterworths, 2001), para. 37; id.: 'The Source of the *Plus Quam Tolerabile* Concept in Nuisance' (2003) 7 *The Edinburgh Law Review*, pp. 218–21.

liability's prominence in this field from the nineteenth century, founded on legal principle whose application was based on some historical laws such as the *Siete Partidas*.[56]

In tort law (Art. 1902 CC), fault liability was the predominant criterion of responsibility, with the exception of Art. 1908 CC which clearly established the strict liability principle. However, early tort law's general rule has branched out over time, and from 1986 on has moved beyond its originally subjective base (with the consequent need for culpability) to an objective foundation.[57] However, it cannot be said that in general there has been a radical shift from fault liability to strict liability, as the case law development (from 1850 until the present day) shows quite clearly.

This point requires further clarification. As regards tort law,[58] there is a contrast between fault liability and strict liability. But it would be impossible to give a definitive answer to one question, namely whether liability produced by nuisance has a subjective or objective cause on the basis of Spanish jurisprudence, because Spanish courts are far from giving a clear and uniform answer to this question, not only in this issue but also in many other kinds of tort law.

Therefore, the situation today is as follows. The basic regulation of tort law in Spanish legislation is Art. 1902 of the Civil Code that without doubt proclaims a fault liability that is based on the guilt of the agent. Together with this, there are some specific Articles, such as Art. 1908 CC, that are exceptions to this general rule of fault liability establishing an objective liability which is based on the existence of a damage, whether the agent is guilty or not. For this reason, by applying Art. 1908 CC, specially aimed at emissions, we would finally conclude that the liability from emissions is objective or strict. The problem is that in many cases the emissions are solved, not by applying Art. 1908 but by wrongly applying Art. 1902.

[56] See, in this respect, the STS Supreme Court 9 April 1866 (JC, vol. 13, 1866, nr. 142, pp. 434 ff.), where different laws of *Partidas* were quoted (P. 7, 33, 11; P. 5, 2, 2–3; P. 5, 3, 4; P. 5, 5, 27; P. 5, 8, 22) to establish the fault liability principle; or STS 17 September 1866 (JC, vol. 14, 1866, nr. 317, pp. 309 ff.). After the promulgation of the Civil Code (1889), the courts kept on applying the same principle, as the case law shows clearly (see, for instance, STS 23 June 1913, JC, vol. 127, 1914, nr. 136, pp. 862 ff.).

[57] In this regard, the STS 22 December 1986 caused an important change of interpretation and established the strict liability principle.

[58] The contrast between fault liability and strict liability fits within the context of tort law, not within the ambit of the *actio negatoria*. As far as I know, there is not and has never been a discussion about whether fault liability is necessary or not for exercising the *actio negatoria* with a basis in Art. 590 Spanish Civil Code.

This would lead, consequently, to a subjective liability. But Spanish jurisprudence has shown an evolution towards an objective interpretation of Art. 1902 without asserting, however, that this rule can support a fully strict liability, and without abandoning totally the criterion of fault liability.[59]

We can conclude that the courts are moving in a blurred zone between strict and fault liability, without knowing if many judgments defend one or the other or if the basis of the judgment is fault or risk. This also happens with nuisance: there are judgments convicting on a basis of fault (fault liability) and others on a basis of the theory of liability by risk (strict liability); by this means, he who does an activity which is able to produce some risk and obtains an economic benefit from it (typically, polluting industries) has to respond to the damage produced by the activity, even if there is no fault at all. There are also judgments that even when they assert that they are based on fault liability, require such extreme diligence that in fact they apply an almost strict liability, as happens in all those judgments that convict corporations even if they have the requested licence and fulfil all the security measures enforced by the administration, on the basis that 'if the damage has been produced, the diligence was not full'.[60]

Therefore, there has not been a radical change from fault to strict liability, but a tendency towards an objective concept of liability without totally leaving aside the fault liability. This is, moreover, a very confusing evolution, because there is no homogeneous jurisprudence asserting the fault or strict liability for nuisance; instead there are judgments in both senses, some of them very ambiguous.

[59] It is usual, in fact, to find in the jurisprudence assertions like this: '....the principle of fault liability is basic in our legal system which is regulated in Art. 1902 of the C.C. Its application requires generally, as a necessary rule, a guilty reprobation to the person who is possibly responsible for the disturbing result, and if it is, however, true that the Supreme Court jurisprudence has evolved by making the liability more objective or strict, it is also true that this change has been moderate, proposing a shift to probing of the facts and hardening the requested diligence, according to the circumstances of each case. This way there has to be extreme care to avoid any damage, but without establishing the risk as the only basis for compensating and without excluding in any case and absolutely the classic principle of fault liability ...' Cf. STS 22 December 1986, above, note 57.

[60] For this reason, we can say that a person is not liable where he usually exploits a zone or business whose purpose is lawful. Where he is held liable, he is required to indemnify and cease the activity, or in some cases only to indemnify, allowing him to continue with the emissive activity depending on the circumstances. In judgments prior to the year 2000, the most usual outcome was to condemn a tortfeasor to pay damages and to take the necessary measures for ceasing the emission, without enforcing the cessation of the activity. Occasions where the closing of the activity is enforced are very rare, but this cannot be totally excluded when it is the only way of stopping the emission.

Actually, the Spanish courts do not refuse to admit at least some consideration of the fault liability principle, because the subjective base continues to play a role in the law of nuisance. For example, in 2003, the Supreme Court stated expressly that the predominance of strict liability does not exclude responsibility based on fault in some cases, for example, when damages were caused, in part, by the proper victim's negligence (or by the negligence of the person who suffered that prejudice). Although the Court recognised in that case the prominence of strict liability, it also declared that 'this principle cannot become the only foundation to claim for compensation, by excluding the classical principle of fault liability'.[61]

What are the causes of the introduction of risk as the basis for compensating (strict liability), without excluding in any case the classic principle of fault liability?

Answering this question is complicated because the extended period of time during which judges brought about all this shift in emphasis makes it difficult to identify the exact causes of it. First, let it be remembered that we are dealing with a tendency towards an objective liability without totally leaving aside the fault liability, i.e. not with an absolute shift from fault to strict liability.

Second, the general development of the principle behind liability took place in a European context, and touched not only private law but also different elements of public law. It seems to me that in this context the process of industrialisation became an important factor that made opportune the gradual introduction of strict liability.

On the role which industrialisation played in the emissions, it should be said that the influence of industrialisation on the regulation of emissions focuses on two basic issues: (a) an increase in the frequency, number and intensity of emissions; and (b) a tendency, produced by this increase, towards objective liability in this area.

Before industrialisation, the key idea of civil liability in Art. 1902 CC was the fact of man as reprehensible and negligent. The aim of civil liability, influenced by medieval canon scholarship and the prevalence of the free will dogma, was not so much to protect the victim from damage and his right to satisfaction, as much as to obtain a moral improvement of individuals' behaviour. But, after the outbreak of the industrial revolution, inventions gave rise to multiple devices and machines (planes, oil-carrying ships, chemical industries, bottled and canned products,

[61] See STS 415/2003 29 April 2003 (*Aranzadi* 2003, vol. III, t. 69, Judgment nr. 4535, pp. 8685–7).

etc.). This led to an increase in risks and damages, in many cases caused through no fault of the agent, but merely by the malfunctioning of the devices. Then a problem arose, namely that by applying the traditional criterion of fault liability, many victims did not obtain their right to a fair compensation. Therefore, from that moment, the main concern was to find a liability system that guaranteed compensation for the damage to all victims, leaving aside the original aim of punishing the reprehensible behaviour. Thus emerged the theory of risk or strict liability.

It was then that the new wrongdoer, industry in various forms with its new capacity for damage, led to a focus on risk and what that risk concerned (the object here), rather than the negligence or fault of the subject. In this regard, the famous STS 12 December 1980, which clearly introduced the strict liability principle, showed the connection between this foundation and industry as 'new wrongdoer'.

Although industry and its new capacity for damage contributed to the shift from fault liability to strict liability, the former principle still plays a role in the Spanish tort law for reasons of *equity*; in other words, to decide some cases applying only the strict liability principle and excluding fault liability would be simply unfair and therefore illegal, as the Supreme Court declared in 2003.[62]

What then were the consequences of industrialisation on the law of nuisance? On the one hand, emissions are no longer limited, in the sense that they are no longer confined to the physical limits of property. On the other hand, the liability principle, this evolves towards an objective system which will coexist with the traditional one based on fault without replacing it.

7.2.3 The legal mechanisms regulating nuisance

It would be of little use to be able to find a 'nuisance' if there were no mechanisms in law to require the cessation of the nuisance and/or compensation for the harm done. It is in the form of personal actions (*actio negatoria*) and duty-based actions (*Aquilian* liability), as well as in abuse of rights, that one finds the legal means to regulate this in private law.

If, as has been said, nuisances are more closely within the realm of tort liability than the law of property,[63] then the regulation of such wrongs will be closely connected to general tort liability. Indeed, owing to the absence of a systematic and exhaustive treatment of nuisance in the CC, it is in

[62] See footnote 61, as well as the principal text. [63] See footnote 27.

this wider area that the mechanisms to protect the rights of the occupier from emanations of neighbours must be found. This is true in practice; the vast majority of legal actions concerning nuisance have been founded on Arts. 1902ff. CC, the tort section of the Code, within which sits the above-mentioned Art. 1908.

The mechanisms of protection coming from these Articles of tort liability are of two types: (1) inhibition, commanding that the harm be avoided before it happens; and (2) compensation, which is an action to recover the value of the harm done. However, in practice, 'the distinction between the two forms of protection does not appear to be easily maintained'.[64]

There is not the space to go into detail on the differences and distinction between the two,[65] but it is submitted that one can avoid confusing the *actio negatoria* with the inhibition, and that there is then a clear place for inhibitionary protection at the margins of tort liability. This is especially the case when one considers the wide leeway possible in the Spanish legal order.

Such preventative protection can act in two fundamentally different ways: (a) owing to the extension of the compensatory award as a means to prevent permanent nuisance; and (b) the *actio negatoria*, which is the clearest example of preventative protection in a purely neighbourly context.

The *actio negatoria*,[66] though recently of particular prominence in the law of nuisance, operates largely outside the ambit of tort liability. This has reached the stage where it is the principal application of Art. 590 CC,[67] whose preventative and inhibitory nature as regards both property and persons is beyond doubt.[68]

In spite of its character and original aim, the *actio negatoria* has branched out over time, and has now been clearly expanded in a new direction: it is now no longer used only to protect an interest in real property, but also for the cessation of a nuisance on property belonging to another.[69]

[64] Macías Castillo, above, n. 26, pp. 304 ff.

[65] On this matter, see Macías Castillo, above, n. 26, pp. 308–9; for a wider view on the *tutela inhibitoria*, see pp. 304–14.

[66] For a bibliography on the *actio negatoria*, see above, n. 4, and particularly the work of Egea Fernández, above, n. 4; see also L. Martín-Ballestero Hernández, *La acción negatoria* (Tecnos, Madrid, 1993); Parra Lucán, 'La defensa civil frente a las inmisiones: la acción negatoria de los artículos 590 Cc y 305 LS', pp. 1963 ff.

[67] Evangelio Llorca, *La acción negatoria de inmisiones en el ámbito de las relaciones de vecindad*, pp. 130–1; Macías Castillo, above, n. 26, p. 315.

[68] J. M. Lacasa Coarasa, *Las actividades peligrosas en la propiedad urbana* (Huesca, 1961), pp. 80–1.

[69] See, in this respect, the STS 5 April 1960 and the *actio negatoria* of the Catalan Act 13/1990, 9 July 1990.

Another characteristic of the *actio negatoria* is that it is not necessary for harm to have occurred for the action to be applicable. This is a typical difference from the protective sphere of tort law. What is more, in a case where there was harm done, the *actio negatoria* of Art. 590 cannot provide reparation for losses suffered; in this case the plaintiff should bring both the *actio negatoria* (Art. 590) and the *Aquilian action* (Art. 1908) cumulatively.[70] Nevertheless it is a rare thing that a Spanish court will apply solely Art. 590 CC *actio negatoria*; that is to say, the injunctive power under Art. 590 is almost always exercised at the same time as the indemnifying action for losses (Art. 1908 CC).[71]

In contrast with the *actio negatoria* relating to property, the tort action does require proof of damage, and the final award will not only satisfy the claimant's need for compensation, but will also include provisions dealing with any possible future harm, by way of an *inhibitoria actio*. Thus, even though there has been a steady expansion of the application of the *actio negatoria*, the tort action is still used most before the courts.

In fact, jurisprudence usually gives priority to the compensation action as a property action; through this action, not only can the damages and disturbances produced by emission be compensated for, but it also enables preventative measures to avoid potential damages in the future, or the cessation of the risk activity when this could also be done through the specific *actio negatoria* of Art. 590 CC (particularly as it is supposed that this action is not necessary when a nuisance has been produced).[72]

Thus, in response to the criticism that civil courts cannot apply preventative measures, courts have responded that the defence of a property right cannot only be limited to the repair of the caused damage, but has to be extended to the prevention measures necessary to avoid further damages.[73]

Finally, there is one further mechanism to complete the arsenal of anti-nuisance measures: in addition to the *actio negatoria* based on Art. 590 and operating out of the law of property, and the tort action based on Arts. 1902 *et seq*, there are other tools, in this case preventative

[70] Evangelio Llorca, *La acción negatoria de inmisiones en el ámbito de las relaciones de vecindad*, p. 227; Macías Castillo, above, n. 26, p. 317.

[71] See, in this respect, the STS 19 December 1963; Parra Lucán: 'La defensa civil frente a las inmisiones: la acción negatoria de los artículos 590 Cc y 305 LS', pp. 1963 ff.

[72] STS 23 June 1913, STS 22 December 1952 and STS 19 December 1971.

[73] SAT Burgos 6 October 1981; SAP Valencia 29 October 1990; see also Parra Lucán, note 4, pp. 1963 ff.

instruments called *interdictos* (or perhaps *injunctions*). Examples of these would be the interdict against new development or against retention of a thing. However, they are, of themselves, rather limited: (1) they can only be imposed for a term of up to a year; (2) there is a certain burden of proof in regard to possession and disturbance (or annoyance); and (3) they do not permit any indemnification for losses suffered.[74]

7.2.4 Nuisance in foral law: the examples of Catalonia and Navarre

As has already been pointed out, the Spanish legal system lacks a norm or principle which brings together relationships between neighbours as a unified whole. The opposite is clearly true in Germany and Italy, for example.

However, there are some amongst the autonomous regions of Spain whose legal work has paid more attention to this area, and they are Catalonia and Navarre.

7.2.4.1 The Act of 13/1990, of 9 July, concerning the *actio negatoria*, nuisance, servitudes and neighbour relations as passed by the Catalan Parliament

Catalan law is the exception that proves the rule. It is the only jurisdiction in Spain to enjoy an exhaustive system of regulation for nuisance.

This chapter will not set out to describe this system in detail, as this is a task which has already been attempted in the literature.[75] Instead, we will leave to one side the history of this system of regulation,[76] as well as the criticisms that have been made against it,[77] and limit ourselves to a brief and concise enumeration of the most interesting aspects: (a) the

[74] For a wider view on different kinds of interdicts, see R. Evangelio Llorca, 'La protección interdictal contra las inmisiones excesivas' (2000) *Actualidad Civil* 15.

[75] Garrido Melero, 'Reflexiones sobre las relaciones de vecindad en Cataluña'; María Eulàlia Amat Llari, 'La protecció del particulars front a les immissions a l'Ordenament català' (2002) 2 *Revista Jurídica de Catalunya*, 229–48; for a relatively recent synthesis on this topic, see Macías Castillo, above n. 26, pp. 121–32.

[76] Jaume Ribalta i Haro 'Immissions i acció negatoria a Catalunya: una lectura històrica i comparativa d'una modernització legislativa', (2001) 1 *Revista de Dret Històric Català* 125–54 (see the English version in (2003) 11.2 *Zeitschrift für Europäisches Privatrecht*, 295–317); by the same author, *Dret urbanístic medieval de la mediterránea* (Barcelona, Universitat Pompeu Fabra – Institut d'Estudis Catalans, 2005).

[77] Evangelio Llorca, above, n. 4, p. 38; Macías Castillo, above, n. 26, pp. 121–32.

systematic and autonomous organisation;[78] (b) German influences;[79] (c) the prominence and wide scope of the *actio negatoria*; and (d) the setting up of a range of limitations on the exercise of rights in property where there are nearby properties.

7.2.4.2 Act 367.1 of the Modern Code of Navarre (*Fuero Nuevo*)

The foral law of Navarre contains a principle which governs the area of nuisance, even though it does not mention it expressly. In other words, while it does not describe nuisance in detail, it does recognise a principle which can be applied to solve disputes between neighbours.[80] This principle can be found in Art. 367.1 of the Modern Code of Navarre,[81] which is located in the section concerning limits on property rights under a community-based approach:

> Owners and other users of land may not risk harm to the property of neighbours, nor cause nuisance which results from an unreasonable exercise of their rights, which should be determined according to the needs of each estate, the nature of the exercise and equity.

First, it should be noted that this provision's limitations apply not only to the owner of land, but also to other users who enjoy such use under some kind of title. Second, it should be noted that the criteria for determining the extent to which acts must be tolerated is defined according to a case-sensitive test of reasonable use. Third, the nuisance must cause damage in order to trigger this section: it cannot be argued that the Act penalises an innocuous interference.[82]

[78] The first chapter of the law covering *actio negatoria* in Arts. 1 and 2 and nuisance in Art. 3 sets out the general framework within which the other legal institutions are developed.

[79] Compare, for instance, some Articles of the Catalan Act with the German BGB (§ 1004, *actio negatoria*; and § 906, emissions); in this respect, see Algarra Prats, above, n. 4, p. 165.

[80] For an abstract on emissions in Navarran law, see Macías Castillo, above, n. 26, pp. 113–20.

[81] Law which historically comes from the *Fuero de Tudela* (cap. 125) and, probably, from the *Fuero Reducido* 6, 6, 33.

[82] Algarra Prats, above, n. 4, pp. 163–4; according to certain doctrine, this law seems to follow certain theories that have arisen over the years for solving emissions: the theory of reasonable use (Ihering), the social necessity theory (Bonfante) and even the theory of normal tolerance from Roman jurisprudence (Alonso Pérez, 'La tutela del Derecho civil frente a las inmisiones molestas y nocivas', p. 4786); the same arguments were used by the STS 12 December 1980.

7.3 The relationship between private law and public law[83]

In Spain, the relationship between private law and public law in relation to nuisance or emissions is not satisfactory at all, as is often noted by civil law commentators especially. The following section will briefly discuss three issues: what the relationship is; the problems that arise because of it; and also some matters relating to administrative licence and the jurisdiction of private law.

According to Art. 590 CC, in order to evaluate the nuisance of a public or administrative body, regulations should be taken into account. In this sense, even the local custom recorded in the CC could repeat or reinforce the administrative regulations. The current public regulation on this matter was enacted in 1961 (*Regulation for Annoying, Unhealthy, Harmful and Dangerous Activities*), a law that is still nowadays in force for the whole country, although other autonomous communities like Castilla-León or Valencia have passed their own legislation as well.[84]

Theoretically, this administrative law should protect the individual's interest by protecting the general interest on topics relating to ecology or environment. However, in practice, public law does not actually manage to protect private interests, sometimes because it also fails to protect the general interest. And even when public law succeeds in its proper function of protecting the general interest, this public interest is not always in accordance with the private or particular one.

Sometimes, public regulations have to face the same interpretative problems as in the private law. For example, it is not entirely clear when a specific nuisance or emission should be tolerated or not. Even when the tolerability's public criterion is precise and certain, it frequently does

[83] Nowadays nuisance concerns not only private law but also public law, and within this part of the law there are different jurisdictions with their own mechanisms of protecting individuals from nuisance: (1) constitutional law: Arts. 10.1, 33.2 and 45 CE); (2) administrative law: the most important law is the Regulation for Annoying, Unhealthy, Harmful and Dangerous Activities 2414/1961, 30 November, which was developed and reformed in 1963 and 1964, respectively; (3) criminal law: the current criminal code punishes wrongdoers against the environment (Art. 305); and (4) European law, thanks to the activity of the European Court of Human Rights, concerned with the protection of the environment (Art. 235 TCEE).

[84] There are also other essential prescriptions from administrative legislation, such as Art. 305 of the *texto refundido de la Ley del Suelo y Ordenación Urbana*, approved by RDL 1/1992, 26 June, and also Art 19.1 of the Law 6/1998 on land regulation, 13 April, on *Régimen del Suelo y Valoraciones*. They are very important because these Acts establish the permitted uses of designated locations for residential purposes, for industry or as parks, thereby also setting certain use limits for preventing emissions.

not ensure that the 'tolerable' nuisance will not produce any harm to individuals.

Let me enunciate some other problems that show the inaccuracy and inefficiency of public law referring to emissions, even though the protection of the environment properly corresponds to the functions of public law:

a) First, there is the sad fact that although – or precisely because – there are a lot of public regulations on the environment and emissions, most of them are not actually observed and applied.
b) Administrative regulation cannot be exhaustive and should not even attempt to be so because of the permanent technical changes, which requires many lists of different activities that, necessarily, become obsolete or out of use. On the contrary, this enumeration of activities should be *ad exemplum*: not closed. What then happens is that the local administration grants licences to undertake some activities that produce harmful emissions or nuisance, or do not control the development of these activities that, while harmless at the moment of granting the licence, later produce harmful nuisance.
c) The administrative procedure is not only extremely slow, but also inefficient. The administration moves too slowly to resolve these problems and does not always seem to have any interest in finding a solution and applying the law. Its 'broadmindedness' in this field is clearly excessive. Thus, 'administrative silence' plays an important role that leaves the citizens out of the protection.
d) Even worse, the administration is not averse to undertaking some activities which are not in accordance with the law. In these cases, the administration becomes the defendant because of its unlawful action or omission, revealing all too frequently its reproachable attitude in this field. The regulator becomes the wrongdoer.
e) It is important to note that a licence from the administration does not preclude the activities being unlawful in civil law. The licence does not operate as presumption *iuris tantum* of the harmful character of the activities to be carried out, according to both commentators and case law. The private law liability system should not be accepted, even less when it refers to the environment and people's health. The principle applicable is that this administrative permission does not exclude fault liability. Where there is damage, there is a civil action, no matter the acquisition of a licence. Conversely, the absence of a licence does not automatically lead to liability; the nuisance must still produce

actionable damage.[85] This shows the extent of liability for nuisance, even within the administrative realm.

f) Furthermore, the citizen usually prefers to take the civil procedure rather than the administrative one because the former is more effective at compensating any losses. Although the administrative jurisdiction can issue measures to prevent further harm, as well as to compensate any damage caused and to impose pecuniary sanctions, seeking damages is in practical terms more difficult than via the civil law route.

The conclusion is that, although the context is more appropriately that of public law, private law seems to be much more responsive to an individual's interests, especially as regards the ease of gaining compensation. Perhaps the eminent lawyer Federico de Castro was right when he pointed out that 'this century suffers from the weight of administrative law, whose power does not seem to consider the individuals'.

Leaving aside the relationship between private law and public law in relation to nuisance, it should be said that the regulatory system currently in force in Spain was set up in 1961, as a consolidated version of dispersed municipal ordinances. From the viewpoint of the material content, there was nothing new in the 1961 Regulation, in that the intention of the rule makers was merely to give a guidance of classified activities whose development was subject to a specific permit to be granted by local authorities.

Depending on the classified activity in question, regional or local authorities are empowered to put the 1961 Regulation into practice by closures, fines, administrative injunctions and so on. A general criterion should be helpful to draw the line: within existing urban areas, local officials are in charge; outside it is regional government. National public agencies are in the field just in exceptional cases (nuclear radiation control).

Spanish zoning regulations used to provide an exhaustive description of uses related to classified activities. Allowed, compatible, non-conforming, prohibited, etc. zoning ordinances continue to be the feeding machinery of Spanish nuisance law.

7.4 Conclusions and possible approaches for the future

There are many issues worthy of note in the Spanish system for regulating nuisance, and, as a consequence, those that have been referred to in this

[85] See on this matter the famous STS 12 December 1980; STS 16 January 1989 (RJ 1989/101); and, more recently, STS 2 February 2001 (RJ 2001/1003, pp. 1643–7).

chapter have been but a small selection. The final section of this chapter will look at some new approaches which appear to be being discussed, or at least which I think should be discussed, concerning the current state and near future of this area.

The Spanish legislative arrangement, with the exception of the autonomous region of Catalonia, lacks any systematic treatment of the law of nuisance. As has been noted above, the consequence of this lacuna is that Arts. 590 and 1908 of the Civil Code have been built upon as the basic regulating instruments of nuisance.[86] At the same time, it is unclear whether one would wish to recognise in these Articles the existence of a general theory concerning nuisance in Spanish law, especially since the relevant discussions of commentators are far from being in agreement.[87]

This legislative inaction has been effectively balanced out by academic work and case law. They have constantly filled in, developed and brought to fruition an area which, far from remaining static, is in a continual state of evolution in line with social and economic as well as cultural and ideological changes. Nevertheless, there still remains the task of drawing the exact line between a lawful and an unlawful nuisance: while criteria exist, there is no unanimous academic or judicial view.[88]

Cases have tended to show the protection against nuisance as revolving around tort liability (Art. 1908 CC),[89] even though there are other more preventative and injunctive mechanisms expressly for use in neighbour disputes, whose exercise does not require proof of damage (Art. 590 CC).

Finally, we have seen how the tort action (Arts 1902 ff.) has evolved from a subjective base to an objective one, but without totally abandoning the criterion of fault liability. In other words, there has not actually been a radical change from subjective (fault) to objective (strict) liability, but, as has already been outlined, a tendency towards an objective

[86] Art. 7.2 CC, which contains the abuse of rights, constitutes an important normative reference in order to base the regulation on relationships between neighbours and distinguish which emissions are indeed illegal and which are not (in this respect, see Macías Castillo, above, n. 26, pp. 101–12).

[87] Macías Castillo, above, n. 26, pp. 93–101.

[88] Although the courts sometimes use normal use standards (the usual tolerance or exercise of rights), those mentioned 'act as certain circumstances considered by the judge' to be appropriate. Those in Spain lack a sufficient autonomy in approach, according to Macías Castillo, above, n. 26, p. 258; with the lack of a clear parameter to solve this matter, Macías, reviving an ancient discussion, proposes to settle *unlawfulness* 'as the key to determine the existence of neighbours' emissions that produce liability' (pp. 268 ff.).

[89] See, in this respect, footnote 27; Macías Castillo, above, n. 26, p. 236.

liability without totally leaving aside fault liability. As has been noted, this is a confused development, with judicial decisions pointing in both directions.

As a foreseeable result of the constant development of the law of nuisance, it seems to be that there are some issues which deserve a detailed examination and discussion. An analysis of the evolution of nuisance liability in the recent history of Spanish law reveals the following threads and trends which we might briefly look at:

1 If one views nuisance from beyond a merely private law standpoint, it can be seen that it touches on many legal spheres (such as European, constitutional, criminal and administrative law), and that therefore it would be wise to have an interdisciplinary approach within the legal world; otherwise the application of the civil norms would become difficult and incomplete.[90]

2 Nuisance, still part of the law relating to neighbours and, more generally, the law of property, has been viewed from a very different perspective in the last fifteen years: from the viewpoint of human or fundamental rights (*derechos de la personalidad*). Due to this new viewpoint, nuisance's legal protection shows a more intensive concern for personal injuries than for physical or property damage, more concern for moral damage than for material harm.[91]

With moral damages, due to the difficulty of evaluating them and because the plaintiff will wish first of all to stop and/or prevent them, the victim usually prefers preventative legal mechanisms (*actio negatoria*),[92] in particular in matters of health and, indeed, of the environment.[93] In

[90] See footnote 84.

[91] R. Evangelio Llorca, 'El perjuicio derivado de las inmisiones. Especial consideración de los daños a la persona' (2000) *Revista Jurídica del Notariado* 35 (July–September), pp. 53–75.

[92] Concerning the increase in the actions devoted to preventing and inhibiting – rather than compensating – the moral damage, see Macías Castillo, above, n. 26, pp. 363 ff. and 397 ff.; shown by jurisprudence since the end of the last century: STS 16 January 1989 (*RJ* 1989/101); STS 16 July 1991 (*RJ* 1991/5393); STS 18 May 1993 (*RJ* 1993/3651); STS 2 February 2001 (*RJ* 2001/1003); SAP Granada 8 February 1990 (*RGD* 1991, pp. 8447–51); SAP Balears 1 December 1994 (*RRCCS* 1997, pp. 645–7, ref. 97); SAP Cáceres 21 November 1997 (*AC Aud.* 1997:721); SAP Asturias 21 May 1997 (*AC Aud.* 1997:1565); SAP León 16 June 1997 (*AC Aud.* 1998:12); SAP Guadalajara 10 December 1994 (*Ar. Civil* 1994/2171); SAP Cáceres 21 November 1996 (*AC Aud.* 1997:721); SAP Asturias 21 May 1997 (*AC Aud.* 1997:1565); SAP León 16 June 1997 (*Ar Civil* 1998/12); SAP Pontevedra 5 April 1999 (*Ar Civil* 1999/913); SAP Segovia 22 December 1999 (*Ar Civil 1999/2413*); SAP Valencia 17 July 1990 (*RGD* 1990, pp. 8033–4).

[93] Díez-Picazo and Ponce de León, above, n. 2, p. 204; on the relationship between the environment, human rights and compensation for moral damage, see STS 2 February 2001 (RJ 2001/1003, pp. 1643–7).

cases of material harm, on the contrary, the plaintiff prefers first of all to be fully compensated for the losses suffered.

However, in the last fifteen years, even moral damages have been claimed to be compensated, as some cases from the Spanish Supreme Court clearly show.[94]

3 This expansion in the ambit of nuisance liability is not free from consequences.

One of these is the diverse, and often antagonistic, doctrinal and judicial interpretations of the ambit of related jurisdictions. While part of the Spanish legal doctrine shows serious doubts over whether the production of noise should be considered an attack against the private life of those disturbed by it,[95] a decision of the European Court of Human Rights (*Tribunal Europeo de Derechos Humanos*) has held exactly to the contrary,[96] and this was eventually followed, with more hesitation to begin with than at present by the Spanish courts, including the Supreme Court.[97]

Another consequence is the vital importance of being able to determine what nuisance levels breach the law. The question of whether the production of noise should give rise to liability can be seen as merely one particular form of this debate, and one of increasing significance.[98]

A further consequence not without implications for private law is 'the flight of private law and the preference for protection under human rights' in the face of nuisance. Harm caused by noise, for example, might enable an action under civil, criminal or administrative law, but the human rights route to protection can be chosen as well. This is because 'such interference can detrimentally affect the physical health of people and be the cause of significant disturbances in sleeping patterns, mental

[94] On compensation for moral damages, see STS 18 May 1993 (RJ 1993/3651); STS 2 February 2001 (RJ 2001/1003, pp. 1643–7).

[95] J. Egea Fernández, 'Ruido ambiental, intimidad e inviolabilidad del domicilio: Stc 119/2001, de 24 de mayo', *InDret* 01/2002 (www.indret.com, 10 August 2005); Macías Castillo, above, n. 26, pp. 391–7.

[96] It considered that the releases from a water purification station produced highly damaging gas and odour emissions in Lorca; they violated Art. 8 of the European Human Rights Convention of the rights of family private life (ECHR 9 December 1994).

[97] STS 28 October 1996, STS 4 November 1996 and, more recently, STS 29 April 2003.

[98] Luis Vacas García-Alos, 'El Derecho de las inmisiones y la protección contra la contaminación acústica', *Diario La Ley* (www.Laley.net, 14 August 2005); Macías Castillo, above, n. 26, which clearly reflects the current importance of this singular emission; Egea Fernández, above, n. 4; see the research published by L. Martín-Retortillo Baquer or the monograph written by J. Pérez Martos, *Ordenación jurídica del ruido* (Montecorvo, Madrid, 2003); the current concern on noise can also be observed on the website www.ruidos.org.

health and can even lead to an increase in blood pressure, arrhythmia, vasoconstriction, etc.'[99]

4 Relationships between neighbours and the area of nuisance, just as within the period of industrialisation itself, have seen vast changes. This transformation in the modern, technological and, one might even say, digital age is of just as large a scope as that which took place during industrialisation. On the one hand, there has been a divergence between the terms 'neighbourhood' and 'closeness': there now exist neighbourhoods which are separated and, what is worse, closeness without neighbourliness. On the other hand, the range of nuisance has expanded to include all nuisances generated by our postmodern society, the harmful nature of many of which we are simply unaware of.[100]

[99] Egea Fernández, above, n. 95, which mentions the report of the World Health Organisation describing the personal damages from excessive noise (www.who.int/peh/noise/noiseold.html); see also J. M. Alvarez-Cienfuegos Suarez, 'La intimidad y el domicilio ante la contaminación acústica: nuevas perspectivas de los derechos fundamentales', *Diario La Ley* 5437 (2001).

[100] Macías Castillo, above, n. 26, pp. 158–62.

APPENDIX: CODE PROVISIONS

The texts provided in this Appendix provide the main texts of national codes dealing with both delict and the protection of neighbours in property law.

1. French Civil Code (1804)

Delict

1382 Any human act whatever which causes damage to another obliges him by whose fault it occurred to make reparation.

1383 Each one is liable for the damage which he causes not only by his own act but also by his negligence or imprudence.

1384 [para. 1] He is liable not only for the damage which he caused by his own act, but also for that which is caused by the act of persons for whom he is responsible, or by things which he has in his keeping.

[para. 2][1] However, he who possesses by whatever right all or part of a building or of personal property in which a fire occurs is liable vis-à-vis third persons for damage caused by such fire only if it is proved that it should be attributed to his fault or to the fault of persons for whom he is responsible.

[para. 3][2] This provision does not apply to relations between owners and tenants, which remain regulated by Articles 1733 and 1734 of the Civil Code.

[para. 4][3] The father and mother, to the extent that they exercise the right of custody, are jointly liable for damage caused by their minor children living with them.

[para. 5] Masters and principals (are liable) for damage caused by their domestics and employees in the functions for which they have been employed.

[para. 6] Teachers and artisans (are liable) for damage caused by their pupils and apprentices during the time when they are under their surveillance.

[1] Text resulting from the law of 7 November 1922. [2] Ibid.

[3] Text resulting from law no 70–459 of 4 January 1970.

[para. 7][4] The above liability arises unless the father and mother and the artisans prove that they could not prevent the act which gave rise to such liability.

[para. 8] As to teachers, the faults, imprudence or negligence alleged against them as having caused the damaging act must be proven according to ordinary law by the plaintiff in the suit.

1385 The owner of an animal or he who avails himself of it while it is being put to his use is liable for the damage which the animal causes, whether the animal was in his keeping or whether it had strayed or escaped.

1386 The owner of a building is liable for damage caused by its ruin, when this occurred through want of maintenance or by a construction defect.

French Code of Building and Dwellings

Art. L. 112–16 The harm caused to the occupants of a building by nuisances (*nuisances*) due to agricultural, industrial or craft activities does not give rise to a right to compensation when the building permit for the building exposed to these nuisances was requested … after the existence of the activities that caused them, as long as these activities were conducted in conformity with the legislative or regulatory provisions in force when they were undertaken and these activities are conducted under the same conditions.

French Planning Code

Art. L. 160–5, para. 1 No indemnity shall be required in the case of servitudes imposed by application of this Code as matters of roads, health and aesthetics or for other purposes, notably, those concerning: land use (*l'utilisation du sol*), the height of buildings, the proportion of the surface of each property on which one may build or not build, the prohibition of building in certain zones and along the side of certain roads, the subdivision of property in various zones.

2. German Civil Code (1900)

Delict

§ **823** (1): A person who wilfully or negligently injures the life, body, health, freedom, property, or other right of another contrary to law is bound to compensate him for any damage arising therefrom.

(2) The same obligation attaches to a person who infringes a statutory provision intended for the protection of others. If according to the purview

[4] Text resulting from the law of 5 April 1937.

of the statute infringement is possible even without fault, the duty to make compensation arises only if some fault can be imputed to the wrongdoer.

§ **826** A person who wilfully causes damage to another in a manner *contra bonos mores* is bound to compensate the other for the damage.

§ **828** (1) A person who has not completed his seventh year of age is not responsible for any damage which he does to another.

(2) A person who has completed his seventh but not his tenth year is not responsible for the harm which he inflicts on another in an accident with a motor vehicle, a railway or a hover rail. This does not apply if he has caused the injury deliberately.

(3) A person who has not yet completed his eighteenth year is, in so far as his responsibility is not excluded under paragraphs 1 or 2, not responsible for the harm which he inflicts on another if, on the commission of the action causing the harm, he does not have the necessary intelligence to realise his responsibility.

§ **831** (1) A person who employs another to do any work is bound to compensate for damage which the other unlawfully causes to a third party in the performance of his work. The duty to compensate does not arise if the employer has exercised ordinary care in the choice of the employee, and, where he has to supply appliances or implements or to superintend the work, has also exercised ordinary care as regards such supply or superintendence, or if the damage would have arisen, notwithstanding the exercise of such care.

(2) The same responsibility attaches to a person who takes over the charge of any of the affairs specified in para. 1, sentence 2, by contract with the employer.

§ **839** (1) If an official wilfully or negligently commits a breach of official duty incumbent upon him towards a third party, he shall compensate the third party for any damage arising therefrom. If only negligence is imputable to the official, he may be held liable only if the injured party is unable to obtain compensation elsewhere.

(2) If an official violates his official duty by a decision in a legal issue, he is only responsible for the harm arising from this if the violation of duty consists of a criminal act. This provision has no application to a refusal or delay which is contrary to duty in exercise of the office.

(3) The duty to compensate does not arise if the victim has intentionally or negligently refrained from averting the harm by the use of a legal remedy.

§ **847** [REPEALED IN 2002. See now § 253 (2)] In the case of injury to body or health, or in the case of deprivation of liberty, the injured party may also demand an equitable compensation in money for damage which is not a pecuniary loss.

Property

§ **903** Insofar as the law or the rights of third parties do not conflict with this, the owner of a thing can deal with the thing at his discretion and can exclude others from any interference with it ....

§ **906** (1) The owner of land cannot forbid the introduction of gases, steam, smells, smoke, soot, heat, noise, vibrations and similar things coming from the land of others insofar as these do not interfere with his use of his land or interfere only to a negligible extent. A negligible interference typically occurs where the limits or targets established by statute or regulation are not exceeded by the interferences laid down and assessed by these provisions. The same applies to standards in general administrative provisions that have been promulgated under Art. 48 of the Federal Environmental Impact Protection Act and represent the state of the art.

(2) The same applies to the extent that a material interference is caused by a use of another plot of land that is usual in that location and cannot be prevented by measures that are economically reasonable for users of this kind. Where an owner is obliged under these provisions to tolerate an interference, he may require the user of the other land to pay compensation, if the interference impairs a use or revenue of the former's land that is usual in that location beyond a degree that the owner can be expected to tolerate....

§ **907** (1) The owner of a plot of land may require that no facilities are created or maintained on a neighbour's plot of land where it can be predicted with certainty that their existence or use will have an impermissible effect on the owner's land. Where an installation satisfies the provisions of the law of the *Land* concerning the distance from the boundary or other protective measures, then the removal of an installation may only be required if the impermissible interference actually occurs.

(2) Trees and bushes are not facilities within the meaning of these provisions.

§ **1004** (1) Where ownership is interfered with through the removal or deprivation of property, the owner can request that the interfering person remove the interference. Where further interferences are anticipated, then the owner can demand a prohibitory injunction.

(2) Such claims are excluded where the owner is bound to tolerate the interference.

3. Netherlands New Civil Code (1992)

Art. 3:13 (1) Whoever has an entitlement cannot invoke it so as to misuse it.

(2) An entitlement can be misused in so far as it is exercised with no purpose other than to harm another or for a purpose other than that for which it

was granted or where there is a marked imbalance between the interest in exercising it and the interest that would be harmed by its exercise, such that it would not be reasonable to exercise it.

(3) By their nature, there can be entitlements which cannot be misused.

Art. 5:37 The owner of land may not cause hindrance by a measure or in any way that is unlawful under [Art. 6:162] to the owners of other land through the spreading of noise, vibration, smell, smoke or gases, or through the withholding of light or the removal of support.

Delict

Art. 6:101 When the damage is partly caused by an occurrence that can be imputed to the injured party, the obligation to pay compensation is reduced by apportioning the damage between the injured party and the liable party in proportion to the degree in which the occurrences that can be imputed to the parties have contributed to the damage, provided that account is taken of the disparity in the seriousness of the respective faults, or other circumstances of the case, to decide whether fairness demands that an alternative apportionment or full recovery takes place or that the obligation to pay lapses.

Art. 6:106 (1) For harm which is not property damage, the victim has the right to compensation fixed according to fairness:

a. where the person responsible had the objective of bringing about such harm;
b. where the victim has suffered physical injury, his honour or good name is harmed or he is affected in any other way in his person; or
c. where the harm relates to the memory of a deceased person and the claim is brought by a spouse who is not separated, a registered partner, or a blood relative to the second degree, that person may take the place of the deceased if, were he still alive, the deceased would have had a right to compensation for injury to his honour or good name.

(2) The right to compensation set out in the previous paragraph is not capable of being transmitted by way of seizure unless an agreement is established or a claim is made in law. The transfer is complete under the general title when the person has informed the other party responsible for making compensation.

Art 6:162 A person who commits an unlawful act towards another, which can be imputed to him, must repair the damage which the other person suffers as a consequence thereof.

Except where there is a ground of justification, the following acts are deemed to be unlawful: the violation of a right, and an act or omission violating a statutory duty or a rule of unwritten law pertaining to proper social conduct.

An unlawful act can be imputed to its author if it results from his fault or from a cause for which he is answerable according to law or common opinion.
Art. 6:163 No duty to compensate arises whenever the violated norm does not protect against the harm that the victim has suffered.
Art. 6:168 (1)The judge may reject a claim to forbid unlawful conduct on the ground that it should be tolerated by reason of pressing social interests. The victim retains his right to compensation under the relevant title [of this Code]...
(3) Where an order for compensation or for conserving a situation is not complied with, then the judge may, if necessary, forbid the conduct.
Art. 6:74 Any failure to perform an undertaking obliges the debtor to compensate the harm suffered by the creditor, unless the failure cannot be attributed to the debtor.

4. Spanish Civil Code (1889)

Property

Art. 7.2[5] The law does not protect the abuse of rights or the antisocial use of them. Every action or omission that, by the intention of its author, by its object or by the circumstances in which it is done, would exceed the normal limits of a right, with nuisance to another individual, will give rise to compensation or to the necessary administrative or judicial measures to prevent the abuse from continuing.
Art. 590 No one may build sewers, aqueducts, ovens, forges, chimneys, stables, stores for corrosive materials, steam-powered machinery or installations which, of themselves or by their outputs, are dangerous or noxious, near to a communal well or a neighbour's well without following the distances prescribed by regulations and local custom and without taking any protective measures necessary for the work, as also laid down by regulations. Where there is no regulation, the builder shall take all precautions which are deemed necessary, according to the established opinion of experts, to avoid harm to descendants or neighbouring buildings.

Delict

Art. 1902 The person who by action or omission causes damage to another by fault or negligence is obliged to repair the damage caused.
Art. 1903 The obligation imposed in the preceding article applies not only for a person's own acts or omissions, but also for those persons for whom a person is responsible.

[5] As inserted by Decree of 31 May 1974.

The father and the mother are responsible for the harm caused by their minor children who are living with them.

Tutors are liable for the harm caused by minors or incapacitated persons under their authority and living with them.

Employers or directors of an establishment or firm are liable for the harm caused by their employees in the performance of tasks that are entrusted to them or of their functions.

The State is liable under this head for the acts of its special agents, but not when the harm has been caused by a civil servant entrusted with practical administration, for which case the preceding paragraph applies.

Masters and directors of arts and trades are liable in respect of the harm caused by their pupils or apprentices, as long as they remain under their control.

The liability under this Article ceases when the persons mentioned prove that they have shown the diligence of the good father of a family to avoid the harm.

Art. 1905 The possessor of an animal or a person who makes use of one is liable for the harm that it causes, even where it had strayed or escaped. This liability only ceases when he proves that the harm resulted from a fortuitous event or from the fault of the person who suffered the harm.

Art. 1906 The owner of a building is liable for the harm caused to neighbouring property when he has not taken the necessary steps to prevent them increasing ....

Art. 1908 The owners of objects causing harm are also liable:

1. By the explosion of machines that had not been kept with due care and by the burning of explosive substances that were not stored in a safe and suitable place.
2. By excessive smoke, that is injurious to the people or the property.
3. By the falling of trees located on thoroughfares, when this is not caused by force majeure.
4. By emanations of sewers or deposits of infected matter, built without the precautions appropriate to the place in which they were.

INDEX

www.ingramcontent.com/pod-product-compliance
Lightning Source LLC
LaVergne TN
LVHW052312200926
848481LV00002B/541

* 9 7 8 1 1 0 7 4 7 5 6 3 2 *